Salt Mines
and Castles

THE DISCOVERY AND RESTITUTION
OF LOOTED EUROPEAN ART

THOMAS CARR HOWE, JR.

with a new Introduction by Steve W. Chadde

To My Mother

Salt Mines and Castles
The Discovery and Restitution of Looted European Art

Thomas Carr Howe, Jr.
with a new Introduction by Steve W. Chadde

Introduction copyright © 2014 by Steve W. Chadde
Printed in the United States of America

ISBN-13: 978-1495443848
ISBN-10: 1495443841

Salt Mines and Castles, by Thomas Howe, Jr., was originally published by Bobbs-Merrill Company in 1946. The original work is now in the public domain.
TYPEFACE: Aragon 10.5/14

∿ NOTE ∿

From May 1945 until February 1946, I served as a Monuments, Fine Arts and Archives Officer in Germany. During the first four months of this assignment, I was engaged in field work which included the recovery of looted works of art from such out-of-the-way places as a monastery in Czechoslovakia, a salt mine in Austria, and a castle in Bavaria. Later, as Deputy Chief of the Monuments, Fine Arts and Archives Section, Office of Military Government, U. S. Zone, I participated in the restitution of recovered art treasures to the countries of rightful ownership.

This book is primarily an account of my own experiences in connection with these absorbing tasks; but I have also chronicled the activities of a number of my fellow officers, hoping thereby to provide the reader with a more comprehensive estimate of the work as a whole than the *resumé* of my own duties could have afforded.

For many helpful suggestions, I am indebted to Captain Edith A. Standen, Lieutenant Lamont Moore and Mr. David Bramble; and for invaluable photographic material, I am particularly grateful to Captain Stephen Kovalyak, Captain P. J. Kelleher, Captain Edward E. Adams and Lieutenant Craig Smyth, USNR.

For permission to reproduce three International News Service photographs, I wish to thank Mr. Clarence Lindner of the San Francisco Examiner.

Thomas Carr Howe, Jr.
San Francisco
July 1946.

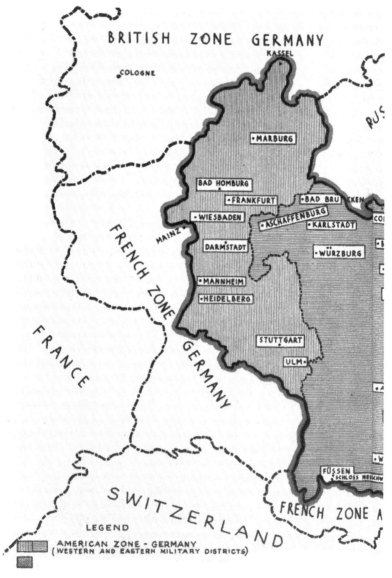

Germany at the end of World War II.

JAN VERMEER, THE ASTRONOMER, 1668. Oil on Canvas, 51 x 45 cm (20 x 17 3/4 in). Recovered from the Alt Aussee salt mine and returned to the Louvre, Paris, France.

∼ *CONTENTS* ∼

C O P Y

ALLIED FORCE HEADQUARTERS

Office of The Commander-in-Chief

AG 000.4-1

29 December 1943

SUBJECT: Historical Monuments

TO   : All Commanders

       Today we are fighting in a country which has contributed a great deal to our cultural inheritance, a country rich in monuments which by their creation helped and now in their old age illustrate the growth of the civilization which is ours. We are bound to respect those monuments so far as war allows.

       If we have to choose between destroying a famous building and sacrificing our own men, then our men's lives count infinitely more and the buildings must go. But the choice is not always so clear-cut as that. In many cases the monuments can be spared without any detriment to operational needs. Nothing can stand against the argument of military necessity. That is an accepted principle. But the phrase "military necessity" is sometimes used where it would be more truthful to speak of military convenience or even of personal convenience. I do not want it to cloak slackness or indifference.

       It is a responsibility of higher commanders to determine through A.M.G. Officers the locations of historical monuments whether they be immediately ahead of our front lines or in areas occupied by us. This information passed to lower echelons through normal channels places the responsibility on all Commanders of complying with the spirit of this letter.

/s/ Dwight D. Eisenhower

DWIGHT D. EISENHOWER,
General, U. S. Army,
Commander-in-Chief.

DISTRIBUTION:
"C"

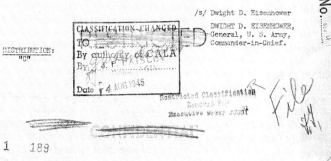

1 189

Allied Commander-In-Chief General Eisenhower communicated to commanders the importance of respecting monuments and artworks so far as the war allowed.

∼ INTRODUCTION ∼

SALT MINES AND CASTLES is a first-hand account of the work of the Monuments, Fine Arts and Archives Section of U.S. Forces, European Theatre (MFA&A), immediately following the end of World War II in 1945. Often referred to simply as the "Monuments Men," this group of unlikely soldiers included art curators, scholars, architects, librarians, and archivists from the U.S. and Great Britain. Their war-time mission was to identify and protect European cultural sites, monuments, and buildings from Allied bombing. After the war, and the focus of this book, their mission was the challenging effort to locate and recover works of art that had been looted by the Nazis.

With the help of civilians such as Rose Valland of the Jeu de Paume Museum in Paris, who had been secretly spying on the Nazis as they removed her beloved art, The Monuments Men soon determined the locations of hidden storage sites. Uncovered were thousands of pieces of art—including priceless paintings by Leonardo DaVinci and Johannes Vermeer, sculptures by Michelangelo, and the Rothschild jewels— hidden across Germany and Austria in underground mines, castles, churches, and monasteries. The Neuschwanstein Castle in Bavaria, for example, was a treasure trove of looted works, requiring six weeks for Allied troops to remove the immense inventory kept there.

Following the recovery of the art, the no less daunting task of inventorying the thousands of items, identification of the owners, restoration of damaged works, and transporting delicate canvases and sculptures to their home countries began.

Salt Mines and Castles details the finding of the looted art, the struggles of removing art from underground vaults or mountain-top castles, the logistical challenges faced by the group due to poor roads, primitive communication, and a lack of transport trucks and storage facilities for interim storage prior to each works' restitution to its original home.

In spite of these hurdles, the dedication, ingenuity, and care shown by the Monuments Men is something for which we can all be grateful and also extremely proud. Their efforts preserved a priceless heritage, much of which is on display at museums around the world today.

ABOUT THE AUTHOR

Thomas Carr Howe, Jr. (1904-1994) was director of the California Palace of the Legion of Honor in San Francisco prior to becoming a naval lieutenant and Monuments officer. He served in Germany from May 1945 through February 1946. He first reported to Lt. Cdr. George Stout who was, at the time, in charge of the MFA&A in Germany at the 12th Army Group Headquarters in Wiesbaden. Howe subsequently traveled to U.S. Third Army Headquarters in Munich before being dispatched to locations across Europe. His first four months of service were spent in the field recovering artworks from their various hiding places.

Under his direction, the Vienna Rothschild collection was evacuated from a monastery in Hohenfurth, Czechoslovakia. Howe also assisted in the packing of the Veit Stoss altar, which was discovered in an underground repository in Nuremberg. At Alt Aussee, Austria, Howe witnessed the removal of many cultural treasures, including the Ghent Altarpiece by Jan van Eyck, Michelangelo's Bruges Madonna, Vermeer's The Artist's Studio, the Rothschild jewels, and 15 cases of stolen Italian artwork removed from Monte Cassino by the Hermann Göring Division as a birthday gift for Reichsmarshall Göring. He also discovered a painting by the 16th century Venetian painter Paris Bordone, entitled Portrait of a Young Woman, which had been on loan to his own mueseum in California. Amazingly, the painting still bore a label from the museum written in his own handwriting.

Howe was later assigned to the Frankfurt USFET Headquarters as the Deputy Chief of the MFA&A to oversee restitution work. During this time he oversaw the return of extraordinary artworks such as the Ghent Altarpiece to Belgium, among many others.

In February of 1946 he returned home and resumed his position as director at the California Palace of the Legion of Honor. At that time he documented his European experience in *Salt Mines and Castles*.

In September 1951, Howe once again returned to Europe, along with S. Lane Faison, to direct the closing of the Collecting Points. He received honors for his work from the Dutch government and was also made a knight of the French Legion of Honor by the French government.

He retired from the Legion of Honor Museum in 1968, and passed away in 1994 at the age of 89.

ABOUT THIS EDITION

Included in this edition are twenty-four pages of photographs illustrating the collection of art by Nazi leaders, plus the recovery of looted pieces by the Allies.

UNCOMMON VALOR SERIES

Salt Mines and Castles is part of a series entitled Uncommon Valor, taken from the quote by Admiral Chester W. Nimitz, U.S. Navy:

"Uncommon valor was a common virtue,"

referring to the hard-won victory by U.S. Marines on Iwo Jima. The intent of the series is to keep alive a number of largely forgotten books, written by men and women who survived extreme hardship and deprivation during immensely trying historical times, or whose efforts were of significance to human culture.

Steve W. Chadde
SERIES EDITOR

Private Paul Oglesby of the 30th Infantry Regiment pauses to observe this severely damaged church in Italy; September 1943.

The Winged Victory of Samothrace is carefully moved down the stairs at the Louvre Museum in Paris. Louvre workers constructed a pulley to position the statue before crating it for shipment. In fall 1939, museums across Europe evacuated their collections to remote locations in the countryside in anticipation of war.

Nazi soldiers unload looted Jewish artwork from trucks for delivery to Hermann Göring.

Germans packaging art for transport.

Germans displaying Botticelli's masterpiece, *Camilla and the Centaur*, from the Uffizi.

A photo taken by the Nazis during World War II shows a room filled with stolen art at the Jeu de Paume museum in Paris.

Rose Valland, Temporary Custodian of the Jeu de Paume. Age: 46. Born: Saint-Etienne-de-Saint-Geoirs, France. Rose Valland, a woman of modest means raised in the countryside of France, was the unlikely hero of the French cultural world. She was a longtime unpaid volunteer at the Jeu de Paume museum, adjacent to the Louvre, when the Nazi occupation of Paris began. An unassuming but determined single woman with a forgettable bland style and manner, she ingratiated herself with the Nazis at the Jeu de Paume and, unbeknownst to them, spied on their activities for the four years of their occupation. After the liberation of Paris, the extent and importance of her secret information, which she fiercely guarded, had a pivotal impact on the discovery of looted works of art from France. (Archives des Musées Nationaux).

PARIS - DECEMBER 2, 1941: At the Jeu de Paume Museum, Reichsmarschall Hermann Göring, painting in his left hand and cigar in his right, sits gazing at two paintings by Henri Matisse being supported by Bruno Lohse. Standing to Göring's left is his art advisor, Walter Andreas Hofer. Note the bottle of champagne on the table at center. Both paintings were stolen from the Paul Rosenberg collection by the Nazis and were recovered and returned after the war. The painting on the left, titled *Marguerites,* today hangs in the Art Institute of Chicago. The other, titled *Danseuse au Tambourin,* is at the Norton Simon Museum in Pasadena, California. (Archives des Musées Nationaux).

Hitler looking at a tiara and a sculpture of Napoleon Bonaparte.

By order of the Führer, more than 16,000 modern works deemed "degenerate" were removed from the walls of German museums. By 1937 works by artists such as Nolde, Kandinsky, Klee, Dix, Chagall, Kokoschka, Beckmann, and many others were collecting dust in various storage facilities pending their new fate. Hitler, accompanied by Goebbels, was seemingly always available when an opportunity arose to see art, especially when it could be used for such effective propaganda purposes. Here they examine art at the Degenerate Art Depot in Berlin.

Adolf Hitler and Hermann Göring examine a painting, likely at the 1937 propaganda exhibition called "Degenerate Art."

Adolf Hitler presents Hermann Göring with *The Falconer* (1880), a painting by the 19th century Austrian academic painter Hans Makart. Hitler bought the painting legitimately from art dealer Karl Haberstock. It is now in the Neue Pinakothek in Munich.

Hitler examining a cache of paintings. Hitler and Göring both had an interest in art, and expanded their personal collections through outright purchase or, during the war years, more commonly by looting and other illegal methods of acquisition.

LA GLEIZE, BELGIUM - FEB 1, 1945: During the Battle of the Bulge, the church in La Gleize was severely damaged. The statue, known as the Madonna of La Gleize, was fully exposed to one of the harshest winters on record. Note the gaping hole in the roof overhead. (Walker Hancock Collection).

LA GLEIZE, BELGIUM - FEB 1, 1945: Monuments Man Walker Hancock (front left, in U.S. Army helmet) assisted residents of the town of La Gleize with the relocation of the Madonna of La Gleize to a more secure site. (Walker Hancock Collection)

BERNTERODE, GERMANY - MAY 1945: The bronze coffin of Friedrich Wilhelm of Prussia was one of four enormous coffins found at the Bernterode repository by Monuments Man Walker Hancock. (Walker Hancock Collection)

The administration buildings at the salt mine at Alt Aussee, Austria. Removal of stolen art treasures from the mine was carried out late in 1945.

Monuments Man Robert Posey, an unidentified U.S. Army officer, and American GIs stand in front of the administration building at the Altaussee salt mine in Austria following the end of the war. May 1945. (Robert Posey Collection)

ALT AUSSEE, AUSTRIA - MAY 1945: One of the many mine chambers in which the Nazis had constructed wooden shelves to house the enormous number of stolen works of art. Note the nine foot ladder in the center right portion of the upper photograph.

ALTAUSSEE, AUSTRIA - JULY 10, 1945: Removal of priceless works of art from the salt mine at Alt Aussee posed problems for Monuments Man George Stout unlike any ever contemplated. Stout constructed a pulley to lift Michelangelo's Bruges Madonna onto the salt cart to begin its long trip home to Belgium. Visible on the far left is Monuments Man Steve Kovalyak, an expert in packing art, who was a key assistant to Stout. (National Gallery, Washington, D.C.).

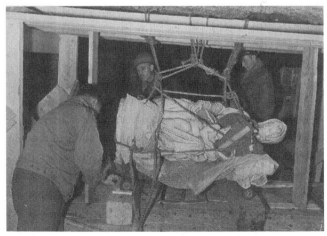

Stephen Kovalyak, George Stout and Thomas Carr Howe moving Michelangelo's sculpture Madonna and child, July 9, 1945, for return to Bruges. The statue was restored to the Church of Notre Dame in September of 1945.

American GIs admire *In the Conservatory,* a masterpiece by Edouard Manet. This painting from Kaiser-Friderich Museum in Berlin, had been brought to the mine for safekeeping.

U.S. soldiers inspecting a Rembrandt self-portrait outside of the Alt Aussee salt mine where it had been stored.

Lt. Gen. Omar N. Bradley, Lt. Gen. George S. Patton, Jr., and Gen. Dwight D. Eisenhower inspect the German museum treasures stored in the Merkers mine on April 12, 1945. Also pictured in the center is Major Irving Leonard Moskowitz.

Hidden inside the Merkers salt mine was the majority of Nazi Germany's gold reserves and paper currency. Most all but the largest paintings from the Kaiser-Friedrich Museum in Berlin were also placed there for safekeeping. In 1946 dollars the value of the gold found in Merkers would be a staggering $5 billion.

Vermeer's *The Astronomer* found in the Alt Aussee mine.

Lt. Daniel Kern and mine worker Max Eder inspect Jan Vermeer's *Portrait of the Artist in His Studio*, found inside the mine at Alt Aussee. The painting was purchased by Hitler for his proposed museum.

OPPOSITE Master Sgt. Harold Maus with a set of Albrecht Dürer engravings found at the Merkers mine.

The Ghent Altarpiece was found in the mine at Altaussee. The central panel of the Ghent Altarpiece, due to its size and weight, proved particularly challenging to move through the narrow passageways. Other panels of the altarpiece are visible in the background behind Monuments Man George Stout. Stout was proud of his U.S. Navy background and usually wore an "N" for Navy on his jacket or helmet.

Race Institute Building. In a corner of the basement were hundreds of Torah scrolls piled 10 feet high. The Race Institute was used by Alfred Rosenberg to research the characteristics of various people overrun by the German Army and under subsequent Nazi rule. American Chaplain Samuel Blinder examines a Sefer Torah as a he begins the overwhelming task of sorting and inspecting. July 1945.

Polish art historian Karol Estreicher with MFAA officer Lt. Frank P. Albright and two American GIs as they prepare to return Leonardo da Vinci's *Lady with an Ermine (Portrait of Cecilia Gallerani,* ca. 1483-88) to the Czartoryski Museum in Cracow, Poland, from which it had been stolen by the Nazis.

The castle of Neuschwanstein in Germany was the key Nazi repository for the greatest works of art stolen from France. Built by "Mad Ludwig" of Bavaria in the 19th century, it contained so many stolen works of art that it took the Monuments Men six weeks to empty it. The extreme vertical height and absence of elevators required most of the works to be carried down the enumerable flights of stairs.

Winter evacuation of looted art from Neuschwanstein, 1945. Snow-covered mountains and a castle turret in the background.

At Schloss Neuschwanstein in southern Bavaria, Captain James Rorimer, who later would become the director of the Metropolitan Museum of Art, supervises the safeguarding of art stolen from French Jews and stored during the war at the castle (April-May, 1945).

Loading recovered art at Neuschwanstein Castle. The many stairs and wintry conditions hampered Allied efforts.

Raymond Lemaire and Edith Standen holding a Rubens portrait at Wiesbaden Collecting Point, 1946.

The celebrated Egyptian sculpture, *Queen Nefertiti*, formerly in the Berlin Museum, discovered in the Merkers salt mine.

~ I ~

PARIS—LONDON—VERSAILLES

"Your name's not on the passenger list," said Craig when I walked into the waiting room of the Patuxent airport. "You'd better see what you can do about it." It was a, hot spring night and I had just flown down from Washington, expecting to board a transatlantic plane which was scheduled to take off at midnight.

'There must be some mistake," I said. "I checked on that just before I left Washington." Craig went with me to the counter where I asked the pretty WAVE on duty to look up my name. It wasn't on her list.

"Let's see what they know about this at the main office," she said with an encouraging smile as she dialed Naval Air Transport in Washington. The next ten minutes were grim. The officer at the other end of the line wanted to know with whom I had checked. Had it been someone in his office? I didn't know. All I knew was that I had to get on that plane. I had important papers which had to be delivered to our Paris office without delay. Was I a courier? Yes, I was—well, that is, almost, I faltered to the WAVE ensign who had been transmitting my replies. "Here, you talk to him," she said, adding, as she handed me the receiver, "I think he can fix it up."

After going through the same questions and getting the same answers a second time, the officer in Washington asked to speak to the yeoman who was supervising the loading of the plane. He was called in and I waited on tenterhooks until I heard him say, "Yes, sir, I can make room for the lieutenant and his gear." Turning the phone over to the WAVE, he asked with a reassuring grin, "Feel better, Lieutenant?"

I was so limp with relief that I scarcely noticed the tall spare man in civilian clothes who had just come up to the counter. "That's Lindbergh," said Craig in a low voice. "Do you suppose he's going over too?"

Half an hour later we trooped out across the faintly lighted field to the C-54 which stood waiting. Lindbergh, dressed now in the olive-drab uniform of a Naval Technician, preceded us up the steps. There were ten of us in all. With the exception of three leather-cushioned chairs, there were only bucket seats. Craig and I settled ourselves in two of these uninviting hollows and began fumbling clumsily with the seat belts. Seeing that we were having trouble, Lindbergh came over and with a friendly smile asked if he could give us a hand. After deftly adjusting our belts, he returned to one of the cushioned seats across the way.

Doors slammed, the engines began to roar and, a few seconds later, we were off. We mounted swiftly into the star-filled sky and, peering out, watched the dark Maryland hills drop away. We dozed despite the discomfort of our bent-over positions and didn't come to again until the steward roused us several hours later with coffee and sandwiches. Afterward he brought out army cots and motioned to us to set them up if we wanted to stretch out As soon as we got the cots unfolded and the pegs set in place, he turned out the lights.

Craig was dead to the world in a few minutes but I couldn't get back to sleep. To the accompaniment of the humming motors, the events of the past weeks began to pass in review: that quiet April afternoon at Western Sea Frontier Headquarters in San Francisco when my overseas orders had come through—those orders I had been waiting for so long, more than a year. It was in March of 1944 that I first learned there was a chance of getting a European assignment, to join the group of officers working with our armies in the "protection and salvaging of artistic monuments in war areas." That was the cumbersome way it was described. The President had appointed a commission with a long name, but it came to be known simply as the Roberts Commission. Justice Roberts of the Supreme Court was the head of it. It was the first time in history that a country had taken such precautions to safeguard cultural monuments lying in the paths of its invading armies.

It was the commission's job to recommend to the War Department servicemen whose professional qualifications fitted them for this work. I had been in the Navy for two years. Before that I had been director of the California Palace of the Legion of Honor, one of San Francisco's two municipal museums of the fine arts. The commission had recommended me, but it was up to me to obtain my own release. I had been in luck on that score. My commanding officer had agreed to let me go. And more important, my wife had too. Only Francesca had wanted to know why Americans should be meddling with Europe's art treasures. Weren't there enough museum directors over there to take care of things? Of course there were in normal times. But now they needed men in uniform—to go in with the armies.

And after all that planning nothing had happened, until three weeks ago. Then everything had happened at once. The orders directed me to report to SHAEF for duty with the Monuments, Fine Arts and Archives Section, G-5, and additional duty with the Allied Control Council for Germany.

The papers had been full of stories about German salt mines—the big one at Merkers where our troops had found the Nazi gold and the treasures from the Berlin museums. I was going to Germany. Would I find anything like that?

I had flown to Washington to receive last-minute instructions. I was to make the trip across by air and was given an extra allowance of twenty-five pounds to enable me to take along a dozen Baedekers and a quantity of photographic paper, for distribution among our officers in the field. I had been introduced to Craig Smyth while in the midst of these final preparations. Like me, he was a naval lieutenant and his orders were identical with mine. He was a grave young Princetonian, formerly on the staff of the National Gallery of Art in Washington.

It was raining when we reached Stevensville, Newfoundland, early the next morning. After an hour's stop we were on our way again. Shortly before noon we struck good weather and all day long sea and sky remained unvaryingly blue. Late in the afternoon we landed on the island of Terceira in the Azores. We had set our watches ahead two hours at Stevensville. Now we set them ahead again. We took off promptly at seven. This was the last lap of the journey—we'd be in Paris in the morning. Presently our fellow passengers settled down for the night. Two of the cushioned chairs were empty, so Craig and I took possession. They were more comfortable than the cots, and as soon as the steward turned out the lights I dropped off to sleep.

It was still dark when I awoke hours later, but there was enough light for me to distinguish two black masses of land rising from the sea. On one, the beacon of a lighthouse revolved with monotonous regularity. We had just passed over two of the Channel Islands. The dawn came rapidly and a pink light edged the eastern horizon. It was not long before we sighted the coast of France. We flew into rosy clouds and, as they billowed about the plane, we caught tantalizing glimpses of the shore line below. The steward pointed out one promontory and told us it was Brest. Soon we had a spectacular view of Mont St. Michel and the long causeway over which I had driven years before on a sketching tour in Normandy. I wondered what had become of Mère Poulard and her wonderful omelettes and lobster. Some people said they had brought more visitors to Mont St. Michel than the architecture. Very likely she was dead and the Germans had probably disposed of her fabulous cuisine.

We had lost two more hours in the course of the night, so it was only seven-thirty when we swooped down at Orly field, half an hour from Paris. It was a beautiful morning and the sun was so bright that it took us a few minutes to get accustomed to the glare. As we walked over to the airport office, we had our first glimpse of war damage at close range—bombed-out hangars and, scattered about the field, the wreckage of German planes. But the airport was being repaired rapidly. Trim new offices had been built and additional barracks were nearing completion. Craig and I booked places on the afternoon plane for London and then climbed onto the bus waiting to take us into Paris.

Thanks to various delays in getting out of Washington, we had missed the Paris celebration of VE-Day by a margin of three days. So we were about to see the wonderful old city at the beginning of a period of readjustment. But a peaceful Sunday morning is no time to judge any city—least of all Paris. Everything looked the same. The arcades along the right side of the Rue de Rivoli and the gardens at the left were empty, as one would expect them to be. We turned into the Rue

Castiglione and came to a halt by the column in the Place Vendôme.

After we had checked our bags at the ATC office, we walked over to the Red Cross Club on the Place de la Concorde. We shaved, washed and then had doughnuts and coffee in the canteen.

Our next move was to call Lieutenant Colonel Geoffrey Webb, the British officer who was head of the MFA&A Section at SHAEF headquarters in Versailles. Before the war, Colonel Webb had been Slade Professor of Art at Cambridge. I explained to him that Smyth and I had arrived but that our orders directed us to report first to Naval Headquarters in London—ComNavEu—and that as soon as we had complied with them we would be back. That was all right with the colonel. He said that Lieutenant Kuhn, USNR, his deputy, was away on a three-day field trip and wouldn't be returning before the middle of the week. And we were primarily Charlie Kuhn's problem.

With that formality out of the way, we retrieved our luggage and wheedled the ATC into giving us transportation to the Royal Monceau, the Navy hotel out near the Étoile. It was time to relax and luxuriate in the thought that it was May and that we were in Paris—that climatic and geographic combination so long a favorite theme of song-writers. I thought about this as we drove along the Champs Élysées. The song writers had something, all right— Paris in May was a wonderful sight. But they had been mooning about a gala capital filled with carefree people, and the Paris of May 1945 wasn't like that. Architecturally, the city was as elegant as ever, but the few people one saw along the streets looked anything but carefree. And there were no taxis. Taxis have always seemed to me as much a part of Paris as the buildings themselves. In spite of a superficial sameness, Paris had an air of empty magnificence that made one think of a beautiful woman struck dumb by shock. I wondered if my thoughts were running away with me, but found that Craig's impressions were much the same.

These musings were cut short by our arrival at the hotel. The Navy had done all right for itself. The same efficient French staff that had presided over this de luxe establishment in prewar days was still in charge. I left the Baedekers and photographic paper for Charlie Kuhn, and then Craig and I walked to Naval Headquarters in the Rue Presbourg. There we attended to routine matters in connection with our orders. It was almost noon by the time we got squared away, so we retraced our steps to the Monceau. Lunch there was a demonstration of what a French chef could do with GI food.

Mid-afternoon found us headed back to Orly in a Navy jeep. Our plane was scheduled to leave at four. This was no bucket-seat job, but a luxurious C-47 equipped with chairs of the Pullman-car variety, complete with antimacassars. We landed at Bovingdon less than two hours later and from there took a bus up to London. Naval Headquarters was in Grosvenor Square. With the American Embassy on one side of it, the Navy on another, and the park in the center used by the Navy motor pool, the dignified old square was pretty thoroughly Americanized.

London was still crowded with our armed forces. The hotels were full, so we were assigned to lodgings in Wimpole Street. These were on the third floor of a pleasant, eighteenth century house, within a stone's throw of No. 50, where Elizabeth Barrett had been wooed and won by Robert Browning. An inspection of our quarters revealed that the plumbing was of the Barrett-Browning period; but the place was clean and, anyway, it wasn't likely that we'd be spending much time there. It had been a long day and we were too tired to think of anything beyond getting a bite to eat and hitting the sack.

For our two days in London we had "Queen's weather"—brilliant sunshine and cloudless skies. Our first port of call early the next morning was the Medical Office, where we were given various inoculations. From there Craig and I went across the square to the American Embassy for a long session with Sumner Crosby, at that time acting as the liaison between the Roberts Commission and its British counterpart, the Macmillan Committee. Sumner provided us with a great deal of useful information. The latest reports from Germany indicated that caches of looted art were being uncovered from day to day. The number of these hiding places ran into the hundreds. The value of their contents was, of course, incalculable. Only a fraction of the finds had as yet been released to the press.

Craig and I began licking our chops at the prospect of what lay ahead. Had we made a mistake in planning to stay two days in London? Perhaps we could get a plane back to Paris that evening. Sumner thought not. There were several things for us to do on the spot, things that would be of use to us in our future activities. One was to call on Colonel

Sir Leonard Woolley, the British archaeologist who, with his wife, was doing important work for the Macmillan Committee. Another was to see Jim Plaut, a naval lieutenant at the London office of OSS. He would probably have valuable information about German museum personnel. It would be helpful to know the whereabouts of certain German scholars, specifically those whose records were, from our point of view, "clean."

Sumner made several appointments for us and then hurried off to keep one of his own. Craig and I stayed on at the office to study the reports. Sumner had already given us the glittering highlights. By noon our heads were filled with facts and figures that made E. Phillips Oppenheim seem positively unimaginative. And The Arabian Nights—that was just old stuff.

It was late afternoon when we finished calling on the various people Sumner had advised us to see, but plenty of time remained to do a little sightseeing before dinner. The cabbie took us past Buckingham Palace, along the Embankment, Birdcage Walk, the Abbey, the Houses of Parliament and finally to St. Paul's. What we saw was enough to give a cruel picture of the damage the Germans had inflicted on the fine old monuments of London.

Craig and I flew back to Orly the following evening, arriving too late to obtain transportation into Paris. We spent an uncomfortable night in the barracks at the airport and drove to the Royal Monceau early the next morning. It was stiflingly hot and I was in a bad humor in spite of the soothing effect of a short haircut— the kind Francesca said needed a couple of saber scars to make it look right. My spirits fell still lower when Craig and I were told that we could stay only two nights at the hotel. Since we were assigned to SHAEF, it was up to the Army to billet us. It seemed rather unfriendly of the Navy, but that's the way it was and there wasn't anything we could do about it.

After lunch we set out for Versailles in a Navy jeep. It was a glorious day despite the heat, and the lovely drive through the Bois and on past Longchamps made us forget our irritation at the Navy's lack of hospitality. The office of the Monuments, Fine Arts and Archives Section was in two tiny "between-floor" rooms in the Grandes ficuries—the big stables which, together with their matching twin, the Petites Écuries, face the main palace.

When we arrived Colonel Webb was deep in conference with a lady war correspondent. The tall, rangy colonel, who reminded me of a humorous and grizzled giraffe, came out to welcome Craig and me. His cordiality was overwhelming at first, but we soon learned the reason. Miss Bonney, the correspondent, was giving the colonel a bad time and he needed moral support. She was firing a rapid barrage of searching questions, and in some cases the colonel didn't want to answer. I was fascinated by his technique. He obviously didn't wish to offend his inquisitor, but on the other hand he wasn't going to be pressed for an expression of opinion on certain subjects. At times he would parry her query with one of his own. At others he would snort some vague reply which got lost in a hearty laugh. Before the interview was over, it was Miss Bonney who was answering the questions—often her own—not the colonel.

Neither Craig nor I could make much of what we heard, but after Miss Bonney's departure the colonel took us into his confidence. Somewhere this indomitable lady had got hold of stray bits of information which, properly pieced together, made one of the most absorbing stories of the war, as far as Nazi looting of art treasures was concerned. The time was not yet ripe to break the story, according to the colonel, so it had been up to him to avoid giving answers which would have filled in the missing pieces of the puzzle.

Then the colonel proceeded to tell us about the *Einsatzstab Rosenberg,* the infamous "task force"—to translate the word literally— organized under the direction of Alfred Rosenberg, the "ideological and spiritual leader" of the Reich, for the methodical plundering of the great Jewish collections and the accumulated artistic wealth of other recognized "enemies of the state." Rosenberg was officially responsible for cultural treasures confiscated in the occupied countries. He had virtually unlimited resources at his command. In the fall of 1940, not long after his appointment, Rosenberg received a congratulatory letter from Göring in which the Reichsmarschall promised to support energetically the work of his staff and to place at its disposal "means of transportation and guard personnel," and specifically assured him the "utmost assistance" of the Luftwaffe. Even before the war, German agents had accumulated exhaustive information concerning collections which were later to be confiscated. The whereabouts of every object of artistic importance was known. Paintings, sculpture, tapestries, furniture, porcelain, enamels, jewels, gold and silver—all were a matter of record. When the Nazis occupied Paris, the Rosenberg Task Force was able to go into operation with clocklike precision. And so accurate was their information that in many instances they even knew the hiding places in which their more foresighted victims had concealed their valuables.

The headquarters of the E.R.R.* had been set up in the Musée du Jeu de Paume, the little museum in the corner of the Tuileries Gardens overlooking the Place de la Concorde. The large staff was composed mainly of Germans, but some of the members were French. Looted treasures poured into the building, to be checked, labeled and shipped off to Germany. But it was more than a clearing house. The choicest things were placed on exhibition and to these displays the top-flight Nazis were invited—to select whatever caught their fancy. Hitler had first choice, Göring second.

It did not occur to the members of the E.R.R. staff that their every move was watched. A courageous Frenchwoman named Rose Valland had ingratiated herself with the "right people" and had become a trusted member of the staff. During the months she worked at the museum, she had two main objectives. One was to sabotage the daily work as much as possible by making intentionally stupid mistakes and by encouraging the French laborers, engaged by the Germans, to do likewise.' The other, and far and away the more important, was the compilation of a file, complete with biographical data and photographs, of the German personnel at the Jeu de Paume. How she ever accomplished this is a mystery. The colonel said that Mile. Valland, now a captain in the French Army, was working with the official French committee for Fine Arts. She had already provided our Versailles office with a copy of her E.R.R. file. Later in the summer I met Captain Valland, a robust woman with gray hair and the most penetrating brown eyes I have ever seen. I asked her how she had ever had the courage to do what she had done. She said with a laugh, "I could never do it again. The Gestapo followed me home every night."

---

* E(insatzstab) R(eichsleiter) R(osenberg)—Reichsleiter meaning realm leader, The Rosenberg Task Force was commonly referred to by these initials.

After regaling us with this account of the E.RJL, Colonel Webb whetted our appetites still further with an outline of what his deputy, Charlie Kuhn, was up to. As the result of a "signal," he had taken off by plane for Germany, and at the moment was either in the eastern part of Bavaria or over the Austrian border, trying to trace two truckloads of paintings and tapestries which two high-ranking Nazis had spirited away from the Laufen salt mine at the eleventh hour. Latest information indicated that the finest things from the Vienna Museum had been stored at Laufen, which was in the mountains east of Salzburg; and it was further believed that the "top cream" of the stuff—the Breughels, Titians and Velásquezes—was in those two trucks. These pictures were world-famous and consequently not marketable, so there was the appalling possibility that the highjackers had carried them off with the idea of destroying them—Hitler's mad Götterdammerung idea. There was also the possibility that they intended to hold the pictures as a bribe against their own safety.

Back at the hotel that night, Craig and I reviewed the events of the day. What we had learned from Colonel Webb was only an affirmation of the exciting things we had gleaned from the reports in the London office. We were desperately anxious to get into Germany where we could be a part of all these unbelievable adventures instead of hearing about them secondhand. Strict censorship was still in force, so we weren't able to share our exuberance with our respective families in letters home. But we could at least exult together over the fantastic future shaping up before us.

We found Charlie Kuhn at the office the next morning. He was a tall quiet fellow with a keen sense of humor, whom I had first known when we had been fellow students at Harvard back in the twenties. During the intervening years we had met only at infrequent intervals. He had remained to teach and had become an outstanding member of the Fine Arts faculty in Cambridge, while I had gone to a museum. His special field of scholarship was German painting and it was this attribute which had led the Roberts Commission to nominate him for his present assignment as Deputy Chief of the MFA&A Section. He had already been in the Navy for two years when this billet was offered him. Notwithstanding his obvious qualifications for his present job, he had so distinguished himself in the earlier work upon which he had been engaged—special interrogation of German prisoners—that it had required White House intervention to "liberate" him for his new duties. No closeted scholar, Charlie chafed under the irritations of administrative and personnel problems which occupied most of his time.

That morning at Versailles he was fresh from his adventures in the field, and we buttonholed him for a firsthand account. Yes, the trucks had been located. They had been abandoned by the roadside, but everything had been found intact. The reports had not been exaggerated: the trucks had contained some of the finest of the Vienna pictures and also some of the best tapestries. They were now in a warehouse at Salzburg and would probably remain there until they could be returned to Vienna. As to their condition, the pictures were all right; the tapestries had mildewed a bit, but the damage wasn't serious.

It was hard to settle down to the humdrum of office routine after his recital of these adventures. Charlie said he wanted to ship us off to Germany as soon as possible because there was so much to be done and so few officers were available.

It turned out that we weren't destined for nearly so swift an invasion of Germany as we had hoped. Later that afternoon Charlie received a letter from the Medical Officer at Naval Headquarters in Paris informing him that Lieutenants Howe and Smyth had not completed their course of typhus shots, and that he would not recommend their being sent into Germany until thirty days after the second and final shot. Charlie wanted to know what this was all about, and we had to admit that we had not been given typhus injections before leaving the States, and had only received the first one in London. After deliberating about it most of the following morning, Colonel Webb and Charlie decided that, if we were willing to take the chance, they'd cut the waiting period to ten days. We were only too willing.

Craig and I made good use of the waiting period. We were put to work on the reports submitted at regular intervals by our officers in the field. These reports contained information concerning art repositories. It was our job to keep the card file on them up to date; to make a card for each new one; to sort out and place in a separate file those which had become obsolete; to check duplications. Each card bore the name of the place, a brief description of the contents, and a map reference consisting of two co-ordinates. In Germany there was much duplication in the names of small towns and villages, so these map references were of great importance.

There was also a file on outstanding works of art which were known to have been carried off by the Germans or hidden away for safekeeping, but the whereabouts of which were as yet unknown— such things, for example, as the crown jewels of the Holy Roman Empire, the Michelangelo *Madonna and Child* from Bruges, the Ghent altarpiece, the treasure from the Cathedral of Metz, the stained glass from Strasbourg Cathedral, and the Veit Stoss altarpiece. The list read like an Almanach de Gotha of the art world.

So far as our creature comforts were concerned, they suffered a great decline when we moved out to Versailles. Our lodging there was a barren, four-story house at No. 1 Rue Berthier. Craig had a room on the ground floor, while I shared one under the eaves with Charlie Kuhn. Judging from the signs still tacked up in various parts of the house, it had been used as a German billet during the occupation; and judging by its meager comforts, only the humblest ranks had been quartered there. No spruce Prussian would have put up with such austerity. A couple of British soldiers also were living there. They were batmen for two officers quartered in a near-by hotel and, for a hundred francs a week, they agreed to do for us as well. They brought us hot water in the morning, polished our shoes each day and pressed our uniforms.

Outwardly our life was rather magnificent, for we usually had our meals at the Trianon Palace Hotel just inside the park grounds. It was a pleasant walk from the Rue Berthier, and an even pleasanter one from the office, involving a short cut behind the main palace and across the lovely gardens. On the whole the gardens had been well kept up and a stroll about the terraces or through the long *allées* was something to look forward to when the weather was fine. Craig and I got into the habit of retiring to a quiet corner of the gardens after work with our German books. There we would quiz each other for an hour or two a day. We made occasional trips into Paris but, more often than not, we followed a routine in which the bright lights—what few there were— played little part.

At the end of our ten-day "incubation" period, Charlie gave us our instructions. We were to go to Frankfurt by air and from there to Bad Homburg by car. At Bad Homburg we were to report to ECAD headquarters, that is, the European Civil Affairs Division, where we would be issued further orders. As members of a pool of officers attached to ECAD, we could be shifted about from one part of Germany to another.

Charlie told us that he and Colonel Webb would be moving to Frankfurt in a few days as SHAEF Headquarters was soon to be set up there. The MFA&A office would continue to function with a joint British and American staff until the dissolution of SHAEF later in the summer. But that would not take place, he said, until the four zones of occupation had been established.

We left for the airport at six-thirty in the morning. Our French driver asked us which airport we wanted. Craig and I looked at each other in surprise. What field was there besides Orly? The answer was Villacoublay. We had never heard of it, so we said Orly. We couldn't have been more wrong. When we finally reached Villacoublay we found great confusion. We couldn't even find out whether our plane had taken off.

After making three attempts to get a coherent answer from the second lieutenant who appeared to be quietly going mad behind the information counter, I gave up.

"This is where you take over, Craig," I said. I had suddenly developed an evil headache and had lost all interest in going any place. I walked over to my luggage, which I had dumped in front of the building, and plunked myself down on top of it, put on dark glasses and went to sleep. An hour later, Craig shook me.

"Come on," he said. "I've found a B-17 that's going to Frankfurt." We piled our gear onto a truck and rumbled out over the bumpy field for a distance of half a mile. One of the B-17's crew was sitting unconcernedly in the grass.

"We'd like to go to Frankfurt," said Craig.

"Okay," he said, "we'll be going along pretty soon." He was disconcertingly casual. But the trip wasn't. We ran into heavy fog and got lost, so it took us nearly three hours to make the run which shouldn't have taken more than two.

We finally landed in a green meadow near Hanau. Craig said he'd look for transportation if I'd stand guard over our luggage. It was an agreeable assignment. The day was warm, the meadow soft and inviting. I took out my German book and a chocolate bar, curled up in the grass and hoped he'd be gone a long time.

Craig came back an hour and a half later with a jeep. We were about twenty miles outside Frankfurt. On the way in the driver said that the city had been eighty percent destroyed. He hadn't exaggerated. As we turned into the Mainzer Landstrasse, we saw nothing but gutted buildings on either side. We continued up the Taunus Anlage and I recognized the Opera House ahead. At first I thought it was undamaged. Then I saw that the roof was gone,' and only the outer walls remained. Most of the buildings were like that. This was just the shell of a city.

Our first stop was SHAEF headquarters, newly established in the vast I. G. Farben building which, either by accident or design, was completely undamaged. There we got another car to take us to Bad Homburg.

The little resort town where the fashionable world of Edward VII's day had gone to drink the waters and enjoy the mineral baths consisted mostly of hotels. Some of them were occupied by our troops. Others were being used as hospitals for wounded German soldiers. The big Kurhaus had received a direct hit, but the rest of the buildings appeared to be undamaged.

At ECAD headquarters we were assigned a billet in the Grand Hotel Parc. That sounded pretty snappy to us—another Royal Monceau, maybe. . The billeting officer must have guessed our thoughts, because he shook his head glumly and said, " 'Tain't anything special. Don't get your hopes up."

It was nice of him to have prepared us for the rat hole which was the Grand Hotel Parc. This shabby structure, built around three sides of a narrow courtyard, had an air of vanished refinement about it, but it could hardly have rated a star in Baedeker. Yet it must have had a certain cachet fifty years ago, for in the entrance hallway hung a white marble plaque. Its dim gold letters told us that Bismarck's widow had spent her declining years "in peaceful happiness beneath this hospitable roof."

Our room was on the fourth floor. The stairs, reminiscent of a lighthouse, might have been designed for a mountain goat. We thought we had struck the ultimate in drabness at the Rue Berthier, but this was worse. The room itself was worthy of its approach. When I opened the big wardrobe I half expected a body to fall out. Two sofas masquerading as beds occupied corners by the window. The window gave onto the dingy courtyard. We silently made up our beds with Army blankets and sprinkled them lavishly with DDT powder.

"Do you suppose there's such a thing as a bathroom?" Craig asked.

"I'd sooner expect to find one in an igloo," I said. "Maybe there's a pump or a trough somewhere out in back. Why don't you go and see?"

When he returned fifteen minutes later he was in high spirits. "There's a bathroom all right and it's got hot water," he said, "but you have to be a combination of Theseus and Daniel Boone to find it. Come along, I'll show you the way."

It was clever of him to find it a second time. I took a piece of red crayon with me and marked little arrows on the walls to show which turns to make. They were a timesaver to us during the next couple days.

After breakfast the next morning, we telephoned 12th Army Group Headquarters in Wiesbaden and talked with Lieutenant George Stout, USNR, who, with Captain Bancel La Farge, was in charge of the advance office of MFA&A in Germany. Stout suggested that we come on over. It was a pleasant drive along the Autobahn, with the blue Taunus mountains in the distance. Parts of Wiesbaden had been badly mauled, but the destruction was negligible compared with Frankfurt. Although many buildings along the main streets had been hit, the colonnaded Kurhaus, now a Red Cross Club, was intact. So was the Opera House.

We found George on the top floor of a dingy building in the center of the town. I hadn't seen him for fifteen years but he hadn't changed. His face was a healthy brown, his eyes were as keen and his teeth as dazzlingly white as ever. George was in his middle forties. His oldest boy was in the Navy but George didn't look a day over thirty. The Roberts Commission had played in luck when they had got him. Of course he was an obvious choice— tops in his field, the technical care and preservation of pictures. He was known and respected throughout the world for his brilliant research work at Harvard, where he presided over the laboratory of the Fogg Museum.

"Bancel's got jobs lined up for you fellows, but I think he'd like to tell you about them himself," George said. "He ought to be back tonight."

"Can't you tell us in a general way what they are?" I asked.

"I think one of them is going to be in Frankfurt and the other will probably be in Munich. You see, all the stuff from the Merkers mine is in the vaults of the Reichsbank at Frankfurt and it ought to be moved to a place where it can be permanently stored."

The "stuff" he referred to was the enormous collection of paintings and sculpture—comprising the principal treasures of the Berlin museums—which George himself had brought out of the Merkers mine in Thuringia. He had carried out the operation virtually singlehanded and in the face of extraordinary difficulties just before the end of hostilities.

"As for Munich," he continued, "repositories are springing up like mushrooms all through Bavaria. Most of it is loot and we're going to have to set up some kind of depot where we can put the things until they can be returned to the countries from which the Nazis stole them."

"What are your plans?" I asked.

"Well, if the trucks show up," he said, "I want to get started for Siegen this afternoon. That's in Westphalia. It's another mine— copper, not salt—and it's full of things from the Rhineland museums. I've got to take them up to Marburg. We have two good depots there."

We lunched with George and then returned to Bad Homburg. There wasn't anything for us to do but wait around until we heard from Captain La Farge. To fill in the time we took our German books and spent the afternoon studying in the Kurpark.

The telephone was ringing in the entrance lobby as we walked in at five. It was Captain La Farge. He had just returned and wanted to see us at once. I said I didn't know whether we could get transportation. He chuckled and said, "Tell them a general wants to see you." Craig and I dashed over to the Transportation Office and tried it out. It worked. So, for the second time that day, we found ourselves on the road to Wiesbaden.

Captain La Farge was waiting for us in the office where we had seen George that morning. He was a tall, slender man in his early forties. With a high-domed head and a long, rather narrow face, he was the classic New Englander. His eyes were hazel and, at that first meeting, very weary. But he had one of the most ingratiating smiles and one of the most pleasant voices I had ever heard. He reminded me of an early Copley portrait.

Without much preamble he launched into a detailed explanation of the plans he had for us.

"I want you to take over the Frankfurt job," he said to me, "and I am sending you down to Munich, Smyth. As George probably told you, we've got to set up two big depots. The one in Frankfurt will be mainly for German-owned art which is now coming in from repositories all over this part of Germany. The one in Munich will be chiefly for loot, though there will be German-owned things down in Bavaria too. Both jobs are equally interesting, equally important and, above all, equally urgent."

We were to get started without delay. Craig would be attached to the Regional Military Government office in Munich, I to the Military Government Detachment in Frankfurt. Captain La Farge suggested that I investigate the possibility of requisitioning the university buildings for a depot, and advised Craig to consider one of the large Nazi party buildings in Munich which he had been 'told was available.

On the way home that night Craig and I compared notes on our new assignments. I was frankly envious of Craig, not only because there was something alluring about all that loot, but because I loved Munich and the picturesque country around it. In turn,

Craig thought I had drawn a fascinating job—one that involved handling the wonderful riches of Berlin's "Kaiser Friedrich," admittedly one of the world's greatest museums.

The following morning we parted on the steps of the Grand Parc Hotel. Craig took off first, in a jeep with trailer attached, a crusty major for his companion. Half an hour later a jeep appeared for me. On the way over to Frankfurt I thought about the experiences of the past three weeks. It had been fun sharing them with Craig and I wished that we might have continued this odyssey together. I didn't realize how soon our paths were to cross again.

∾ 2 ∾

ASSIGNED TO FRANKFURT

The Military Goverment Detachment had its headquarters in a gray stone building behind the Opera House. It was one of the few in the city that had suffered relatively little damage. I reported to the Executive Officer, a white-haired major named James Franklin. After I had explained the nature of the work I was expected to do, he took me around to the office of Lieutenant Julius Buchman, the Education and Religious Affairs Officer, who had also the local MFA&A problems as part of his duties. Buchman couldn't have been more pleasant, and said he'd do everything he could to help. There was an air of quiet good humor about him that I liked at once. I learned that he was an architect by profession and had studied at the Bauhaus in Dessau before the war. He spoke fluent German. I told him that first of all I'd like to get settled, so he guided me to Captain Wyman Ooley, the Billeting Officer.

Ooley was a happy-go-lucky fellow, the only Billeting Officer I ever met who was always cheerful. He had been a schoolteacher in Arkansas. Together we drove out to the residential section where a group of houses had been set aside for the Military Government officers. This part of the city had not been heavily bombed and each one of the houses had a pretty garden.

"I'll tell you, I've got a real nice room in that house over there," he said, pointing to a gray stucco house partly screened by a row of trees.

"But it's for lieutenant colonels. It's empty right now, but I might have to throw you out later." Thinking that lieutenant colonels would be very likely to have ideas about good plumbing, I quickly said I'd take the chance.

The front door was locked. Ooley called, "Lucienne!" One of the upper windows was instantly flung open and a woman, dustcloth in hand, leaned out, waved and disappeared. A moment later she reappeared at the front door. Lucienne, all smiles, was as French as the tricolor. Ooley explained in pidgin French, with gestures, that I was to have a room on the second floor, wished me luck and departed. Lucienne bustled up to the second floor chattering away at a great rate, expressing surprise and delight that I was "officier de la Marine" and also taking considerable satisfaction in having recognized my branch of the service.

She threw open a door and then dashed off to the floor above, still chattering and gesticulating. I was left alone to contemplate the splendor before me—an enormous, airy bedroom looking out on a garden filled with scarlet roses. This couldn't be true. Even lieutenant colonels didn't deserve this. The room had cream-colored walls, paneled and decorated with chinoiserie designs. A large chest of drawers and a low table were decorated in the same manner. In one corner was an inviting chaise longue, covered in rose brocade. Along the end wall stood the bed—complete with sheets and a pillow. The built-in wardrobe had full-length mirrors which reflected the tall French windows and the garden beyond.

As I stood there trying to take it all in, Lucienne appeared again. With her was a dapper little fellow whom she introduced as her husband, René. He acknowledged the introduction and then solemnly introduced Lucienne. After this bit of mock formality, he explained that he and Lucienne had charge of all the houses in the block. If anything was not to my liking I was to let them know and it would be righted at once.

Further conversation revealed that the two of them had been deported from Paris early in 1941 and been obliged to remain in Frankfurt, working for the Germans, ever since. All through the bombings, I asked? But of course, and they had been too terrible. During one of the worst raids they had been imprisoned in the bomb shelter. The falling stones had blocked the exit. They had had to remain under the ground for forty-eight hours. They had been made deaf by the noise, yes, for two months. And the concussion had made them bleed from the nose and the ears. I asked if they expected to go back to Paris. Yes, of course, but they were in no hurry. It was very nice in Germany, now that the Americans were there. With that they left me to unpack and get settled.

When I had finished, I decided to explore a bit. There were two other bedrooms on the second floor. Neat labels on the doors indicated that they were occupied by lieutenant colonels. There were two other doors at the end of the hall. Neither one was labeled, so I peered in. They were the bathrooms. And what bathrooms! Marble floors, tiled walls, double washbasins and built-in tubs. Although it was only the middle of the morning, I had to sample one of those magnificent tubs. And as a kind of tribute to all this elegance, I felt constrained to discard my khakis and put on blues.

Captain La Farge had stressed the urgency of setting up an art depot, so the next ten days were given over to that project. Buchman generously shelved his own work to help me with it. Together we inspected" the University of Frankfurt. The newest of the German universities, it had opened its doors at the outbreak of the first World War. The main administration building, an imposing structure of red sandstone, had been badly damaged by incendiaries but could be repaired. It would be a big job, but we could worry about that later. The first step was to have it allocated for our use. That had to be done through the proper Army "channels." Buchman steered me through. Then we had to obtain an estimate of the repairs. It took three days to get one from the university architect. It was thorough but impractical and had to be completely revised. We took the revised estimate to the Army Engineers and asked them to make an inspection of the building and check the architect's figures. They were swamped with work. It would be a week before they could do anything. I said it was a high priority job, hoping to speed things along. But the Engineers had heard that one before. We'd have to be patient.

Charlie Kuhn and Colonel Webb had moved up to Frankfurt and were established at SHAEF headquarters in the I. G. Farben building.

Their office was only a few blocks from mine, and during my negotiations for the use of the university building I was in daily communication with them.

While waiting for the Engineers to make the promised inspection, I made a couple of field trips with Buchman. The first was a visit to Schloss Kronberg, a few kilometers from Frankfurt. It was a picturesque medieval castle, unoccupied since the first part of the seventeenth century. Valuable archives were stored there. We wanted to see if they were in good condition, and also to make sure that the place had been posted with the official "Off Limits" signs.

A flock of geese scattered before us as we drove up to the entrance at the end of a narrow, winding road. We knocked on the door of the caretaker's cottage and explained the purpose of our visit to the old fellow who timidly appeared with a large bunch of keys. He limped ahead of us across the cobbled courtyard, and we waited while he fitted one of the keys into the lock.

A wave of heavy perfume issued from the dark room as the door swung open. When our eyes had become accustomed to the dim light, we saw that we were in the original *Waffenraum* of the castle. But, in addition to the clustered weapons affixed to the walls, there were five sarcophagi in the center of the vaulted room. Around them stood vases filled with spring flowers. On the central sarcophagus rested a spiked helmet of the first World War. The others were unadorned.

The old caretaker explained that the central tomb was that of the Landgraf of Hesse who had died thirty years ago. Those on either side contained the remains of his two sons who had likewise died in the first World War. The other two coffins were those of the elder son's wife and of a princess of Baden who had been killed in one of the air raids on Frankfurt in 1944. All five sarcophagi had originally stood in the little chapel across the courtyard. It had been destroyed by an incendiary bomb the winter before.

We left this funerary chamber with a feeling of relief and continued our inspection of the castle. A winding ramp in one of the towers led to the floors above. From the top story we had a superb view of the broad Frankfurt plain spread out below. The caretaker told us he had watched the bombings from that vantage point. The great banqueting hall, with a musicians' gallery at one end, had been emptied of its original furnishings and was now a jumble of papers stacked in piles of varying heights. These were part of the Frankfurt archives. Others were stored in two rooms on the ground floor. All of the rooms were dry and weatherproof, so there was nothing further to be done about them for the present. There was no place in Frankfurt as yet to which they could be moved. "Off Limits" signs had been posted. They would discourage souvenir hunters from unauthorized delving.

On our way back to the car the caretaker told us that the castle still belonged to Margarethe, Landgrafin of Hesse, the youngest sister of the last Kaiser. Although she was now in her seventies, she came every day to put fresh flowers beside the tombs of her husband and her two sons. She lived at a newer castle, Schloss Friedrichshof, only a few kilometers away. He apparently didn't know that Schloss Friedrichshof had been taken over by the Army and was being used as an officers' country club. The old Landgrafin was living modestly in one of the small houses on the property. Her scapegrace son, Prince Philip, as I learned later, had played an active role in the artistic depredations of the Nazi ringleaders. I was to hear more of the Hesse family before the end of the year.

A second excursion took us still farther afield. On an overcast morning two days later, Buchman, Charlie Kuhn, Captain Rudolph Vassalle (who was the Public Safety Officer of the detachment) and I set out in the little Opel sedan which had been assigned the MFA&A office. We struck out to the east of Frankfurt on the road to Gelnhausen. We stopped at this pleasant little town with its lovely, early Gothic church and went through the formality of obtaining clearance from the local Military Government Detachment to make an inspection in that area.

From there we continued by a winding secondary road which led us through increasingly hilly country to Bad Brückenau. Our mission there was twofold: Captain Vassalle wanted to track down a young Nazi officer, reportedly a member of the SS, and to find a warehouse said to contain valuable works of art. I had gathered from Buchman that many such reports petered out on investigation. Still, there was always the chance that the one you dismissed as of no importance would turn out to be something worth while.

After making several inquiries, we eventually located a small house on the edge of town. In response to our insistent hammering, the door of the house was finally opened by a pallid young man probably in his late twenties. If he was the object of the captain's search he had certainly undergone a remarkable metamorphosis, for he bore little resemblance to the dapper officer of whom Captain Vassalle carried a photograph for identification. The captain seemed satisfied that he was the man. So leaving them in conversation, the three of us followed up the business of the reported works of art. The other two occupants of the house— an old man and a young woman who may have been the wife of the man who had opened the door—responded to our questions with alacrity and took us to the cellar. There we were shown a cache of pictures, all of them unframed and none of them of any value. They appeared to be what the old man claimed—their own property, brought to Bad Brückenau when they had left Frankfurt to escape the bombings. In any case, we made a listing of the canvases, identifying them as best we could and making notations of the sizes, and also admonishing the couple not to remove them from the premises.

After that the old man took us across the back yard to a large modern bam which was heavily padlocked. Once inside he unshuttered a row of windows along one side of the main, groundfloor room. It was jammed to the ceiling with every conceivable item of household furnishings: chairs, tables, beds, bedding, kitchen utensils and porcelain. But no pictures. We poked around enough to satisfy ourselves that first appearances were not deceiving. They weren't, so, having made certain that the old fellow, who claimed to be merely the custodian of these things, understood the regulations forbidding their removal, we picked up Captain Vassalle.

He had completed his interrogation of the alleged SS officer and placed him under house arrest.

Our next objective was an old Schloss which, according to our map, was still a good hour's drive to the northeast. As it was nearly noon and we were all hungry, we decided to investigate the possibilities of food in the neighborhood. On our way back through Bad Brückenau we stopped at the office of a small detachment of troops and asked where we could get some lunch. The hospitable second lieutenant on duty in the little stucco building, which had once been part of the Kurhaus establishment, gave us directions to the sprawling country hotel, high up above the town, where his outfit was quartered. He said that he would telephone ahead to warn the mess sergeant of our arrival.

For a little way we followed along the Sinn, which flows through the grassy valley in which Bad Brückenau nestles. Then we began to mount sharply and, for the next fifteen minutes, executed a series of hairpin turns and ended abruptly beside a rambling structure which commanded a wonderful view of the valley and the wooded hills on the other side. Our hosts were a group of friendly young fellows who seemed delighted to have the monotony of their rural routine interrupted by our visit. They asked Charlie and me the usual question—what was the Navy doing in the middle of Germany—and got our stock reply: we are planning to dig a canal from the North Sea to the Mediterranean.

We had a heavy downpour during lunch, and we waited for the rain to let up before starting out again. Then we took the winding road down into town, crossed the river and drove up into the hills on the other side of the valley. An hour's drive brought us to upland meadow country and a grove of handsome lindens. At the end of a long double row of these fine trees stood Schloss Rossbach. "Castle" was a rather pompous name for the big seventeenth century country house with whitewashed walls and heavily barred ground-floor windows.

We were received by the owners, a Baron Thüngen and his wife, and explained that we had come to examine the condition of the works of art, which, according to our information, had been placed there for safekeeping. They ushered us up to a comfortable sitting room on the second floor where we settled down to wait while the baroness went off to get the keys. In the meantime we had a few words with her husband. His manner was that of the haughty landed proprietor, and he looked the part. He was a big, burly man in his sixties. He was dressed in rough tweeds and wore a matching hat, adorned with a bushy "shaving brush," which he hadn't bothered to remove indoors. That may have been unintentional, but I idly wondered if it weren't deliberate discourtesy and rather wished that I had kept my own cap on. I wished also that I could have matched his insolent expression, but thought it unlikely because I was frankly enjoying the obvious distaste which our visit was causing die old codger.

However, his attitude was almost genial compared with that of his waspish wife, who reappeared about that time, armed with a huge hoop from which a great lot of keys jangled. The baroness, who was much younger than her husband, had very black hair and discontented dark eyes. She spoke excellent English, without a trace of accent. I felt reasonably sure that she was not German but couldn't guess her nationality. It turned out that she was from the Argentine. She was a sullen piece and made no effort to conceal her irritation at our intrusion. She explained that neither she nor her husband had anything to do with the things stored there; that, in fact, it was a great inconvenience having to put up with them.

She had asked the young woman who knew all about them to join us.

The young woman in question arrived and was completely charming. She took no apparent notice of the baroness' indifference, which was that of a mistress toward a servant whom she scarcely knew. Her fresh, open manner cleared the atmosphere instantly. She introduced herself as Frau Holzinger, wife of the director of Frankfurt's most famous museum, the Staedelsches Kunstinstitut, Because of conditions in Frankfurt, and more particularly because their house had been requisitioned by the American military authorities, she had come to Schloss Rossbach with her two young children. Country life, she continued, was better for the youngsters and, besides, her husband had thought that she might help with the things stored at the castle. I had met Dr. Holzinger when I went one day to have a look at what remained of the museum, so his wife and I hit it off at once. I was interested to learn that she was Swiss and a licensed physician. She smilingly suggested that we make a tour of the castle and she would show us what was there.

The first room to be inspected was a library adjoining the sitting room in which we had been waiting. Here we found a quantity of excellent French Impressionist paintings, all from the permanent collection of the Staedel, and a considerable number of fine Old Master drawings. Most of these were likewise the property of the museum, but a few—I remember one superb Rembrandt sketch— appeared to have come from Switzerland. Those would, of course, have to be looked into later, to determine their exact origin and how they came to be on loan at the museum. But for the moment we were concerned primarily with storage conditions and the problem of security. In another room we found an enormous collection of books, the library of one of the

Frankfurt museums. In a third we encountered an array of medieval sculpture—saints of all sizes and description, some of carved wood, others of stone, plain or polychromed. These too were of museum origin.

The last storage room was below ground, a vast, cavernous chamber beneath the house. Here was row upon row of pictures, stacked in two tiers down the center of the room and also along two sides. From what we could make of them in the poor light, they were not of high quality. During the summer months they would be all right in this underground room, but we thought that the place would be very damp in the winter. Frau Holzinger assured us that this was so and that the pictures should be removed before the bad weather set in.

The baroness chipped in at this point and affably agreed with that idea, undoubtedly happy to further any scheme which involved getting rid of these unwelcome objects. She also warned us that the castle was far from safe as it was, what with roving bands of Poles all over the countryside. As we indicated that we were about to take our leave, she elaborated upon this theme, declaring that their very lives were in danger, that every night she and her husband could hear prowlers in the park. Since they—as Germans—were not allowed to have firearms, they would be at the mercy of these foreign ruffians if they should succeed in breaking into the castle. By this time we were all pretty fed up with the whining baroness. As we turned to go, Charlie Kuhn, eyeing her coldly, asked, "Who brought those Poles here in the first place, madam? We didn't."

To our delight, the weather had cleared and the sun was shining. Ahead of us on the roadway, the foliage of the lindens made a gaily moving pattern. Our work for the day was done and we still had half the afternoon. I got out the map and, after making some quick calculations, proposed that we could take in Würzburg and still get back to Frankfurt at a reasonable hour. We figured out that, with the extra jerry can of gas we had with us, we could just about make it. We would be able to fill up at Würzburg for the return trip. So, instead of continuing on the road back to Bad Brückenau, we turned south in the direction of Karlstadt.

It was pleasant to be traveling a good secondary road instead of' the broad, characterless Autobahn, on which there were no unexpected turns, no picturesque villages. There was little traffic, so we made very good time. In half an hour we had threaded our way through Karlstadt-on-the-Main. In this part of Franconia the Main is a capricious river, winding casually in and out of the gently undulating hills. A little later we passed the village of Veitschochheim where the Prince-Bishops of Würzburg had an elaborate country house during the eighteenth century. The house still stands, and its gardens, with a tiny lake and grottoes in the Franco-Italian manner, remain one of the finest examples of garden planning of that day. As we drove by we were glad that this inviting spot had not attracted the attention of our bombers.

Alas, such was not the case with Würzburg, as we realized the minute we reached its outskirts! The once-gracious city, surely one of the most beautiful in all Germany, was an appalling sight. Its broad avenues were now lined with nothing but the gaping, ruined remnants of the stately eighteenth century buildings which had lent the city an air of unparalleled distinction and consistency of design. High on its hilltop above the Main, the mellow walls of the medieval fortress of Marienberg caught the rays of the late afternoon sun. From the distance, the silhouette of that vast structure appeared unchanged, but the proud city of the Prince-Bishops which it overlooked was laid low.

We drove slowly along streets not yet cleared of rubble, until we came to the Residenz, the great palace of the Prince-Bishops, those lavish patrons of the arts to whom the city owed so much of its former grandeur. This magnificent building, erected in the first half of the eighteenth century by the celebrated baroque architect, Johann Balthasar Neumann, for two Prince-Bishops of the Schönborn family, was now a ghost palace, its staring glassless windows and blackened walls pathetic vestiges of its pristine splendor.

We walked up to the main entrance wondering if it could really be true that the crowning glory of the Residenz—the glorious ceiling by Tiepolo, representing Olympus and the Four Continents— was, as we had been told, still intact. With misgivings we turned left across the entrance hall to the Treppenhaus and mounted the grand staircase. We looked up and there it was—as dazzling and majestically beautiful as ever—that incomparable fresco, the masterpiece of the last great Italian painter. Someone with a far greater gift for words than I may be able to convey the exaltation one experiences on seeing that ceiling, not just for the first time but at any time. I can't. It leaves artist and layman alike absolutely speechless. I think that, if I had to choose one great work of art, it would be this ceiling in the Residenz. You can have even the Sistine ceiling. I'll take the Tiepolo.

For the next half hour we examined every comer of it. Aside from a few minor discolorations, the result of water having seeped through the lower side of the vault just above the cornice, the fresco was undamaged. Considering the destruction throughout the rest of the building, I could not understand how this portion of the palace could be in such a remarkable state of preservation. The explanation was an interesting example of how good can sometimes come out of evil. Some forty years ago, as I remember the story, there was a fire in the Residenz. The wooden roof over a large portion, if not all, of the building was burned away. When it came to replacing the roof, the city fathers decided it would be a prudent idea to cover the part above the Tiepolo with steel and concrete. This was done, and consequently, when the terrible conflagration of March 1945 swept Würzburg—following the single raid of twenty minutes which destroyed the city—the fresco was spared. As we wandered through other rooms of the Residenz— the Weisser Saal with its elaborate stucco ornamentation and the sumptuous Kaiser Saal facing the garden, once classic examples of the Rococo—I wished that those city fathers had gone a little farther with their steel and concrete.

We stopped briefly to examine the chapel in the south wing. Here, miraculously enough, there had been relatively little damage, but the caretaker expressed concern over the condition of the roof and said that if it weren't repaired before the heavy rains the ceiling would be lost. Knowing how hard it was to obtain building materials for even the most historic monuments when people didn't have a roof over their heads, we couldn't reassure him with much conviction.

The spectacle of ruined Würzburg had a depressing effect upon us, so we weren't very talkative on our way back to Frankfurt. We passed through only one town of any size, Aschaffenburg, which, like Würzburg, had suffered severe damage. Although I had not been long in Germany and had seen but few of her cities, I was beginning to realize that the reports of the Allied air attacks had not been exaggerated. I was ready to believe that there were only small towns and villages left in this ravaged country.

One morning Charlie Kuhn rang up to say that I should meet him at the Reichsbank early that afternoon. This was something I had been looking forward to for some time, the chance to look at the wonderful things from the Merkers mine which were temporarily stored there. With Charlie came two members of the MFA&A organization whom I had not seen since Versailles and then only briefly. They had been stationed at Barbizon, as part of the Allied Group Control Council for Germany (usually referred to simply as "Group CC") the top level policy-making body as opposed to SHAJEF, which dealt with the operational end of things. These two gentlemen were John Nicholas Brown, who had come over to Germany with the assimilated rank of colonel as General Eisenhower's adviser on cultural affairs, and Major Mason Hammond, in civilian life professor of the Classics at Harvard.

It had been decided, now that we were about to acquire a permanent depot in which to store the treasures, to make one Monuments officer responsible for the entire collection. By this transfer of custody, the Property Control Officer in whose charge the things were at present, could be relieved of that responsibility. Major Hammond had with him a paper designating me as custodian. Knowing in a general way what was stored in the bank, I felt that I was on the point of being made a sort of director, pro tem, of the Kaiser Friedrich Museum.

The genial Property Control Officer, Captain William Dunn, was all smiles at the prospect of turning his burden over to someone else. But before this transfer could be made, a complete check of every item was necessary. Major Hammond knew just how he wanted this done. I was to have two assistants, who could come over the next morning from his office in Hoechst, twenty minutes from Frankfurt. The three of us, in company with Captain Dunn, would make the inventory.

We wandered through the series of rooms in which the things were stored. In the first room were something like four hundred pictures lined up against the wall in a series of rows. In two adjoining rooms were great wooden cases piled one above another. In a fourth were leather-bound boxes containing the priceless etchings, engravings and woodcuts from the Berlin Print Room. Still another room was filled with cases containing the renowned Egyptian collections. It was rumored that one of them held the world-famous head of Queen Nefertiti, probably the best known and certainly the most beloved single piece of all Egyptian sculpture. It had occupied a place of special honor in the Berlin Museum, in a gallery all to itself.

Still other rooms were jammed with cases of paintings and sculpture of the various European schools. In a series of smaller alcoves were heaped huge piles of Oriental rugs and rare fabrics. And last, one enormous room with bookshelves was filled from floor to ceiling with some thirty thousand volumes from the Berlin Patent Office. Quite separate and apart from all these things was a unique collection of ecclesiastical vessels of gold and silver, the greater part of them looted from Poland. These extremely precious objects were kept in a special vault on the floor above.

Captain Dunn brought out a thick stack of papers. It was the complete inventory. Major Hammond said that the two officers who would help with the checking were a Captain Edwin Rae and a WAC lieutenant named Standen. Aside from having heard that Rae had been a student of Charlie Kuhn's at Harvard, I knew nothing about him. But the name Standen rang a bell: was she, by any chance, Edith Standen who had been curator of the Widener Collection? Major Hammond smilingly replied, "The same." I had known her years ago in Cambridge where we had taken Professor Sachs' course in Museum Administration at the same time. I remembered her as a tall, dark, distinguished-looking English girl. To be exact, she was half English: her father had been a British Army officer, her mother a Bostonian. Recalling her very reserved manner and her scholarly tastes, I found it difficult to imagine her in uniform.

Early the following morning, I met my cohorts at the entrance to the Reichsbank. I was pleasantly surprised to find that Captain Rae was an old acquaintance if not an old friend. He also had been around the Fogg Museum in my time. Edith looked very smart in her uniform. She had a brisk, almost jovial manner which was not to be reconciled with her aloof and dignified bearing in the marble halls of the Widener house at Elkins Park. We hunted up Captain Dunn and set to work. Our first task was to count and check off the paintings stacked in the main room. We got through them with reasonable speed, refraining with some difficulty from pausing to admire certain pictures we particularly fancied. Then we tackled the Oriental rugs, and that proved to be a thoroughly thankless and arduous task. We had a crew of eight PWs—prisoners of war—to help us spread the musty carpets out on the floor. Owing to the fact that the smaller carpets—in some cases they were hardly more than fragments—had been rolled up inside larger ones, we ended with nearly a hundred more items than the inventory called for. That troubled Captain Dunn a bit, but I told him that it didn't matter so long as we were over. We'd have to start worrying only if we came out short. By five o'clock we were' tired and dirty and barely a third of the way through with the job.

The next day we started in on the patent records. There had been a fire in the mine where the records were originally stored. Many of them were slightly charred, and all of them# had been impregnated with smoke. When we had finished counting the whole thirty thousand, we smelled just the way they did. As a matter of fact we hadn't wanted to assume responsibility for these records in the first place. Certainly they had nothing to do with art. But Major Hammond had felt that they properly fell to us as archives. And of course they were archives of a sort.

On the morning of the third day, as I was about to leave my office for the Reichsbank, I had a phone call from Charlie Kuhn. He asked me how the work was coming along and then, in a guarded voice, said that something unexpected had turned up and that he might have to send me away for a few days. He told me he couldn't talk about it on the telephone, and anyway, it wasn't definite. He'd probably know by afternoon. I was to call him later. This was hardly the kind of conversation to prepare one for a humdrum day of taking inventory, even if one were counting real treasure. And for a person with my curiosity, the morning's work was torture.

When I called Charlie after lunch he was out but had left word that I was to come to his office at two o'clock. When I got there he was sitting at his desk. He looked up from the dispatch he was reading and said with a rueful smile, "Tom, I am going to send you out on a job I'd give my eyeteeth to have for myself." Then he explained that certain developments had suddenly made it necessary to step up the work of evacuating art repositories down in Bavaria and in even more distant areas. For the first time in my life I knew what was meant by the expression "my heart jumped a beat"—for that was exactly what happened to mine! No wonder Charlie was envious. This sounded like the real thing.

Charlie told me that I was to fly down to Munich the next morning and that I would probably be gone about ten days. To save time he had already had my orders cut. All I had to do was to pick them up at the AG office. I was to report to Third Army Headquarters and get in touch with George Stout as soon as possible. Charlie didn't know just where I'd find George. He was out in the wilds somewhere. As a matter of fact he wasn't too sure about the exact location of Third Army Headquarters. A new headquarters was being established and the only information he had was that it would be somewhere in or near Munich. The name, he said, would be "Lucky Rear" and I would simply have to make inquiries and be guided by signs posted along the streets.

I asked Charlie what I should do about die completion of the inventory at the Reichsbank, and also about the impending report from the Corps of Engineers on the University of Frankfurt building. He suggested that I leave the former in Captain Rae's hands and the latter with Lieutenant Buchman. Upon my return I could take up where I had left off.

That evening I threw my things together, packing only enough clothes to see me through the next ten days. Not knowing where I would be billeted I took the precaution of including my blankets. Even at that my luggage was compact and light, which was desirable as I was traveling by air.

MUNICH AND THE BEGINNING OF FIELD WORK

The next morning I was up before six and had early breakfast. It was a wonderful day for the trip, brilliantly clear. The corporal in our office took me out to the airfield, the one near Hanau where Craig Smyth and I had landed weeks before. It was going to be fun to see Craig again and find out what he had been up to since we had parted that morning in Bad Homburg. The drive to the airfield took about forty-five minutes. There was a wait of half an hour at the field, and it was after ten when we took off in our big C-47. We flew over little villages with red roofs, occasionally a large town—but none that I could identify—and now and then a silvery lake.

Just before we reached Munich, someone said, "There's Dachau." Directly below us, on one side of a broad sweep of dark pine trees, we saw a group of low buildings and a series of fenced-in enclosures. On that sunny morning the place looked deserted and singularly peaceful. Yet only a few weeks before it had been filled with the miserable victims of Nazi brutality.

In another ten minutes we landed on the dusty field of the principal Munich airport. Most of the administration buildings had a slightly battered look but were in working order. It was a welcome relief to take refuge from the blazing sunshine in the cool hallway of the main building. The imposing yellow brick lobby was decorated with painted shields of the different German states or "Länder." The arms of Bavaria, Saxony, Hesse-Nassau and the rest formed a colorful frieze around the walls.

A conveyance of some kind was scheduled to leave for town in a few minutes. Meanwhile there were sandwiches and coffee for the plane passengers. By the time we had finished, a weapons carrier had pulled up before the entrance. Several of us climbed into its dust-encrusted interior. It took me a little while to get my bearings as we drove toward Munich. I had spotted the familiar pepper-pot domes of the Frauenkirche from the air but had recognized no other landmark of the flat, sprawling city which I had known well before the war.

It was not until we turned into the broad Prinz Regenten-Strasse that I knew exactly where I was. As we drove down this handsome avenue, I got a good look at a long, colonnaded building of white stone. The roof was draped with what appeared to be an enormous, dark green fishnet. The billowing scallops of the net flapped about the gleaming comice of the building. It was the Haus der Deutschen Kunst, the huge exhibition gallery dedicated by Hitler in the middle thirties to the kind of art of which he approved—an art in which there was no place for untrammeled freedom of expression, only the pictorial and plastic representation of all the Nazi regime stood for. The dangling fishnet was part of the elaborate camouflage. I judged from the condition of the building that the net had admirably served its purpose.

In a moment we rounded the corner by the Prinz Karl Palais. Despite the disfiguring coat of ugly olive paint which covered its classic fagade, it had not escaped the bombs. The little palace, where Mussolini had stayed, had a hollow, battered look and the formal garden behind it was a waste of furrowed ground and straggling weeds. We turned left into the wide Ludwig-Strasse and came to a grinding halt beside a bleak gray building whose walls were pockmarked with artillery fire. I asked our driver if this were Lucky Rear headquarters and was told curtly that it wasn't, but that it was the end of the line. It was MP headquarters and I'd have to see if they'd give me a car to take me to my destination, which the driver said was " 'way the hell" on the other side of town.

Before going inside I looked down the street to the left. The familiar old buildings were still standing, but they were no longer the trim, cream-colored structures which had once given that part of the city such a clean, orderly air. Most of them were burned out. Farther along on the right, the Theatinerkirche was masked with scaffolding. At the end of the street the Feldherren-Halle, Ludwig I's copy of the Loggia dei Lanzi, divested of its statuary, reared its columns in the midst of the desolation.

It was gray and cool in the rooms of the MP building, but the place was crowded. Soldiers were everywhere and things seemed to be at sixes and sevens. After making several inquiries and being passed from one desk to another, I finally got hold of a brisk young sergeant to whom I explained my troubles. At first he said there wasn't a chance of getting a ride out to Lucky Rear. Every jeep was tied up and would be for hours. They had just moved into Munich and hadn't got things organized yet. Then all at once he relented and with a grin said, "Oh, you're Navy, aren't you? In that case I'll have to fix you up somehow. We can't have the Navy saying the Army doesn't co-operate."

He walked over to a window that looked down on the courtyard below, shouted instructions to someone and then told me I'd find a jeep and driver outside. "Think nothing of it, Lieutenant," he said in answer to my thanks. "Maybe I'll be wanting a ship to take me home one of these days before long. Have to keep on the good side of the Navy."

On my way out I gathered up my luggage from the landing below and climbed into the waiting jeep. We turned the comer and followed the Prinz Regenten-Strasse to the river. I noticed for the first time that a temporary track had been laid along one side. This had been done, the driver said, in order to cart away the rubble which had accumulated in the downtown section. We turned right and followed the Isar for several blocks, crossed to the left over the Ludwig bridge, then drove out the Rosenheimer-Strasse to the east for a distance of about three miles. Our destination was the enormous complex of buildings called the Reichszeugmeisterei, or Quartermaster Corps buildings, in which the rear echelon of General Patton's Third Army had just established its headquarters.

Even in the baking sunlight of that June day, the place had a cold, unfriendly appearance. We halted for identification at the entrance, and there I was introduced to Third Army discipline. One of the guards gave me a black look and growled, "Put your cap on." Startled by this burly order, J hastily complied and then experienced a feeling of extreme irritation at having been so easily cowed. I could at least have asked him to say "sir."

The driver, sensing my discomfiture, remarked good-naturedly, "You'll get used to that sort of thing around here, sir. They're very, very fussy now that the shooting's over. Seems like they don't have anything else to worry about, except enforcing a lot of regulations." This was my first sample of what I learned to call by its popular name, "chicken"—a prudent abbreviation for the exasperating rules and regulations one finds at an Army headquarters.

Third Army had its share of them—perhaps a little more than its share. But I didn't find that out all at once. It took me all of two days.

My driver let me out in front of the main building, over the central doorway of which the emblem of the Third Army was proudly displayed—a bold "A" inside a circle. The private at the information desk had never heard of the "Monuments, Fine Arts and Archives Section," but said that if it was a part of G-5 it would be on the fifth floor. I found the office of the Assistant Chief of Staff and was directed to a room at the end of a corridor at least two blocks long. I was told that the officer I should see was Captain Robert Posey. I knew that name from the reports I had studied at Versailles, as well as from a magazine article describing his discovery, months before, of some early frescoes in the little Romanesque church of Mont St. Martin which had been damaged by bombing. The article had been written by an old friend of mine, Lincoln Kirstein, who was connected with the MFA&A work in Europe.

When I opened the door of the MFA&A office, George Stout was standing in the middle of the room. The expression of surprise on his face changed to relief after he had read the letter I handed him from Charlie Kuhn.

"You couldn't have arrived at a more opportune time," he said. "I came down from Alt Aussee today to see Posey, but I just missed him. He left this morning for a conference in Frankfurt. I wanted to find out what had happened to the armed escort he promised me for my convoys. We're evacuating the mine and desperately shorthanded, so I've got to get back tonight. It's a six-hour drive."

"Charlie said you needed help. What do you want me to do?" I asked. I hoped he would take me along.

"I'd like to have you stay here until we get this escort problem straightened out. I was promised two half-tracks, but they didn't show up this morning. I've got a call in about them right now. It's three o'clock. I ought to make Salzburg by five-thirty. There'll surely be some word about the escort by that time, and I'll phone you from there."

Before he left, George introduced me to Lieutenant Colonel William Hamilton, the Assistant Chief of Staff, and explained to him that I had come down on special orders from SHAEF to help with the evacuation work. George told the colonel that I would be joining him at the mine as soon as Captain Posey returned and provided me with the necessary clearance. After we had left Colonel Hamilton's office, I asked George what he meant by "clearance." He laughed and said that I would have to obtain a written permit fr6m Posey before I could operate in Third Army territory. As Third Army's Monuments Officer, Posey had absolute jurisdiction in all matters pertaining to the fine arts in the area occupied by his Army. At that time it included a portion of Austria which later came under General Mark Clark's command.

"Don't worry," said George. "I'll have you at the mine in a few days, and you'll probably be sorry you ever laid eyes on the place."

I went back to the MFA&A office and was about to settle down at Captain Posey's vacant desk. I looked across to a corner of the room where a lanky enlisted man sat hunched up at a typewriter. It was Lincoln Kirstein, looking more than ever like a world-weary Rachmaninoff. Lincoln a private in the U. S. Army! What a far cry from the world of modem art and the ballet! He was thoroughly enjoying my astonishment.

"This is a surprise, but it explains a lot of things," I said, dragging a chair over to his desk. "So you are the Svengali of the Fine Arts here at Third Army."

"You mustn't say things like that around this headquarters," he said apprehensively.

During the next two hours we covered a lot of territory. First of all, I wanted to know why he was an enlisted man chained to a typewriter. With his extraordinary intelligence and wide knowledge of the Fine Arts, he could have been more useful as an officer. He said that he had applied for a commission and had been turned down. I was sorry I had brought up the subject, but knowing Lincoln's fondness for the dramatic I thought it quite possible that he had wanted to be able to say in later years that he had gone through the war as an enlisted man. He agreed that he could have been of greater service to the Fine Arts project as an officer. Then I asked him what his "boss"—he was to be mine too—was like. He said that Captain Posey, an architect in civilian life, had had a spectacular career during combat. In the face of almost insurmountable obstacles, such as lack of personnel and transportation and especially the lack of any real co-operation from the higher-ups, he had accomplished miracles. Now that the press was devoting more and more space to the work the Monuments officers were doing—the discovery of treasures in salt mines and so on— they were beginning to pay loving attention to Captain Posey around the headquarters.

I gathered from Lincoln that the present phase of our activities appealed to the captain less than the protection and repair of historic monuments under fire. If true, this was understandable enough. He was an architect. Why would he, except as a matter of general cultural interest, find work that lay essentially in the domain of a museum man particularly absorbing? It seemed reasonable to assume that Captain Posey would welcome museum men to shoulder a part of the burden. But I was to learn later that my assumption was not altogether correct.

Eventually I had to interrupt our conversation. It was getting late, and still no word about the escort vehicles. Lincoln told me where I would find the officer who was to have called George. He was Captain Blyth, a rough-and-ready kind of fellow, an ex-trooper from the state of Virginia. The outlook was not encouraging. No vehicles were as yet available. Finally, at six o'clock, he rang up to say that he wouldn't know anything before morning.

Lincoln returned from chow, I gave him the message in case George called while I was out and went down to eat. It was after eight when George telephoned. The connection from Salzburg was bad, and so was his temper when I told him I had nothing to report.

Lincoln usually spent his evenings at the office. That night we stayed till after eleven. Here and there he had picked up some fascinating German art books and magazines, all of them Nazi publications lavishly illustrated. They bore eloquent testimony to Hitler's patronage of the arts. The banality of the contemporary work in painting was stultifying—dozens of rosy-cheeked, buxom maidens and stalwart, brown-limbed youths reeking with "strength through joy," and acres of idyllic landscapes. The sculpture was better, though too often the tendency toward the colossal was tiresomely in evidence. It was in recording the art of the past, notably in the monographs dealing with the great monuments of the Middle Ages and the Baroque, that admirable progress had been made. I asked Lincoln enviously how he had got hold of these things. He answered laconically that he had "liberated" them.

Captain Blyth had good news for me the next morning. Two armored vehicles had left Munich for the mine. I gave the message to George when he called just before noon.

"They're a little late," he said. "Thanks to the fine co-operation of the 11th Armored Division, I am being taken care of from this end of the line. I'll try to catch your fellows in Salzburg and tell them to go back where they came from. I am sending you a letter by the next convoy. It's about a repository which ought to be evacuated right away. I can't give you any of the details over the phone without violating security regulations. As soon as Posey gets back, you ought to go to work on it. After that I want you to help me here."

After George had hung up, I asked Lincoln if he had any idea what repository George had in mind. Lincoln said it might be the monastery at Hohenfurth. It was in Czechoslovakia, just over the border from Austria. While we were discussing this possibility, Craig Smyth walked in.

As soon as he had recovered from the surprise of finding me at Captain Posey's desk, he explained the reason for his visit. Something had to be done right away about the building he was setting up as a collecting point. He had been promised a twenty-four-hour guard. He had been promised a barrier of barbed wire. So far, Third Army had failed to provide either one. A lot of valuable stuff had already been delivered to the building, and George was sending in more. He couldn't wait any longer.

"Let's have a talk with Colonel Hamilton," I said. As we walked down to the Assistant Chief of Staff's office, Craig told me that the buildings he had requisitioned were the ones Bancel La Farge had suggested when we saw him at Wiesbaden a month ago.

"Can't this matter wait until Captain Posey returns?" the colonel asked.

"I am afraid it can't, sir," said Craig. "As you know, the two buildings were the headquarters of the Nazi party. The Nazis meant to destroy them before Munich fell. Having failed to do so, I think it quite possible that they may still attempt it. Both buildings are honeycombed with underground passageways. Only this morning we located the exit of one of them. It was half a block from the building. We hadn't known of its existence before. The works of art stored in the building at present are worth millions of dollars. In the circumstances, I am not willing to accept the responsibility for what may happen to them. I must have guards or a barrier at once."

The colonel reached for the telephone and gave orders that a cordon of guards was to be placed on the buildings immediately. He made a second call, this time about the barbed wire. When he had finished he told Craig that the guard detail would report that afternoon; the barbed wire would be strung around the building the next morning. We thanked the colonel and returned to Posey's office.

We found two officers who had just come in from Dachau. They were waiting to see someone connected with Property Control. They had brought with them a flour sack filled with gold wedding rings; a large carton stuffed with gold teeth, bridgework, crowns and braces (in children's sizes) ; a sack containing gold coins (for the most part Russian) and American greenbacks. As we looked at these mementos of the concentration camp, I thought of the atrocity film I had seen at Versailles and wondered how anyone could believe that those pictures had been an exaggeration.

I went back with Craig to his office at the Königsplatz. The damage to Munich was worse than I had realized. The great Deutsches Museum by the river was a hollow-eyed specter, but sufficiently intact to house DPs. Aside from its twin towers, little was left of the Frauenkirche. The buildings lining the Brienner-Strasse had been blasted and burned. Along'the short block leading from the Carolinen Platz to the Königsplatz, the destruction was total: on the left stood the jagged remnants of the little villa Hitler had given D'Annunzio; on the right was a heap of rubble which had been the Braun Haus. But practically untouched were the two Ehrentempel—the memorials to the "martyrs" of the 1923 beer-hall "putsch." The colonnades were draped with the same kind of green fishnet that had been used to camouflage the Haus der Deutschen Kunst. The classic façades of the museums on either side of the square—the Glyptothek and the Neue Staatsgalerie— were intact. The buildings themselves were a shambles.

I followed Craig up the broad flight of steps to the entrance of the Verwaltungsbau, or Administration Building. It was three stories high, built of stone, and occupied almost an entire block. True to the Nazi boast, it looked as though it had been built to "last a thousand years." And it was so plain and massive that I didn't see how it could change much in that time. There was nothing here that could "grow old gracefully." The interior matched the exterior. There were two great central courts with marble stairs leading to the floor above.

Although the building had not been bombed, it had suffered severely from concussion. Craig said that when he had moved in two weeks ago the skylights over the courts had been open to the sky. On rainy days one could practically go boating on the first floor. There had been no glass in the windows. Now they had been boarded up or filled in with a translucent material as a substitute. All of the doors had been out of line and would not lock. But the repairs were already well under way and, according to Craig, the place would be shipshape in another month or six weeks. He said that his colleague, Hamilton Coulter, a former New York architect now a naval lieutenant, was directing the work and doing a magnificent job. Even under normal conditions it would have been a staggering task. With glass and lumber at a premium, to say nothing of the scarcity of skilled labor, a less resourceful man would have given up in despair.

Craig was rapidly building up a staff of German scholars and museum technicians to assist him in the administration of the establishment. It would soon rival a large American museum in complexity and scope. Storage rooms on the ground floor had been made weatherproof. Paintings and sculpture were already pouring in from the mine at Alt Aussee—six truckloads at a time. In accordance with standard museum practice, Craig had set up an efficient accessioning system. As each object came in, it was identified, marked and listed for future reference. Quarters had been set aside for a photographer. Racks were being built for pictures. A two-storied record room was being converted into a library.

Craig had also requisitioned the "twin" of this colossal building—the Fuhrerbau, where Hitler had had his own offices. This was only a block away on the same street and also faced the Königsplatz. It was connected with the Verwaltungsbau by underground passageways. It was in the Fuhrerbau that the Munich Pact of 1938—the pact that was to have guaranteed "peace in our time"— had been signed. Craig showed me the table at which Mr. Chamberlain had signed that document. Craig was using it now for a 1 conference table.

Repairs were being concentrated on the Administration Building, since its "twin" was being held in reserve for later use. At the moment, however, a few of the rooms were occupied by a small guard detail. The truck drivers and armed guards who came each week with the convoys from the mine were also billeted there.

Just as Craig and I were finishing our inspection of the Fuhrerbau, a convoy of six trucks, escorted by two half-tracks, pulled into the parking space behind the building. The convoy leader had a letter for me. It was the one George Stout had mentioned on the telephone. Lincoln was right. The repository George had in mind was the monastery at Hohenfurth. In his letter he stressed the fact that the evacuation should be undertaken at once. He suggested that I try to persuade Posey to send Lincoln along to help me.

Craig had a comfortable billet in the Kopemikus-Strasse, a four-room flat on the fourth floor of a modem apartment building. The back windows looked onto a garden. Over the tops of the poplar trees beyond, one could see the roof of the Prinz Regenten Theater where, back in the twenties, I had seen my first complete performance of Wagner's *Ring*. Craig told me that the theater was undamaged except for the Speisesaal where, in prewar days, lavish refreshments were served during intermissions. That one room had caught a bomb.

I accepted Craig's invitation to share the apartment with him while in Munich and made myself at home in the dining room. It had a couch, and there was a sideboard which I could use as a chest of drawers. The bathroom was across the hall and he said that the supply of hot water was inexhaustible. By comparison, the officers' billets at Third Army Headquarters were tenements.

Ham Coulter had similar quarters on the ground floor. We * stopped there for a drink on our way to supper at the Military Government

Detachment. "Civilized" was the word that best described Ham. He was a tall, broad-shouldered fellow with sleek black hair, finely-chiseled features and keen, gray eyes. When he smiled, his mouth crinkled up at the corners, producing an agreeably sarcastic expression. Ham poured out the drinks with an elegance the ordinary German cognac didn't deserve. They should have been dry martinis. I liked him at once that first evening, and when I came to know him better I found him the wittiest and most amiable of companions. He and Craig were a wonderful combination. They had the greatest admiration and respect for each other, and during the many months of their work together there was not the slightest disagreement between them.

The officers' dining room that evening was a noisy place. The clatter of knives and forks and the babble of voices mingled with the rasping strains of popular American tunes pounded out by a Bavarian band. As we were about to sit down, the music stopped abruptly and a second later struck up the current favorite, "My Dreams Are Getting Better All the Time." Colonel Charles Keegan, the commanding officer, had entered the dining hall. I was puzzled by this until Ham told me that it happened every night. This particular piece was the colonel's favorite tune and he had ordered it to be played whenever he came in to dinner. The colonel was a colorful character—short and florid, with a shock of white hair. He had figured prominently in New York politics and would again, it was said. He had already helped Craig over a couple of rough spots and if some of his antics amused the MFA&A boys, they seemed to be genuinely fond of him.

While we were at dinner, three officers came and took their places at a near-by table. Craig identified one of them as Captain Posey. I had been told that he was in his middle thirties, but he looked younger than that. He had a boyish face and I noticed that he laughed a great deal as he talked with his two companions. When he wasn't smiling, there was a stubborn expression about his mouth, and I remembered that Lincoln had said something about his "deceptively gentle manner." On our way out I introduced myself to him. He was very affable and seemed pleased at my arrival. But he was tired after the long drive from Frankfurt, so, as soon as I had arranged to meet him at his office the next day, I joined Ham and Craig back at the apartment.

I got out to Third Army Headquarters early the following morning and found Captain Posey already at his desk, going through the papers which had accumulated during his absence. We discussed George's letter at considerable length, and I was disappointed to find that he did not intend to act on it at once. Somehow it had never occurred to me that anyone would question a proposal of George's.

For one thing, Captain Posey said, he couldn't spare Lincoln; and for another, there was a very pressing job much nearer Munich which he wanted me to handle. He then proceeded to tell me of a small village on the road to Salzburg where I would find a house in which were stored some eighty cases of paintings and sculpture from the Budapest Museum. He showed me the place on the map and explained how I was to go about locating the exact house upon arrival. I was to see a certain officer at Third Army Headquarters without delay and make arrangements for trucks. He thought I would need about five. It shouldn't take more than half a day to do the job if all went well. After this preliminary briefing, I was on my own.

"My first move was to get hold of the officer about the trucks. How many did I need? When did I want them and where should he tell them to report? I said I'd like to have five trucks at the Königsplatz the following morning at eight-thirty. The officer explained that the drivers would be French, as Third Army was using a number of foreign trucking companies to relieve the existing shortage in transportation.

Later in the day I had a talk with Lincoln about my plans and he gave me a piece of advice which proved exceedingly valuable—that I should go myself to the trucking company which was to provide the vehicles, and personally confirm the arrangements. So, after lunch I struck out in a jeep for the west side of Munich, a distance of some seven or eight miles.

I found a lieutenant, who had charge of the outfit, and explained the purpose of my visit. He had not been notified of the order for five trucks. There was no telephone communication between his office and headquarters, so all messages had to come by courier, and the courier hadn't come in that day. He was afraid he couldn't let me have any trucks before the following afternoon. I insisted that the matter was urgent and couldn't wait, and, after much deliberating and consulting of charts, he relented. I told him a little something about the expedition for which I wanted the trucks and he showed real interest. He suggested that I ought to have extremely careful drivers. I replied that I should indeed, as we would be hauling stuff of incalculable value.

Thereupon he gave me a harrowing description of the group under his supervision. All of them had been members of the French Resistance Movement—ex-terrorists he called them—and they weren't afraid of God, man or the Devil. Well, I thought, isn't that comforting! "Oh, yes," he said, "these Frenchies drive like crazy men. But," he continued, "one of the fellows has got some sense. I'll see if I can get him for you." He went over to the window that looked out on a parking ground littered with vehicles of various kinds. Here and there I saw a mechanic bent over an open hood or sprawled out beneath a truck. The lieutenant bellowed, "Leclancher, come up here to my office!"

A few seconds later a wiry, sandy-haired Frenchman of about forty-five appeared in the doorway. Leclancher understood some English, for he reacted with alert nods of the head as the lieutenant gave a brief description of the job ahead, and then turned and asked me if I spoke French. I told him I did, if he had enough patience. This struck him as inordinately funny, but I was being quite serious. What really pleased him was the fact that I was in the Navy. He said that he had been in the Navy during the first World War. Then and there a lasting bond was formed, though I didn't appreciate the value of it at the time.

Eight-thirty the next morning found me pacing the Königsplatz. Not a truck in sight. Nine o'clock and still no trucks. At nine thirty, one truck rolled up. Leclancher leaped out and with profuse apologies explained that the other four were having carburetor trouble. There had been water in the gas, too, and that hadn't helped. For an hour Leclancher and I idled about, whiling away the time with conversation of no consequence, other than that it served to limber up my French. At eleven o'clock Leclancher looked at his watch and said that it would soon be time for lunch. It was obvious that he understood the Army's conception of a day as a brief span of time, in the course of which one eats three meals. If it is not possible to finish a given job during the short pauses between those meals, well, there's always the next day. I told him to, go to his lunch and to come back as soon as he could round up the other trucks. In the meantime I would get something to eat near by.

When I returned shortly after eleven thirty—having eaten a K ration under the portico of the Verwaltungsbau in lieu of a more formal lunch—my five trucks were lined up ready to go. 3 appointed Leclancher "chef de convoi"—a rather high-sounding title for such a modest caravan—and he assigned positions to the other drivers, taking the end truck himself. Since my jeep failed to arrive, I climbed into the lead truck. The driver was an amiable youngster whose name was Roger Roget. During the next few weeks he was the lead driver in all of my expeditions, and I took to calling him "Double Roger," which I think he never quite understood.

To add to my anxiety over our belated start, a light rain began to fall as we pulled out of the Kdnigsplatz and turned into the Brienner-Strasse. We threaded our way cautiously through the slippery streets choked with military traffic, crossed the bridge over the Isar and swung into the broad Rosenheimer-Strasse leading to the east.

Once on the Autobahn, Roger speeded up. The speedometer needle quivered up to thirty-five, forty and finally forty-five miles an hour. I pointed to it, shaking my head. "We must not exceed thirty-five, Roger."

He promptly slowed down, and as we rolled along, I forgot the worries of the morning. I dozed comfortably. Suddenly we struck an unexpected hole in the road and I woke up. We were doing fifty. This time I spoke sharply, reminding Roger that the speed limit was thirty-five and that we were to stay within it; if we didn't we'd be arrested, because the road was well patrolled. With a tolerant grin Roger said, "Oh, no, we never get arrested. The MPs, they stop us and get very angry, but—" with a shrug of the shoulders—"we do not understand. They throw the hands up in the air and say 'dumb Frenchies* and we go ahead."

"That may work with you," I said crossly, "but what about me? I'm not a 'dumb Frenchy.' "

For the next hour I pretended to doze and at the same time kept an eye on the speedometer. This worked pretty well. Now and again I would look up, and each time, Roger would modify his speed.

Presently we came to a bad detour, where a bridge was out. We had to make a sharp turn to the left, leave the Autobahn and descend a steep and tortuous side road into a deep ravine. Hiat day the narrow road was slippery from the rain, so we had to crawl along. The drop into the valley was a matter of two or three hundred feet and, as we reached the bottom, we could see the monstrous wreckage of the bridge hanging drunkenly in mid-air. The ascent was even more precarious, but our five trucks got through.

We had now left the level country around Munich and were in a region of rolling hills. Along the horizon, gray clouds half concealed the distant peaks. Soon the rain stopped and the sun came out. The mountains changed to misty blue against an even bluer sky. The road rose sharply, and when we reached the crest, I caught a glimpse of shimmering water. It was Chiemsee, largest of the Bavarian lakes.

In another ten minutes the road flattened out again and we came to the turnoff marked "Prien." There we left the Autobahn for a narrow side road which took us across green meadows. Nothing could have looked more peaceful than this lush, summer countryside. Reports of SS troops still hiding out in the nearby forests seemed preposterous in the pastoral tranquillity. Yet only a few days before, our troops had rounded up a small band of these die-hards in this neighborhood. The SS men had come down from the foothills on a foraging expedition and had been captured while attempting to raid a farmhouse. It was because of just such incidents, as well as the ever-present fire hazard, that I had been sent down to remove the museum treasures to a place of safety.

The road was dwindling away to a cow path and I was beginning to wonder how much farther we could go with our two-and-a-half-ton trucks, when we came to a small cluster of houses. This was Grassau. I had been told that a small detachment of troops was billeted there, so I singled out the largest of the little white houses grouped around the only crossroads in the village. It had clouded over and begun to rain again. As I entered the gate and was crossing the yard, the door of the house was opened by a corporal.

He didn't seem surprised to see me. Someone at Munich had sent down word to Prien that I was coming, and the message had reached him from there. I asked if he knew where the things I had come for were stored. He motioned to the back of the house and said there were two rooms full of big packing cases. He explained that he and one other man had been detailed to live in the house because of the "stuff" stored there. They had been instructed to keep an eye on the old man who claimed to be responsible for it. That would be Dr. Csanky, director of the Budapest Museum, who, according to my information, would probably raise unqualified hell when I came to cart away his precious cases. The corporal told me that the old man and his son occupied rooms on the second floor.

I was relieved to hear that they were not at home. It would make things much simpler if I could get my trucks loaded and be on my way before they returned. It was already well after two and I wanted to start back by five at the latest. I asked rather tentatively about the chances of getting local talent to help with the loading, and the corporal promptly offered to corral a gang of PWs who were working under guard near by.

While he went off to see about that, I marshaled my trucks. There was enough room to back one truck at a time to the door of the house. A few minutes later the motley "work party" arrived. There were eight of them in all and they ranged from a young fellow of sixteen, wearing a faded German uniform, to a reedy old man of sixty. By and large, they looked husky enough for the job.

I knew enough not to ask my drivers to help, but knew that the work would go much faster if they would lend a hand. Leclancher must have read my thoughts, for he immediately offered his services. As soon as the other four saw what Leclancher was doing, they followed suit

There were eighty-one cases in all. They varied greatly in size, because some of them contained sculpture and, consequently, were both bulky and heavy. Others, built for big canvases, were very large and fiat but relatively light. We had to "design" our loads in such a way as to keep cases of approximately the same type together. This was necessary for two reasons: first, the cases would ride better that way, and second, we hadn't any too much space. As I roughly figured it, we should be able to get them all in the five trucks, but we couldn't afford to be prodigal in our loading.

The work went along smoothly for an hour and we were just finishing the second truck when I saw two men approaching. They were Dr. Csanky and his son. This was what I had hoped to avoid. The doctor was a dapper little fellow with a white mustache and very black eyes. He was wearing a corduroy jacket and a flowing bow tie. The artistic effect was topped off by a beret set at a jaunty angle. His son was a callow string bean with objectionably soulful eyes magnified by horn-rimmed spectacles. They came over to the truck and began to jabber and wave their arms. We paid no attention whatever—just kept on methodically lifting one case after another out of the storage room. The dapper doctor got squarely in my path and I had to stop. I checked his flow of words with a none too civil "Do you speak English?" That drew a blank, so I asked if he spoke German. No luck there either. Feeling like an ad for the Berlitz School, I inquired whether he spoke French. He said "Yes," but the stream of Hungarian-French which rolled out from that white mustache was unintelligible. It was hopeless. At last I simply had to take him by the shoulders and gently but firmly set him aside. This was the ultimate indignity, but it worked. At that juncture he and the string bean took off. I didn't know what they were up to and I didn't care, so long as they left us alone.

Our respite was short-lived. By the time we had the third truck ready to move away, they were back. And they had come with reinforcements: two women were with them. One was a rather handsome dowager who looked out of place in this rural setting. Her gray hair, piled high, was held in place by a scarlet bandanna, and she was wearing a shabby dress of green silk. Despite this getup, there was something rather commanding about her. She introduced herself as the wife of General Ellenlittay and explained in perfect English that Dr. Csanky had come to her in great distress. Would ɪ be so kind as to tell her what was happening so that she t could inform him?

"I am removing these cases on the authority of the Commanding General of the Third United States Army," I said. If she were going to throw generals' names around, I could produce one too— and a better one at that.

Her response to my pompous pronouncement was delivered charmingly and with calculated deflationary effect. "Dear sir, forgive me if I seemed to question your authority. That was not my intention. It is quite apparent that you are removing the pictures, but where are you taking them?"

"I am sorry, but I am not at liberty to say," I replied. That too sounded rather lordly, but I consoled myself by recalling that Posey had admonished me not to answer questions like that.

She relayed this information to Dr. Csanky and the effect was startling. He covered his face with his hands and ɪ thought he was going to cry. Finally he pulled himself together and let forth a flood of unintelligible consonants. His interpreter tackled me again.

"Dr. Csanky is frantic. He says that he is responsible to his government for the safety of these treasures and since you are taking them away, there is nothing left for him to do but to blow his brains out." My patience was exhausted. I said savagely, "Tell Dr. Csanky for me that he can blow his brains out if he chooses, but I think it would be silly. If you must know, Madame, I am a museum director myself and you can assure him that no harm is going to come to his precious pictures."

I should never have mentioned that I had even so much as been inside a museum, for, from that moment until we finished loading the last truck, the little doctor never left my side. I was his "cher coll&gue," and he kept up a steady barrage of questions which the patient Madame Ellenlittay tried to pass along to me without interrupting our work. •

As we lined the trucks up, preparatory to starting back to Munich, Dr. Csanky produced several long lists of what the cases contained. He asked me to sign them. This I refused to do but explained to him through the general's wife that if he cared to have the lists translated from Hungarian and forwarded to Third Army Headquarters, they could be checked against the contents and eventually returned to him with a notation to that effect.

Our little convoy rolled out of Grassau at six o'clock, leaving the group of Hungarians waving forlornly from the comer. Just before we turned onto the Autobahn, Leclancher signaled from the rear truck for us to stop. He came panting up to the lead truck with a bottle in his hand. With a gallant wave of the arm he said that we must drink to the success of the expedition. It was a bottle of Calvados—fiery and wonderful. We each took a generous swig and then—with a rowdy "en voiture!"—we were on our way again. It was a nice gesture. '

The trip back to Munich was uneventful except for the extraordinary beauty of the long summer evening. The sunset had all the extravagance of the tropics. The sky blazed with opalescent clouds. As we drove into Munich, the whole city was suffused with a coral light which produced a more authentic atmosphere of Götterdammerung than the most ingenious stage Merlin could have contrived.

It was nearly nine when we rolled into the parking area behind the Fuhrerbau—too late to think about unloading and also, I was afraid, too late to get any supper. We had pieced out with K rations and candy bars, but were still hungry. A mess sergeant, lolling on the steps of the building, reluctantly produced some lukewarm stew. After we had eaten, I prevailed on one of the building guards to take my five drivers out to their billets south of town. It was Saturday night. I told Leclancher we would probably be making a longer trip on Monday and that I would need ten drivers. He promised to select five more good men, and we arranged to meet in the square as we had that morning. But Monday, he promised, they would be on time.

After checking the tarpaulins on my five trucks, I sauntered over to the Central Collecting Point on the off-chance that Craig might be working late. I found him looking at some of the pictures which George had sent in that day from the mine. The German packers whom Craig had been able to hire from one of the old established firms in Munich— one which had worked exclusively for the museums there—had finished unloading the trucks only a couple of hours earlier. Most of the things in this shipment had been found at the mine, so now the pictures were stacked according to size in neat rows about the room. In one of them we found two brilliant portraits by Mme. Vigée-Lebrun. Labels on the front identified them as the likenesses of Prince Schuvalov and of the Princess Golowine. Marks on the back indicated that they were from the Lanckoroncki Collection in Vienna, one of the most famous art collections in Europe. Hitler was rumored to have acquired it en bloc— through forced sale, it was said—for the great museum he planned to build at Linz. In another stack we came upon a superb Rubens landscape, a fine portrait by Hals and two sparkling allegorical scenes by Tiepolo. These had no identifying labels other than the numbers which referred to lists we didn't have at the moment However, Craig said that the documentation on the pictures, as a whole, was surprisingly complete. Then we ran into a lot of nineteenth century German masters—Lenbach, Spitzweg, Thoma and the like. These Hitler had particularly admired, but they didn't thrill me. I was getting sleepy and suggested that we had had enough art for one day. I still had a report of the day's doings to write up for Captain Posey before I could turn in, so we padlocked the room and took off.

Even though the next day was Sunday, it was not a day of rest for me. The trek to Hohenfurth, scheduled for Monday, involved infinitely more complicated preliminary arrangements than the easy run of yesterday. Captain Posey got out maps of the area into which the convoy would be traveling; gave me the names of specific outfits from whom I would have to obtain clearance as well as escorts along the way; and, most important of all, supplied information concerning the material to be transported. None of it, I learned, was cased. He thought it consisted mainly of paintings, but there was probably also some furniture. This wasn't too definite. Nor did we have a very clear idea as to the exact number of trucks we would need. I had spoken for ten on the theory that a larger number would make too cumbersome a convoy. At least I didn't want to be responsible for more at that stage of the game, inexperienced as I was. In the circumstances, two seasoned packers might, I thought, come in handy, so I was to see if I could borrow a couple of Craig's men. There was the problem of rations for the trip up and back. Posey procured a big supply of C rations, not so good as the K's, but they would do. While at Hohenfurth we would be fed by the American outfit stationed there. It was a good thing that there was so much to be arranged, because it kept me from worrying about a lot of things that could and many that did happen on that amazing expedition.

In the afternoon I went out to make sure of my trucks and on the way back put in a bid for the two packers. My request wasn't very popular, because Craig was shorthanded, but he thought he could spare two since it was to be only a three-day trip—one day to go up, one day at Hohenfurth, and then back the third day.

Craig gloomily predicted that I'd never get ten trucks loaded in one day, but I airily tossed that off with the argument that we had loaded five trucks at Grassau in less than four hours. "But that stuff was all in cases," he said. "You'll find it slow going with loose pictures." Of course he was right, but I didn't believe it at die time.

ᘐ 4 ᘑ
MASTERPIECES IN A MONASTERY

We woke up to faultless weather the following morning, and on the way down to the Königsplatz with Craig I was in an offensively optimistic frame of mind. All ten of my trucks were there. This was more like it—no tiresome mechanical delays. We were all set to go. Leclancher had even had the foresight to bring along an extra driver, just in case anything happened to one of the ten. That was a smart idea and I congratulated him for having thought of it.

It wasn't till I started distributing the rations that I discovered our two packers were missing. But that shouldn't take long to straighten out. Craig's office was just across the way. I found them cooling their heels in the anteroom. They looked as though they had come right out of an Arthur Rackham illustration—stocky little fellows with gnarled hands and wizened faces as leathery as the *Lederhosen* they were wearing. Each wore a coal-scuttle hat with a jaunty feather, and each had a bulging bandanna attached to the end of a stick. There was much bowing and scraping. The hats were doffed and there was the familiar "Grüss Gott, Herr Kapitan," when I walked in.

Craig appeared and explained the difficulty. Until the last minute, no one had thought to ask whether the men had obtained a Military Government permit to leave the area—and of course they hadn't. With all due respect to the workings of Military Government, I knew that it would take hours, even days, to obtain the 80 permits. So, what to do? I asked Craig what would happen if they went without them. He didn't know. But if anyone found out about it, there would be trouble. I didn't see any reason why anyone should find out about it. The men would be in my charge and I said I'd assume all responsibility.

Meanwhile the two Rackham characters were shifting uneasily from one foot to the other, looking first at Craig and then at me, without the faintest idea what the fuss was all about. Craig reluctantly left it up to me. Not wanting to waste any more time, I told the little fellows that everything was "in Ordnung" and bundled them off to the waiting trucks.

Again our way led out to the east, the same road we had taken two days before; and again I was perched up in the lead truck with Double Roger. The country was more beautiful than ever in the morning sunlight. We skirted the edge of Chiemsee and sped on through Traunstein. The mountains loomed closer, their crests gleaming with snow. Roger commented that it was *"la neige éternelle"* and I was struck by the unconscious poetry of the phrase.

To save time we ate our midday rations en route, pulling off to one side of the Autobahn in the neighborhood of Bad Reichenhall. Farther on we came to a fork in the highway. A sign to the right pointed temptingly to Berchtesgaden, only thirty kilometers away. But our road was the one to the left—to Salzburg. In another few minutes we saw its picturesque fortress, outlined against the sky, high above the town.

I had to make some inquiries in Salzburg. Not knowing the exact location of the headquarters where I could obtain the information I needed, I thought it prudent to park the convoy on the outskirts and go on ahead with a single truck. It probably wasn't going to be any too easy, even with exact directions, to get all ten of them through the narrow streets, across the river and out the other side. This was where a jeep would have come in handy. I had been a fool not to insist on having one for this trip.

Leclancher asked if he might go along with Roger and me. The three of us drove off, leaving the other nine drivers and the two little packers to take their ease in the warm meadow beside which we had halted. It was about three miles into the center of town and the road was full of confusing turns. But on the whole it was well marked with Army signs.

Before the end of the summer I became reasonably proficient in translating the cabalistic symbols on these markers, but at that time I was hopelessly untutored and neither of my companions was any help. After driving through endless gray archways and being soundly rebuked by the MPs for going the wrong direction on several one-way streets, we found ourselves in a broad square paved with cobblestones. It was the Mozartplatz.

The lieutenant colonel I was supposed to see had his office in one of the dove-colored buildings facing the square. It was a big, high-ceilinged room with graceful rococo decorations along the walls and a delicate prism chandelier in the center. I asked the colonel for clearance to proceed to Linz with my convoy. After I had explained the purpose of my trip to Hohenfurth, he offered to expedite the additional clearance I would need beyond Linz.

He rang up the headquarters of the 65th Infantry Division which was stationed there. In a few minutes everything had been arranged. The colonel at the other end of the line said that he would send one of his officers to the outskirts of the city to conduct us to his headquarters on our arrival. There would be no difficulty about billets. He would also take care of our clearance across the Czechoslovakian border the following day. I thanked the colonel and hurried down to rejoin Leclancher and Roger.

Since the proposed Autobahn to Linz had never been finished, we had to take a secondary highway east of Salzburg. Our road led through gently rolling country with mountains in the distance. I was grateful for the succession of villages along the way. They were a relief after the monotony of the Autobahn and also served to control the speed of the convoy. We wound through streets so narrow that one could have readied out and touched the potted geraniums which lined the balconies of the cottages on either side. Laughing, towheaded children waved from the doorways as we passed by. Roger, intent on his driving, didn't respond to the exuberance of the youngsters, and I wondered if he might be thinking of the villages of his own country, where the invaders had left a bitter legacy of wan faces.

It was after seven when we reached the battered outskirts of Linz, the city of Hitler's special adoration. He had lavished his attention on the provincial old town, his mother's birthplace, hoping to make it a serious rival of Vienna as an art center. To this end, plans for a magnificent museum had been drawn up, and already an impressive collection of pictures had been assembled against the day when a suitable building would be ready to receive them.

We approached the city from the west—its most damaged sector. It was rough going, as the streets were full of chuckholes and narrowed by piles of rubble heaped high on both sides. There was no sign of an escort, so we drew up beside an information post at a main intersection. Our cavalcade was too large to miss, as long as we stayed in one place. We waited nearly an hour before a jeep came along. A jaunty young lieutenant came over, introduced himself as the colonel's "emissary" and said that he had been combing the town for us. The confusion of the debris-filled streets had caused us to take a wrong turn and, consequently, we had missed the main thoroughfare into town. The lieutenant, whose name was George Anderson, led us by a devious route to a large, barrackslike building with a forecourt which afforded ample parking space for the trucks. Billets had already been arranged, as promised, but to get food at such a late hour was another matter. However, by dint of coaxing in the right quarter, Anderson even contrived to do that.

As we drove off in his jeep to the hotel where the officers were billeted, he remarked with a laugh that he wouldn't be able to do as well by me but thought he could dig up something. The hotel was called the "Weinzinger," and Anderson said that Hitler had often stayed there. Leaving me to get settled, he went off on a foraging expedition. He returned shortly with an armful of rations, a bottle of cognac and a small contraption that looked like a tin case for playing cards. This ingenious little device, with a turn of the wrist, opened out into a miniature stove. Fuel for it came in the form of white lozenges that resembled moth balls. Two of these, lighted simultaneously, produced a flame of such intensity that one could boil water in less than a quarter of an hour. I got out my mess kit while Anderson opened the rations, and in ten minutes we whipped up a hot supper of lamb stew. With a generous slug of cognac for appetizer, the lack of variety in the menu was completely forgotten.

While we topped off with chocolate bars, I asked him about conditions up the line in the direction of Hohenfurth.

"You won't have any trouble once you reach Hohenfurth, because it's occupied by our troops," he said, "but before swinging north into Czechoslovakia you'll have to pass through Russian-held Austrian territory."

This was bad news, for I had no clearance from the Russians. I hadn't foreseen the need of it. Captain Posey couldn't have known about it either because he was punctilious and would never have let me start off without the necessary papers. '

I had heard stories of the attitude of the Russians toward anyone entering their territory without proper authorization. An officer in Munich told me that his convoy had been stopped. He had been subjected to a series of interrogations and not allowed to proceed for a week.

"Could your colonel obtain clearance for me from the Russians?" I asked.

"He could try, but it would probably take weeks," Anderson said. "If you're in a hurry, your best bet is to take a cHance and go on through without clearance. You never can tell about the Russians. They might stop you and again they might not."

Then I mentioned my problem children—my German packers. Anderson didn't think the Russians would look on them with much favor, if my trucks were stopped and inspected. I asked about another road to Hohenfurth. Perhaps there was one to the west of the Russian lines. He didn't know about any other route but said that we could take a look at the big map in the O.D.'s office on the next floor.

To my great relief, it appeared that there was another road—one which ran parallel with the main road, four or five miles to the west of it. But Anderson tempered enthusiasm with the remark that it might not be wide enough for my two-and-a-half-ton trucks. There was nothing on the map to indicate whether it was much more than a cow path and the duty officer didn't know. One of the other officers might be able to tell me. I could ask in the morning.

That night I worried a good deal about the hazards that seemed to lie ahead, and woke up feeling depressed. Things, I reflected,. had been going too well. I should have guessed that there would be rough spots here and there. After early breakfast I called to thank the colonel, Anderson's chief, for his kindness, and while in his office had a chance to inquire about the alternate route.

"The back road is all right," he said without hesitation. "Take it by all means. You will cross the Czech frontier just north of Leonfelden. A telephone call to our officer at the border control will fix that up. You should be able to make Hohenfurth in about two hours. The C.O. at Hohenfurth is Lieutenant Colonel Sheehan of the 263rd Field Artillery Battalion."

On my way through the outer office I stopped for a word with Lieutenant Anderson, and while there the colonel gave instructions about the call to the border-control post. That done, Anderson said, "If you've got a minute, there's something I want to show you." I followed him down the stairs and through the back entrance of the hotel to the broad esplanade beside the Danube. The river was beautiful that morning. Its swiftly flowing waters were really blue.

We walked over to the river where a white yacht tugged at her moorings. She was the *Ungaria,* presented by Hitler to Admiral Horthy, the Hungarian Regent. Anderson took me aboard and we made a tour of her luxurious cabins. She was about a hundred twenty feet over all and her fittings were lavish to the last detail. The vessel was now in the custody of the American authorities, but her original crew was still aboard.

After this unexpected nautical adventure, Anderson took me to my trucks and saw us off on the last lap of the journey. Beyond Urfahr, the town across the Danube from Linz, we turned north. It was slow going for the convoy because the road was steep and winding. Our progress was further impeded by an endless line of horse-drawn carts and wagons, all moving in the direction of Linz. Most of them were filled with household furnishings. Presently the road straightened out and we entered a region of rolling, upland meadows and deep pine forests. After an hour and a half's drive we reached Leonfelden, a pretty village with a seventeenth century church nestling in a shallow valley. Just beyond it was the frontier. We identified ourselves to the two officers—one American, the other Czech—and continued on our way. Our entry into Czechoslovakia had been singularly undramatic. In another twenty minutes we pulled into Hohenfurth.

It was not a particularly prepossessing village on first sight. Drab, one-story houses lined the one main street. The headquarters of the 263rd Field Artillery Battalion occupied an unpretentious corner building. Lieutenant Colonel John R. Sheehan, the CO., was a big, amiable fellow, with a Boston-Irish accent.

"If you've come for that stuff in the monastery," he said, "just tell me what you need and I'll see that you get it. I'm anxious to get the place cleared out because we're not going to be here much longer. When we leave, the Czechs are going to take over." The colonel called for Major Coleman W. Thacher, his "Exec," a pleasant young Bostonian, and told him to see that I was properly taken care of. The major, in turn, instructed his sergeant to show me the way to the monastery and to provide billets for my men.

It was after eleven, but the sergeant said we'd have time to take a look at the monastery before chow. He suggested that we take the trucks to the monastery, which was not more than three-quarters of a mile from headquarters. We drove down a narrow side street to the outskirts of town. The small villas on either side were being used for officers' billets. The street ended abruptly, and up ahead to the left, on a slight eminence, I saw the cream-colored walls of the monastery.

A curving dirt road wound around to the entrance on the west side. The monastery consisted of a series of rambling buildings forming two courtyards. In the center of the larger of these stood a chapel of impressive proportions. An arched passageway, leading through one of the buildings on the rim of the enclosure, provided the only means of access to the main courtyard. It had plenty of "Old World charm" but looked awfully small in comparison with our trucks.

Leclancher pooh-poohed my fears and said he'd take his truck through. He did—that is, part way through. With a hideous scraping sound the truck came to a sudden stop. The bows supporting the tarpaulin had not cleared the sloping sides of the pointed arch. This was a fine mess, for it was a good two hundred yards from the entrance to the building, behind the chapel, in which the things were stored. It would prolong the operation beyond all reason if we had to carry them all that way to the trucks. And what if it rained? As if in answer to my apprehension, it suddenly did rain, a hard drenching downpour. I should have had more faith in the resourcefulness of my Frenchmen; at that critical juncture Leclancher announced that he had found the solution. The bows of the trucks could be forced down just enough to dear the archway.

As soon as this had been done, nine of the trucks filed through and lined up alongside the buttresses of the chapel. The tenth remained outside to take the drivers and the two packers to chow.

After seeing to it that they were properly cared for, the sergeant deposited me at the officers' mess.

At lunch, Colonel Sheehan introduced me to the military Government Officer of his outfit, Major Lewis W. Whittemore, a bluff Irishman, who gave me considerable useful information about the setup at the monastery.

"Mutter, an elderly Austrian, is in charge of the collections stored there—a custodian appointed by the Nazis. He is a dependable fellow so we've allowed him to stay on the job. You'll find him thoroughly cooperative," said the major. "One of the buildings of the monastery is being used as a hospital for German wounded."

"Are there any monks about the place?" I asked.

"Hitler ran them all out, but a few have returned. When Hohenfurth is turned over to the Czechs, it will make quite a change in this Sudetenland community. Even the name is going to be changed—to its Czech equivalent, Vysi Brod. All the signs in town will be printed in Czech, too. It will be the official language. Except for a few families, the entire population is German."

"How will that work?" I asked.

The major apparently interpreted my question as an expression of disapproval of the impending change-over, for he said rather belligerently, "The Czechs in this region have had a mighty raw deal from the Germans during the past few years." I rallied weakly with the pious observation that two wrongs had never made a right and that I hoped some satisfactory solution to the knotty problem could be reached.

By the time we had finished lunch the rain had dwindled to a light drizzle. I started out on foot to the monastery, leaving word at the colonel's quarters for the sergeant to meet me in the courtyard of the *Kloster*. He got there about the same time I did, and together we started looking for Dr. Mutter, the Austrian custodian. We went first to the library of the monastery—a beautiful baroque room lined with sumptuous bookcases of burled walnut surmounted with elaborate carved and gilded scroll-shaped decorations. The room was beautifully proportioned, some seventy feet long and about forty feet wide. Tall French windows looked out on the peaceful monastery garden, which, for lack of care, was now overgrown with tangled vines and brambles. Along the opposite side of the handsome room stood a row of massive sixteenth century Italian refectory tables piled high with miscellaneous bric-a-brac: Empire candelabra, Moorish plates, Venetian glass, Della Robbia plaques and Persian ceramics. Across one end, an assortment of Louis Quinze sofas and chairs seemed equally out of place. What, I wondered, were these incongruous objects doing in this religious establishment?

The explanation was soon forthcoming. The sergeant found Dr. Mutter in a small room adjoining the library. He was a lanky, studious individual with a shock of snow-white hair, prominent teeth and a gentle manner which just missed being fawning. Hohenfurth's Uriah Heep, I thought unkindly. The moment he began to speak in halting English, I revised my estimate of him. He was neither crafty nor vicious. On the contrary, he was just a timid, and, at the moment, frightened victim of circumstance. What German I know has an Austrian flavor, and when I trotted this out he was so embarrassingly happy that I wished I had kept my tongue in my head. But it served to establish an *entente cordiale* which proved valuable during the next few days. They were to be more hectic than I had even faintly imagined.

After a little introductory palaver, I explained that I had come to remove the collections which had been brought to the monastery by the Germans, and that I would like to make a preliminary tour of inspection. I suggested that we look first at the paintings.

"Paintings?" he asked doubtfully. "You mean the modern pictures? They are not very good—just the work of some of the Nazi artists. They were brought here—and quite a lot of sculpture too—when it was announced that Hitler was coming to Hohenfurth to see the really important things."

Then I learned what he meant by the "really important things"— room after room, corridor after corridor, all crammed with furniture and sculpture, methodically looted from two fabulous collections, the Rothschild of Vienna and the Mannheimer of Amsterdam. By comparison, the Hearst collection at Gimbel's was trifling. The things I had seen in the library were only a small part of this melange. In an adjoining chamber—a vaulted gallery, fifty feet long—there were a dozen pieces of French and Dutch marquetry. And stacked against the walls were entire paneled rooms, coffered ceilings and innumerable marble busts. Next to that was a room crowded with more of the same sort of thing, except that the pieces were small and more delicate. In one corner I saw an extraordinary table made entirely of tortoise shell and mounted with exquisite ormolu.

It was an antique-hunter's paradise, but for me quite the reverse. How was I going to move all of this stuff? Dr. Mutter could see that I was perplexed, and apologetically added that I had seen only a part of the collections. Remembering that I had asked to see the pictures, he took me to a corner room containing approximately a hundred canvases. As he had said, they were a thoroughly dull lot—portraits of Hitler, Hess and some of the other Nazi leaders, tiresome allegorical scenes, a few battle subjects and a group of landscapes. The labels pasted on the backs indicated that they had all been shown at one time or another in ' exhibitions at the Haus der Deutschen Kunst in Munich. While I was looking at them, Dr. Mutter shyly confessed that he was a painter but that he didn't admire this kind of work.

On the floor below, there was a forest of contemporary German sculpture—plaster casts, for the most part, all patinated to resemble bronze. In addition there were a few portrait busts in bronze and one or two pieces in glazed terra cotta. The terracotta pieces had some merit. The sculpture occupied one entire side of a broad corridor which ran around the four sides of a charming inner garden. The corridor had originally been open but the archways were now glassed in. Turning a corner, we came upon a jumble of architectural fragments—carved Gothic pinnacles, sections of delicately chiseled moldings, colonnettes, Florentine wellheads and wall fountains. At one end was a pair of elaborate gilded wrought-iron doors and at either side wefe handsome wall lanterns, also of wrought iron. These too were Mannheimer, Dr. Mutter replied, when I hopefully asked if they were not a part of the monastery fittings.

As final proof of the looters' thorough methods, I was shown a vaulted reception hall, into the walls of which had been set a large and magnificent relief by Luca della Robbia, a smaller but also very beautiful relief of the *Madonna and Child* by some Florentine sculptor of the fifteenth century, and an enormous carved stone fireplace of Renaissance workmanship. The hall was stacked with huge cases as yet unpacked, and from the ceiling were suspended two marvelous Venetian glass chandeliers—exotic accents against a background of chaste plaster walls.

This partial tour of inspection ended with a smaller room across from the reception hall where Dr. Mutter proudly exhibited what he considered the finest thing of all—a life-sized, seated marble portrait by Canova. It was indeed a distinguished piece of work. Hitler had bought the statue in Vienna, so Dr. Mutter said, from the Princess Wmdischgratz. It had been destined for the Führer Museum at Linz.

I learned afterward that the statue had belonged at one time to the Austrian emperor, Franz Josef. Canova began the statue in 1812 as a portrait of Maria-Elisa, Princess of Lucca—a sister of Napoleon. The sculptor's more celebrated portrait of Napoleon's sister Pauline had been carved a few years earlier. When Maria-Elisa lost her throne and fortune, she was unable to pay for the portrait But Canova was resourceful: he changed the portrait into a statue of Polyhymnia, the Muse of poetry and song. He accomplished this metamorphosis by idealizing the head and adding the appropriate attributes of the Muse. Later the statue was given to Franz Josef. Eventually it passed into the collection of his granddaughter—the daughter of Rudolf, who died at Mayerling— the Princess Windischgratz.

The statue was one of the most delicate and graceful examples of the great neoclassic master's style, and I marveled both at its cold perfection and the fact that it had come through its travels completely unscathed. For all her airy elegance, the Muse must weigh at least a ton and a half, I calculated—suddenly coming down to earth with the realization that I would be expected to take her back to Munich!

Over Dr. Mutter's protest that I had not yet seen everything, I said that I should get my men started. There was no time to be lost. Colonel Sheehan provided eight men and, after cautioning them about the value and fragility of the objects, I detailed Dr. Mutter to supervise their work. The first job was to bring some of the furniture down to the ground floor. As yet we had no packing materials, so we could do no actual loading. The next step was to show the packers what we were up against. At first they went from room to room shaking their heads and muttering, but after I had explained that we would only select certain things, they cheered up and set to work. Luckily, some of the furniture had a fair amount of protective padding—paper stuffed with excelsior— and that could be used until we were able to get more. We had enough, they agreed, to figure on perhaps two truckloads. Leaving them to mull over that, I went off to round up a couple of the trucks. Here was another problem. Not only did the furniture have to be brought down a long flight of stone stairs, but to reach the stairs in the first place it had to be carried a distance of two hundred yards. Once down the stairs it had to be carried another two hundred yards down a long sloping ramp to the only doorway opening onto the courtyard. I told Leclancher to bring one of the trucks around to that doorway and then took off in search of paper, excelsior, rope and blankets. In one of the near-by sheds I found only a small supply of paper and some twine. We would need much more.

Major Whittemore came to the rescue and drove me to a lumber and paper mill several kilometers away. As we drove along he told me that he had been having trouble with the German managers of the mill, but they knew now that he meant business, so I was not to *ask* for what I wanted, I was to *tell* them. At the mill I got a generous supply of paper, excelsior and rope and, on my return to the monastery, sent one of the trucks back to pick it up. But there wasn't a spare blanket to be had in all of Hohenfurth.

When I got back, it looked like moving day. The ramp was already lined with tables, chairs and chests. Dr. Mutter was running back and forth, cautioning one GI not to drop a delicate cabinet, helping another with an overambitious armful of equal rarity and all the while trying in vain to check the numbers marked on the pieces as they flowed down the stairs in a steady stream. Meanwhile, my two packers trudged up and down the ramp, lugging heavy chests and monstrous panels which looked more than a match for men twice their size.

In spite of their concerted efforts, we didn't have anything like enough help, so I appealed to Leclancher. With discouraging independence, he indicated that his men were drivers, not furniture movers, and that he couldn't order them to help. But he would put it up to them. After a serious conference with them, Leclancher reported that they had agreed to join the work party. Now, with a crew of twenty, things moved along at a faster pace. With a couple of the GIs, the two packers and I set to work loading the first truck. Here was where the little Rackhamites shone. In half an hour the first truck was packed and ready to be driven back to its place beside the chapel wall. The second truck was brought up and before long joined its groaning companion, snugly parked against a buttress.

Presently, the eight GIs trooped out into the courtyard. It was half past five and time for chow. The Frenchmen knocked off too, leaving Dr. Mutter, the two packers and me to take stock of the afternoon's accomplishment. While we were thus engaged, Leclancher came to tell me that my driver, the one I called "Double Roger," was feeling sick and wanted to see a doctor. In the confusion of the afternoon's work I hadn't noticed that he was not about. We found him curled up in the back of the truck and feeling thoroughly miserable. I drove him down to the Medical Office in the village and there Dr. Sverdlik, the Battalion Surgeon, examined him. Roger's complaint was a severe pain in the midriff and the doctor suggested heat treatments. He said that the German surgeon up at the monastery hospital had the necessary equipment.

That seemed simple enough, since the drivers were billeted in rooms adjoining the hospital wing. But I reckoned without Roger. What? Be treated by a German doctor? He was terrified at the prospect, and it required all my powers of persuasion to talk him into it. Finally he agreed, but only after Dr. Sverdlik had telephoned to the hospital doctor and given explicil instructions. I also had to promise to stand by while the doctor ministered to him.

The German, Major Brecker, was methodical and thorough. He found that Roger had a kidney infection and recommended that he be taken to a hospital as soon as possible. I explained that we would not be returning to Munich for at least two days and asked if the delay would be dangerous. He said that he thought not. In the meantime he would keep Roger under a "heat basket." Roger eyed this device with suspicion but truculently allowed it to be applied. When I went off to my supper, twenty minutes later, he was sleeping peacefully—but not alone. Three of his fellow drivers were sprawled on cots near by, just in case that Boche had any intentions of playing tricks on their comrade. Maybe not, but they were taking no chances! What a lot of children they were, I thought, as I walked wearily down to supper.

That evening I asked the colonel if I could get hold of some PWs to help out with the work the following day. He said that there was a large camp between Hohenfurth and Krummau and that I could have as many as I wanted. So I put in a bid for sixteen. After arranging for them to be at the monastery at eight the next morning, I went to my own quarters which were in a house just across the way.

I had one little errand of mercy to take care of before I turned in. There was a recreation room on the first floor and adjoining it a makeshift bar. Most of the officers had gone to the movies, so I managed to slip in unobserved and pilfer two bottles of beer. Tucking them inside my blouse, I made off for the monastery. There, after some difficulty in finding my way around the dark passageways, I located the rooms occupied by my two little packers. They were making ready for bed, but when they saw what I had for them, their leathery old faces lighted up with ecstatic smiles. If I had been a messenger from heaven, they couldn't have been happier. Leaving them clucking over their unexpected refreshments, I went back to my own billet and fell into bed. I hadn't had exactly what one would call a restful day myself.

That beer worked wonders I hadn't anticipated. When I arrived at the monastery a little before eight the next morning I found that my two packers, together with Dr. Mutter, had been at work since seven. As yet there was no sign of the Frenchmen, but I thought that they would probably show up before long. At eight my gang of PWs appeared and the sergeant who brought them explained that I wouldn't be having the crew of GIs who had helped out the day before. When I protested that I needed them more urgently than ever, he informed me that the combination of GI and PW labor simply wouldn't work out; that I certainly couldn't expect to have them both doing the same kind of work together. I said that I most certainly could and did expect it. Well, my protest was completely unavailing, and if I had to make a choice I was probably better off with the sixteen PWs. Perhaps my two packers could get enough work out of them to compensate for the loss of the GIs.

I had just finished assigning various jobs to the PWs when Leclancher turned up. "May I have a word with you?" he asked. "It is about Roger."

"What about Roger? Is he any worse?" I asked.

"No, but he is not any better either," he said. "Is it possible that we shall be returning to Munich tomorrow morning?"

"Not the ghost of a chance," I said. "We shan't be through loading before tomorrow night. We're too shorthanded."

"But if we all pitched in and worked, even after supper?" he asked.

"It would make a big difference," I said. "But it's entirely up to you. It's certainly worth a try if the drivers are willing."

I'll never forget that day. I never saw Frenchmen move with such rapidity or with such singleness of purpose. When five o'clock came, we had finished loading the fifth truck. Taking into account the two from the preceding day, that left only three more trucks to fill. Leclancher came to me again. The drivers wanted to work until it got dark. That meant until nine o'clock. Knowing that the two packers were equally eager to get back to Munich, I agreed. I hurried off to call the sergeant about the PWs. Special arrangements would have to be made to feed them if we were keeping on the job after supper. Also, I had to make sure that someone at Battalion Headquarters would be able to provide a vehicle to take them back to their camp.

While the drivers went off to chow and the PWs were being fed in the hospital kitchen, I joined Dr. Mutter and the packers to discuss these new developments. I felt sure that I would be returning to Hohenfurth in another few days with additional trucks to complete the evacuation. That being the case, some preliminary planning was necessary. I instructed Dr. Mutter to call in a stonemason to remove the Della Robbia relief and the other pieces which had been set into the walls, so that they would be ready for packing when we came back. I gave him a written order which would enable him to lay in a supply of lumber for packing cases which would have to be built for some of the more fragile pieces. Lastly, the four of us surveyed the storage rooms and made an estimate of the number of trucks we would need for the things still on hand.

To save time I had a couple of chocolate bars for my supper and was ready to resume work when our combined forces reappeared. The next two hours and a half went by like a whirlwind and by eight o'clock we knotted down the tarpaulin on the last truck. Everybody was content. Even the PWs seemed less glum than usual, but that was probably because they had been so well fed in the hospital kitchen.

If we were to make it through to Munich in the one day, we would have to start off early the next morning. Accordingly I left word that the trucks were to be lined up outside the monastery entrance at seven-thirty sharp. Then I went down to the colonel's quarters to see about an armed escort for the convoy. I found Colonel Sheehan and Major Thacher making preparations to "go out on the town." They looked very spruce in their pinks and were in high spirits.

"We missed you at supper," said the colonel. "How's the work coming along?"

"My trucks are loaded and ready to roll first thing in the morning if I can have an escort," I said.

"That calls for a celebration," he said. "Pour yourself a drink. I'll make a bargain with you. You can have the escort on one condition—that you join our party tonight."

I didn't protest. I thought it was a swell idea. A few minutes later, the captain with whom I was billeted arrived and the four of us set out for an evening of fun.

In the short space of two days I had grown very fond of these three officers, although we had met only at mealtime. They were, in fact, characteristic of all the officers I had encountered at Hohenfurth—friendly, good-natured and ready to do anything they could to help. That they were all going home soon may have had something to do with their contented outlook on life, and they deserved their contentment. As members of the 26th Division, the famous "Yankee Division," they had seen plenty of action, and as we drove along that night in the colonel's car, my three companions did a lot of reminiscing.

While they exchanged stories, I had a chance to enjoy the romantic countryside through which we were passing. We were, the colonel had said, headed for Krummau, an old town about fifteen miles away.

The road followed along the winding Moldau River, which had 'an almost supernatural beauty in the glow of the late evening light. The bright green banks were mirrored, crystal clear, on its unrippled surface, as were the rose-gold colors of the evening clouds.

We crossed the river at Rosenberg, and as we went over the bridge I noticed that it bore—as do all bridges in that region—the figure of St. John Nepomuk, patron saint of Bohemia. The castle, perched high above the river, was the ancestral seat of the Dukes of Rosenberg who ruled this part of Bohemia for hundreds of years. One of them murdered his wife and, according to the legend, she still haunted the castle. Robed in white, she was said to walk the battlements each night between eleven-thirty and twelve. Major Thacher thought that we should test the legend by paying a visit to the castle on our return from Krummau later that evening.

When we arrived in Krummau it was too dark to see much of the old town except the outline of the gray buildings which lined the narrow streets. Our objective was a night club operated by members of an underground movement which was said to have flourished there throughout the years of Nazi oppression. There was nothing in any way remarkable about the establishment, but it provided a little variety for the officers stationed thereabouts. My companions were popular patrons of the place. They were royally welcomed by the proprietor, who found a good table for us, not too near the small noisy orchestra. Two pretty Czech girls joined us and we all took turns dancing. There were so many more men than girls that we had to be content with one dance each. Then the girls moved on to another table.

We whiled away a couple of hours at the club before the colonel said that we should be starting back. I hoped that we would be in time to pay our respects to the phantom duchess, but the clock in the square was striking twelve when we rumbled through the empty streets of Rosenberg. It had begun to rain again.

At six the next morning, I looked sleepily out the window. It was still raining. We would have a slow trip unless the weather cleared, and I thought apprehensively of the steep road leading into Linz. Fresh eggs—instead of the usual French toast—and two cups of black coffee brightened my outlook on the soggy morning and I was further cheered to find the convoy smartly lined up like a row of circus elephants when I reached the monastery at seven-thirty. Leclancher had taken the lead truck and the ailing Roger was bundled up in the cab of one of the others.

Dr. Mutter waved agitated farewells from beneath the ribs of a tattered umbrella as we slid slowly down the monastery drive. At the corner of the main street of the village we picked up our escort, two armed jeeps. They conducted us to the border where we gathered in two similar vehicles which would set the pace for us into Linz. The bad weather was in one respect an advantage: there was practically no traffic on the road.

At Linz I stopped long enough to thank Anderson and his colonel for the escort vehicles they had produced on a moment's notice that morning in response to a call from Colonel Sheehan. This third pair of jeeps were very conscientious about their escort duties. The one in the vanguard kept well in the lead and would signal us whenever he came to a depression in the road. This got on Leclancher's nerves, for I heard him muttering under his breath every time it happened. But I was so glad to have an escort of any kind that I pretended not to notice his irritation.

When we reached Lambach, midway between Linz and Salzburg, we lost this pair of guardians but acquiitd two sent on from the latter city. While waiting for them to appear, I scrounged lunch for myself and the drivers at a local battery. As soon as the new escorts arrived we started on again and pulled into Salzburg at two-thirty. This time there were no delays and we threaded our way through the dripping streets and out on to the Autobahn without mishap.

I now had only one remaining worry—the bad detour near Rosenheim. Again, perhaps thanks to the weather, we were in luck and found this treacherous by-pass free of traffic. As we rolled into Munich, the rain let up and by the time we turned into the Königsplatz, the sun had broken through the clearing skies.

My first major evacuation job was finished. As soon as I got my drivers fixed up with transportation back to their camp and the members of our escort party fed and billeted I could relax with a clear conscience. It was a little after five-thirty, and Third Army's inflexible habits about the hour at which all enlisted men should eat didn't make this problem such an easy one. Third Army Headquarters was a good twenty minutes away, so I took the men to the Military Government Detachment where the meal schedule was more elastic. Afterward I shepherded them to their billets and went off to my own. I would have to write up a report of the expedition for Captain Posey, but that could wait.

~ 5 ~

SECOND TRIP TO HOHENFURTH

The first order of business the next morning was a conference with Captain Posey. I gave him a complete account of the Hohenfurth trip and presented ray recommendations for a second and final visit to complete the evacuation. It was my suggestion that I return to the monastery with the same trucks—as soon as they could be unloaded and serviced—and that he send up another officer with at least eight additional trucks, the second convoy to arrive by the time I had completed the loading of my own. I proposed taking four packers this time instead of two, the idea being that two of the packers could help me with the loading while the others were building cases for the fragile objects which would have to be crated. I mentioned also the impending withdrawal of our troops from Hohenfurth, which would make later operations of such nature impossible.

This was of course no news to Captain Posey as, presumably, it had been the determining factor in the removal of the Hohenfurth things in the first place. He approved my plan and advised me to get my trucks lined up, and said he would see what he could do about sending an additional officer. I didn't like the sound of that. Too often I had used those same words myself when confronted with a difficult request Furthermore, it had been my experience with the Army in general thus far—and with Third Army in particular—that "out of sight, out of mind" was a favorite motto. I had no intention of going back to Hohenfurth until I had a definite promise that reinforcements would be forthcoming. I think that my insistence piqued the captain a bit. But at that point I was feeling exceedingly brisk and businesslike—a mood which I found new and stimulating. It would be better to have a clear understanding now as to who would join me in Hohenfurth; as I explained to Captain Posey, I would like to give the officer some detailed instructions, preferably oral ones, before I started off.

I spent the rest of that day and most of the following one at the Verwaltungsbau supervising the unloading of the ten trucks from Hohenfurth and making trips out to the trucking company headquarters to conclude arrangements for continued use of the vehicles. Also, I had to put in a request for eight others. It was gratifying to find that every piece we had packed at Hohenfurth came through without a scratch. My two packers, to whom all credit for this belonged, were equally elated. My request for the services of four packers was met with black looks, but when I promised that we'd not be gone more than four or five days, Craig acquiesced.

Late in the afternoon of the second day, I went again to Posey's office. He was not there but I found Lincoln, as usual hunched morosely over his typewriter. He said he had good news for me. Captain Posey had pulled a fast one and snatched a wonderful guy away from Jim Rorimer, Monuments Officer at Seventh Army— a fellow named Lamont Moore. Moore was already, he thought, on his way down to Munich to make the trip to Hohenfurth. When I said I didn't know Moore, Lincoln proceeded to tell me about him.

"Lamont was director of the educational program at the National Gallery in Washington before he went into the Army. Before that he had a brilliant record at the Newark Museum. The two of you ought to get along famously. Lamont's got a wonderful sense of humor. He's exceedingly intelligent and he's had a lot of experience in evacuation work."

"Where did you know him?" I asked.

"We were in France last winter. That was before he was commissioned. He's a lieutenant now," Lincoln said.

"That sounds perfect. But I want to ask you a question about something else and I want a truthful answer. I have a sneaking notion that you knew all the time time what was in that monastery at Hohenfurth. How about it?"

"Furniture and sculpture, you mean, instead of paintings?" he asked. "Of course I didn't."

"Well, maybe you didn't, but perhaps you can imagine how I felt when I found that the Mannheimer collection alone contained more than two thousand items, and that the Rothschild pieces totaled up to a similar figure."

Lincoln's chuckle belied his protestations. "I've got another piece of news for you," he said. "John Nicholas Brown and Mason Hammond are arriving tomorrow. I thought you might like to see them before you return to Hohenfurth."

"You told me once that Captain Posey, like many another officer, doesn't relish visitors from higher headquarters," I said. "Am I to infer a connection between his absence from the office and the impending arrival of these two distinguished emissaries from the Group Control Council?"

He assured me that I was not, but I left the office wondering about it all the same.

That evening George Stout paid one of his rare and fleeting visits to Munich. On these occasions he stayed either with Craig or Ham Coulter. This time the four of us—all "strays" from the Navy— gathered in Ham's quarters.

"The work at the mine," George said, "is going along as rapidly as can be expected in the circumstances. But it's got to be stepped up. I came down to find out how soon you could join me."

"I'm going back to Hohenfurth again," I said. "Lamont Moore is to meet me there."

George was glad to hear this and said that he and Lamont had worked together at the Siegen mine in Westphalia. He confirmed all of the good things Lincoln had told me about Lamont and said that he'd like to have both of us at Alt Aussee. He promised to have a talk with Posey about it, because he was of the opinion that these big evacuation jobs should be handled by a team rather than by a single officer. According to George, a team of at least three—and preferably four— officers would be the perfect setup. Then the work could be divided up. Each officer would have specific duties, assigned to him on the basis of his particular talents. But all members of the team would have responsibilities of equal importance. It would be teamwork in the real sense of the term.

Like all of George's proposals, this one sounded very sensible. At the same time, when I recalled the haphazard way I had been obliged to conduct operations thus far myself, I wondered if it weren't Utopian. That didn't discourage George. When he had a good idea he never let go of it. And, if we had only been a larger group, I am convinced that his brain child about teams would have had wonderful results. As it was, the events of the next few weeks were to demonstrate how effective the scheme was on a small scale.

When I got out to Third Army Headquarters the next morning, George had already come and gone. I would have liked to ask Posey about their conversation but he didn't seem to be in a chatty mood—at least not on that subject. However, he did have a few caustic things to say about "people from high headquarters who have nothing better to do than travel around and interrupt the work of others."   -

Knowing that he was referringto Messrs. Brown and Hammond— Lincoln's assurance of the night before to the contrary notwithstanding—I piously observed that high-level visitors to the field might do quite a lot of good. For one thing, the fact that they had taken the trouble to visit it emphasized the importance of tfie work they had come to inspect; and, for another, it pleased the/officer in the field to have his job noticed by the boys at the top. I thought I sounded pretty convincing, but sensing that I was not, I turned to other topics.

About that time John and Mason arrived. Our last meeting had taken place in the vaults of the Reichsbank at Frankfurt several weeks before. Mason referred to that and jokingly accused me of having run out on him. When I told him that I was about to return to Hohenfurth he announced loudly that that was perfect—he and John would drop in to see me there. I said that would be fine but, when I noted the expression on Captain Posey's face, I added to myself, "fine, if they get the clearance." Before coming up to see me, they expected to visit one or two places south of Munich, so they wouldn't reach Hohenfurth before the end of the week.

Captain Posey was a great believer in the old theory that the Devil finds work for idle hands, at least as far as I was concerned. That same afternoon he casually suggested that I take a "little run down into the Tyrol" for him and inspect a castle about which he had been asked to make a report. He proposed the trip with such pre-war insouciance that it sounded like a pleasant holiday excursion. As a matter of fact it was an appealing suggestion, despite my plans for an early morning start to Hohenfurth.

It was a beautiful summer day and my jeep driver asked if a friend of his, a sergeant who was keen about photography, might come along. I agreed and the three of us headed out east of Munich on the Autobahn. It was fun to be riding in an open jeep instead of an enclosed truck.

We reached Rosenheim in record time and there struck south into the mountains. Our objective was the little village of Brixlegg, between Kufstein and Innsbruck, We were on the main road to the Brenner Pass. Italy was temptingly close. We stopped from time to time so that the sergeant could get a snapshot of some particularly dramatic vista. But there was an embarrassment of riches—every part of the road was spectacularly beautiful.

Brixlegg was a tiny cluster of picturesque chalets, but it had not been tiny enough to elude the attentions of the air force. On the outskirts we saw the shattered remains of what had been an important factory for the manufacture of airplane parts. Happily, the bombers had concentrated their efforts on the factory. The little village had suffered practically no damage at all.

We located our castle without difficulty. It was Schloss Matzen, one of the finest castles of the Tyrol—the property of a British officer, Vice-Admiral Baillie-Grohman. This gentleman had requested a report on the castle from the American authorities. We found everything in perfect order. The admiral's cousin—a Hungarian baron named Von Schmedes who spoke excellent English— was in residence. He showed us over the place. The castle was an example of intelligent restoration. According to the inscription on a plaque over the entrance, the aunt of the present owner had devoted her life to this task.

Although an "Off Limits" sign was prominently displayed on the premises, the baron was fearful of intruders. As the castle stood some distance from the main highway, I thought he was being unduly apprehensive. He said that an official letter of warning to unwelcome visitors would be an added protection. To please him I wrote out a statement to the effect that the castle was an historic monument, the property of a British subject, etc., and signed it in the name of the Commanding General of the Third U. S. Army.

On our way out we were shown two rooms on the ground floor which were filled with polychromed wood sculpture from the museum at Innsbruck. The baron said that additional objects from the Innsbruck museum were stored in a near-by castle, Schloss Lichtwert.

It was but a few minutes' drive from Schloss Matzen, so I decided to have a look at it. Schloss Lichtwert, though not nearly so picturesque either in character or as to site, was the more interesting of the two. It stood baldly in the middle of a field and was actually a big country house rather than a castle.

We were hospitably received by a courtly old gentleman, Baron von Iname, to whom I explained the reason for our visit. One of his daughters offered to do the honors, saying that her father was extremely deaf. We followed her to a handsome drawing room on the second floor, where several other members of the family were gathered in conversation around a large table set with coffee things. In one of the wall panels was a concealed door, which the daughter of the house opened by pressing a hidden spring. Leading the way, she took us into a room about twenty feet square filled with violins, violas and 'cellos. They hung in rows from the ceiling, like hams in a smokehouse. Fraulein von Iname said that the collection of musical instruments at Innsbruck was a very fine one. We were standing in a Stradivarius forest.

When we passed back into the drawing room, the father whispered a few words to his daughter. She turned to us smiling and said, "Father asked if I had pointed out to you the thickness of the walls in this part of the castle. He is very proud of the fact that they date from the fourteenth century and that our family has always lived here. He also asks me to invite you to take coffee with us."

Knowing that coffee was valued as molten gold, I declined the invitation on the grounds that we had a long trip ahead of us. Thanking her for her courtesy, we left. It was after eleven when we got back to Munich. We had driven a little more than three hundred miles.

Bad weather and bad luck attended us all the way to Hohenfurth the next day. Less than an hour out on the Autobahn, we came upon a gruesome accident—an overturned jeep and the limp figures of two GIs at one side of the road, the mangled body of a German soldier in the center of the pavement. An, ambulance had already arrived and a doctor was ministering to the injured American soldiers. The German was obviously beyond medical help. As soon as the road was cleared, we continued—but at a very sober pace.

On the other side of Salzburg we had carburetor trouble which held us up for nearly two hours. It was after five thirty when we reached Linz. We stopped there for supper and I had a few words with the colonel who had looked after us so well a few days before. He seemed surprised to see me again, and rather agitated.

"You can get through this time," he said, "but don't try to come back this way."

"What do you mean, sir?" I asked, puzzled by his curt admonition.

Apparently annoyed by my query, he said brusquely, "Don't ask any questions. Just do as I say—don't come back this way."

At supper I saw Lieutenant Anderson again and I broached the subject to him. "Does the colonel mean that the Russians are expected to move up to the other side of die Danube?" I asked.

"Take a good look at the bridge when you cross over tonight," he said.

It was my turn to be nettled now. "Look here, I don't mean to be intruding on any precious military secret, but I am expecting a second convoy to join me at Hohenfurth in two days; if the other trucks aren't going to be able to get through I ought to let the people at Third Army Headquarters know."

"Well, frankly I don't know just what the score is, but the colonel probably has definite information," he said. "What I meant about the bridge is that it's jammed with people and carts, all coming over to the west side of the Danube. It's been like that for the past two days and it can mean only one thing—that the Russians aren't far behind."

This wasn't too reassuring, but I decided to take a fatalistic attitude toward it. If I had to find some other route back from Hohenfurth, I'd worry about it when the time came. I did, however, try to get through to Third Army Headquarters on the phone. Posey's office didn't answer, so I asked Anderson to put in a call for me in the morning.

It was slow going over the bridge, but we finally forced our way through the welter of carts and wagons. Once we were in open country, the traffic thinned out and we moved along at a faster pace. The Czech and American officers at the frontier recognized us and waved us through without formality. We arrived in Hohenfurth a little before nine. I knew the ropes this time, so it was a simple matter to get the men billeted in the monastery. After that I went on to my own former billet. When I reached the house, I found a group of officers in the recreation room. They were holding an informal meeting. Colonel Sheehan was presiding and motioned to me to join the group. He had just returned from the headquarters at Budweis with important news. His own orders had come through, so he would be pulling out for home in a few days. But of greater concern to me was the news that the Czechs would definitely take over at the end of the week. We would still have some troops in the area, but their duties would be greatly curtailed. I would have to finish the job at the monastery as fast as possible and head back to Munich.

We resumed our work at the monastery with surprisingly few delays. It was almost as if there had been no interruption of our earlier operations. This time I had double the number of PWs, so I did not have to call on the drivers to help with the loading. During my absence, Dr. Mutter had put a stonemason to work on the pieces which had been set into the wall, and these now lay like parts of a puzzle in a neat pattern on the floor of the reception hall, ready to be packed. He had also procured lumber and nails, so my two extra packers were able to get to work on the cases which had to be built. By evening, seven of the trucks were loaded, leaving only one more to do the next day.

That night I consulted one of the officers, who had a wide knowledge of the roads in that area, about an alternate route to Munich. He showed me, on the map, a winding back road which would take me through Passau—instead of Linz and Salzburg—to Munich. It was, he said, a very "scenic route" but longer than the way I had come. He felt sure, though, that I could get my trucks through, that there were no bad detours, etc. It was comforting to know that this route existed as a possibility—just in case. But I still had hopes of being able to go back by way of Linz, in spite of the colonel's warning.

The next day was the Fourth of July—not that I expected either my French or German associates to take special notice of the fact. Still I was glad that I had only one truck to load on the holiday. I took advantage of the later breakfast hour, knowing that my faithful German packers would be on the job at seven o'clock as usual. When I arrived at the monastery at nine-thirty, I found that the last truck was already half loaded. There was enough room to add the two cases containing the Della Robbia plaque and the Renaissance fireplace taken out of the wall; and, if we were careful, we might find a place for the fifteenth century Florentine relief which the stonemason had also painstakingly removed. Once that was done, there was nothing to do but wait for the arrival of Lieutenant Moore and the additional trucks.

I called the workmen together. In halting German, I explained the significance of the Fourth of July and announced that there would be no more work that day. It was providentially near the lunch hour. I could send the PWs back to their camp as soon as they had eaten. The German packers, intent on returning to Munich as soon as possible, chose to get on with the cases they were building. Dr. Mutter and I retired to his study to take stock of the receipts we had thus far made out. As for the French drivers, they had disappeared to their quarters.

After lunching at the officers' mess, I decided to celebrate the Glorious Fourth in my own quiet way. Major Whittemore had lent me a car, so I set out on an expedition of my own devising. Ever since the night of our trip to Krummau, I had wanted to explore the castle of Rosenberg, and this seemed the logical time to do it. Rosenberg was only eight kilometers away.

It was a sleepy summer afternoon. Not a leaf was stirring as I followed the winding Moldau into the pretty village with its storybook castle. The road to the castle was rough and tortuous, reminding me of a back road in the Tennessee mountain country. Just as I was beginning to wonder if the little sedan were equal to the climb, the road turned sharply into a level areaway before the castle courtyard.

I parked the car and went in search of the caretaker. When I found no one, I ascended a flight of stone steps which led from the courtyard to the second floor. The room at the head of the stairs was empty, but I heard voices in the one adjoining. Two cleaning women were scrubbing the floor, chattering to each other as they worked. They were startled to see me, but one of them had the presence of mind to scurry off and return a few minutes later with the archetype of all castle caretakers. He had been custodian for the past fifty-six years. Lately there hadn't been many visitors.

He took me first to the picture gallery—a long high-ceilinged room with tall windows looking out over the river. There were a dozen full-length canvases around the rough plaster walls, past Dukes of Rosenberg and their sour-faced Duchesses. The *clou* of the collection was a tubercular lady in seventeenth century costume. The caretaker solemnly informed me that she was the ill-fated duchess who paced the ramparts of the castle every night just before twelve. She had lived, he told me, in the fourteenth century. When I mentioned as tactfully as possible that her gown indicated she had been a mere three hundred years ahead of the styles, he gave me a dirty look as much as to say, *'a disbeliever.'* I did my best to erase this unfortunate impression and proceeded to the next series of apartments. They included a weapon room, a sumptuous state bedchamber reserved for royal visitors, several richly furnished reception rooms, and a long gallery called the Crusaders' Hall—a copy, the caretaker said, of a room in the Palace at Versailles. Here hung full-length portraits of such historic personages as Godefroy de Bouillon, Robert Guiscard and Frederick Barbarossa—all done by an indifferent German painter of the last century. Notwithstanding its ostentatious atmosphere, the gallery had a dignity quite in keeping with the musty elegance of the castle.

I thanked the old man, gave him a couple of cigarettes and returned to the car. It was time for me to be getting back to the monastery.

I gauged my arrival nicely. As I pulled up to the entrance, the guard at the archway came over to the car to tell me that eight trucks had just driven through. When I reached the courtyard the last of them was backing up against the chapel wall.

A tall, rangy lieutenant, wearing the familiar helmet liner prescribed by Third Army regulations, walked up to the car as I was getting out and said, "Good afternoon, sir. Dr. Livingstone, I presume?"

So this was Lamont Moore. Just as Lincoln had predicted, I liked him at once. There was a quiet self-possession about him, coupled with a quizzical, humorous expression, which was pleasantly reassuring. I have never forgotten the impression of Olympian calm I received at that first meeting. In succeeding months, there were many times when Lamont got thoroughly riled, but his composure never deserted him.

His even temper and his sense of humor could always be depended upon to leaven the more impetuous actions of his companions.

Without wasting breath on inconsequential conversation, he suggested that we "case the joint." After introducing him to Dr. Mutter, who was still hovering around like a distracted schoolmaster, we made a tour of the premises. By the time we had finished I had the comforting, if somewhat unflattering, feeling that he had a clearer understanding of the work there than I, notwithstanding the time I had spent at the monastery.

On our way down to the village afterward, I asked Lament if he had had any difficulty coming up through Linz. He said no, but that he also had been warned not to return that way.

As soon as he had found a billet, we settled down to talk over the loading of his trucks. "The colonel says that we'll have to finish the job in a hurry. The Czechs are taking over at the end of the week," I said. "And if the Russians move up to the Danube, we won't be able to go back by way of Linz. We'll have to return by way of Passau."

"I understand that there isn't any bridge over the Danube at Passau," Lamont said quietly. At that I got excited, but in the same quiet voice Lamont said, "Don't worry. We've got more important things to think about—something to drink, for example."

We went over to the officers' club, arriving just in time to be offered a sample of the Fourth of July punch which two of the officers had been mixing that afternoon. From the look of things, they had perfect confidence in their recipe, which called for red wine, armagnac and champagne. After the first sip I didn't have to be told there would be fireworks in Hohenfurth that evening.

Lamont and I began to discuss mutual friends and acquaintances in the museum world, a habit deeply ingrained in members of our profession. We agreed that a mutual "hate" often brought people together more quickly than a mutual admiration. Then inconsistently— it was probably the punch—we started talking about Lincoln, whom we both liked very much.

"It was Lincoln who told me what a fine fellow you are, Lamont," I said.

"That's interesting," he said with a noiseless laugh. "He said the same thing about you."

Comparing notes, we found that Lincoln had given us identical vignettes of each other.

"Tell me something about the work you've been doing in MFA&A. This is my first real job, so I'm still a neophyte," I said.

Lamont rolled his eyes wearily and said, "Oh, I've been evacuating works of art for the past four months, and I wonder sometimes if it's ever going to end. Siegen was my big show. It was the foul and dripping copper mine in Westphalia where the priceless treasures from the Rhineland museums were stored. The shaft was two thousand feet deep and some of the mine chambers were more than half a mile from the shaft. Walker Hancock of First Army and George Stout had inspected it originally and advised immediate evacuation. But no place was available. First Army was pushing eastward, so all Walker could do was to reassure himself from time to time that the contents were adequately guarded.

"Shortly before VE-Day, I received a cryptic telegram at Ninth Army Headquarters stating that, as of midnight that particular night, Siegen was my headache. Then followed weeks of activity in which Walker, Steve and I were involved."

"Who is Steve?" I asked.

"Steve Kovalyak of Punxsutawney, Pennsylvania," said Lamont. "I think he's with George at Alt Aussee now. I hope you'll meet him. He's a great character.

"A bunker at Bonn was approved as a new repository for the Siegen treasures. I surveyed the roads to Bonn and found them impossible for truck transport. George was called to Alt Aussee. Walker went off to see about setting up a collecting point at Marburg.

"Then I was called back to Ninth Army Headquarters. The evacuation of Siegen was momentarily at a standstill.

"Later I returned and, with Walker's and Steve's assistance, completed the evacuation. We moved everything to Marburg, except the famous Romanesque doors from the church of Santa Maria im Kapitol. Walker took them to the cathedral at Cologne, along with the Aachen crown jewels.

"Siegen was the second major evacuation—perhaps you could say it was the first carried out by a *team* of MFA&A officers."

"What was the first?" I asked.

"The Merkers mine, where the Nazi gold and the Berlin Museum things were stored. That was the most spectacular of the early evacuations—that and Bernterode."

"What about Bernterode?" I asked. I had read Hancock's official report of the operation and had seen some snapshots taken in the mine, so I was curious to have a firsthand account.

"Walter Hancock was the officer in charge of the evacuation," said Lamont. "Like Siegen, it was a deep-shaft mine, so the contents had to be brought up by an elevator. It was a hell of a job to get the elevator back in working order. The dramatic thing about Bernterode was the discovery of a small chapel, or shrine, constructed in one of the mine chambers and then completely walled up.

"In this concealed shrine, the Nazis had placed the bronze sarcophagi of Frederick the Great, Frederick William—the Soldier King—and those of Von Hindenburg and his wife. On the coffins had been laid wreaths, ribbons and various insignia of the Party. Around and about them were some two hundred regimental banners, many of them dating from the early Prussian wars.

"When Walker was ready to take the coffins out of the mine, he found they were so large and heavy that they'd have to come up one at a time. He was standing at the top of the shaft as the coffin of Frederick the Great rose slowly from the depths. As it nearedı the level, a radio in the distance blared forth the 'Star-Spangled Banner.' And just as the coffin came into view, the radio band struck up 'God Save the King.' The date," Lamont added significantly, "was May the eighth."

If I thought I was going to get much sleep that night, I reckoned without the patriotic officers of the Yankee Division, who were hell-bent on making it a really Glorious Fourth. It had been my mistake in the first place to move into quarters directly over the recreation room. It wasn't much of a bedroom anyway—just an alcove with an eighteenth century settee for a bed. I was resting precariously on this spindly collector's item when the door was flung open and Major Thacher shouted that I was wanted below. I told him to go away. To my surprise he did—but only to return a few minutes later with reinforcements. I must come down at once— colonel's orders, and if I wouldn't come quietly, they'd carry me down. Before I could get off my settee, it was pitched forward and I sprawled on the floor. What fun it was for everybody— except me! I put on a dressing gown and was marched down the stairs. I had been called in, as a naval officer, to settle an argument: Who had won the Battle of Jutland? The Battle of Jutland, of all things! At that moment I wasn't at all sure in what war it had been fought, let alone who had won it. But assuming an assurance I was far from feeling I declared that it had been a draw. My luck was with me that night after all, for that had been the colonel's contention. So I was allowed to return to my makeshift bed.

Lamont took some of the wind out of my sails by assuring me the next morning that the British had defeated the German fleet at Jutland in 1916.

But we were having our own battle of Hohenfurth that morning, so I was too preoccupied to give Jutland more than a passing thought. Just before noon, as we finished our fourth truck, John Nicholas Brown and Mason Hammond arrived. Mason, as was his custom when traveling about Germany, was bundled up in a great sheepskin coat—the kind used by the Wehrmacht on the Russian front—and looked like something out of *Nanook of the North.* John, less arctically attired, hailed us gaily from the back seat of the command car.

Lamont and I suspended operations to show them around. We were pleased by their comments on our work—how admirably it was being handled and so on—but we struck a snag when we showed them Canova's marble Muse. Lamont and I had just about decided to leave her where she was. Our two visitors thought that would be a pity, a downright shame. We pointed out that to transport the statue would be a hazardous business, even if we succeeded in getting it onto a truck in the first place. We had no equipment with which to hoist anything so heavy. On our inspection tour they kept coming back to the subject of the Canova, and Lamont gave me an irritated look for having called their attention to it at all.

At lunch, which we had with the colonel, they fixed us. When the subject of the statue was brought up, the colonel instantly agreed to provide us with a winch and also two extra trucks. We needed the trucks all right, but we weren't particularly happy about the winch.

As soon as we got back to the monastery, we broke the news to Dr. Mutter. The Muse was about to take a trip. He held up his hands in dismay and said it would take us half a day to get the statue loaded.

When we told the German packers what we had in mind, they made a few clucking noises, and then began the necessary preparations. The first thing they did was to get hold of two logs, each about six feet in length and five inches in diameter.

With the help of a dozen PWs, they got them placed beneath the base of the statue. From that point on, it was a matter of slowly rolling the statue as the logs rolled. It was arduous work. A distance of well over four hundred yards was involved, and the last half of it was along a sloping ramp where it was particularly difficult to keep the heavy marble under control.

Once the truck was reached, it was necessary to set up a stout runway from the ground to the bed of the truck. This done, the next move was to place heavy pads around the base of the statue, so that the cable of the winch would not scratch the surface of the marble. It was a tense moment. Would the winch be strong enough to drag its heavy burden up the runway? It began to grind, and slowly the Muse slid up the boards, paused for a quivering instant and then glided majestically along the bed of the truck. There were cheers from the PWs who had gathered around the truck to watch. We all sighed with relief, and then congratulated the little packers who had engineered the whole operation. Dr. Mutter kept shaking his head in disbelief. He told us that when the statue had been brought to the monastery in the first place, it had taken three hours to unload it. The present operation had taken forty-five minutes.

After this triumph, the loading of the remaining trucks seemed an anticlimax, but we kept hard at it for the next six hours. By seven o'clock, all ten of them were finished. All told, we would be a convoy of eighteen trucks.

We were on the point of starting down to the village for supper, when Dr. Mutter, even more agitated than he had been before, rushed up and implored us to grant him a great favor. Would we, out of the kindness of our hearts—oh, he knew he had no right to ask such a favor—would we take him and his wife and little girl along with us to Linz the next day? Linz was his home, he had a house there. He had brought his family to Hohenfurth only because the Nazis wouldn't allow him to give up his duties as custodian of the collections at the monastery. Now the Czechs were going to be in complete control. He and his family were Austrians and there was no telling what would happen to them.

How news does get around, I thought to myself. We hadn't said a word about the Czechs taking over, but when I expressed the proper surprise and asked him where he had heard *that* rumor, he wagged his head as much as to say, "Oh, I know what I am talking about, all right!"

My heart wasn't exactly bleeding for Dr. Mutter, but at the thought of his little girl, who was about the age of my own, I couldn't say no. I told him to be ready to leave at seven the next morning. I didn't tell him how uncertain it was that we would ever get to Linz at all.

It was pouring when I crawled out of my bed at six a.m. I seemed to specialize in bad weather, particularly when starting out with a convoy! At the monastery everything was in order. At the last minute I decided to tell Dr, Mutter there was a possibility—even a probability—that we would not be able to cross over at Linz, and I told him why. He was terrified when I mentioned the prospect of being stopped by the Russians. I assured him that we would drop him and his family off at one of the villages on the other side of the Austrian border, if we found there was going to be trouble. It was cold comfort but the best I had to offer.

I climbed into the lead truck, Lamont into the tenth, and Leclancher, as usual, took over the last truck. Leclancher, with his customary ability to pull a rabbit out of a hat at a critical juncture, had found among his drivers one who spoke some Russian, so we had put him at the controls of the first truck. It might make a good impression.

Once again we had a jeep escort to the border, and there we picked up three others to conduct us as far as Linz. The cocky little sergeant in the jeep that was to lead came over to my truck, squinted up at me and said, "You look nervous this morning, Lieutenant."

Well, I thought, if it's that apparent, what's the use of denying it? "I am," I said. "This is a big convoy and it's filled with millions of dollars' worth of stuff. I'd hate to have anything happen to it."

He whistled at that. Then, rubbing his hands briskly, he retorted, "And nothing is going to happen to it."

He took off and we swung in behind him. The first hour was a long one. There was more traffic than ever before—a steady stream of carts all moving toward Linz. At last we shifted into low gear, and I knew that we were on the steep grade leading down to Urfahr. If there were going to be trouble, we'd know it in a minute. At that moment, the sergeant in the lead jeep turned around and waved. I thought, There's trouble ahead. But he was only signaling that the road was clear.

We rolled over the rough cobblestones onto the bridge. I saw the gleaming helmet liners of the new escort awaiting us as we drew up to the center of the span. I motioned to one of our new guardians that we would stop at the first convenient place on the other side.

We were such a long convoy that I thought we'd be halfway through Linz before our escort directed us to pull over to the curb. There we unloaded the Mutter family and their luggage. The doctor and his wife were tearfully grateful and the little girl smiled her thanks.

I was feeling relaxed and happy and wanted to share my relief with someone, so I suggested to Lamont that we pay our respects to the colonel who had warned us not to come through Linz. It was a letdown to find only a warrant officer in the colonel's anteroom. But he remembered us and was surprised to see us again. He said we had been lucky; the latest news was that the Russians would move up to the opposite side of the Danube by noon. We left appropriate messages for the colonel and his adjutant, returned to our trucks and headed west toward Lambach.

As on the previous trip, the escort turned back at that point. A new one—this time an impressive array of six armed jeeps—shepherded us from there. We stopped for lunch with a Corps of Engineers outfit of the 11th Armored Division on the outskirts of Schwannenstadt. The C.O., Major Allen, and his executive officer, Captain Myers, welcomed us as warmly as if we had been commanding generals instead of a motley crew of eighteen French drivers, plus twelve "noncoms" from the escorting jeeps—a total of thirty-two, including Lamont and me. We doled out K rations to our four packers, for we couldn't take civilians into an Army mess.

After lunch I telephoned ahead to Salzburg to ask for an escort from there to Munich, requesting that it meet us on the edge of tcrwn, east of the river. The weather had cleared, and drying patches of water on the road reflected a blue sky. By the time we had sighted Salzburg it was actually hot. As we rolled into the outskirts we were enveloped in clouds of dust from the steady procession of military vehicles. We waited in vain for our new escort. After an hour we decided to proceed without one. I didn't like the idea very much, but it was getting on toward five o'clock, and we wanted to reach Munich in time for supper. We fell far short of our goal, being forced to stop once because of a flat tire, and a second time because of carburetor trouble. These two delays cost us close to two hours. At seven o'clock we halted by the placid waters of Chiemsee and ate cold C rations in an idyllic setting. It was after nine when we lumbered into the parking area behind the Gargantuan depot at the Königsplatz. Lamont and I had twin objectives—hot baths and bed. It didn't take us long to achieve both!

We had had every intention of making an early start the next morning, not so much because of any blind faith in Benjamin Franklin's precepts, but simply because they stopped serving breakfast in the Third Army mess shortly before eight o'clock. In fact, the first thing one saw on entering the mess hall was a large placard which stated peremptorily, "The mess will be cleared by 0800. By order of the Commanding General." And such was Third Army discipline—we had a different name for it—that the mess hall was completely devoid of life on the stroke of eight.

It was a little after seven when I woke up. Lamont was still dead to the world, so I shaved and dressed before waking him. There was a malevolent gleam in his eyes when he finally opened them. He asked frigidly, "Are you always so infernally cheerful at this hour of the morning?" I told him not to confuse cheerfulness with common courtesy, and mentioned the peculiar breakfast habits of the Third Army.

We arrived at the mess hall with a few minutes to spare. The sergeant at the entrance asked to see our mess cards. We had none but I explained that we were attached to the headquarters.

"Temporary duty?" he asked.

"Yes, just temporary duty," I said with a hint of thankfulness.

"Then you can't eat here. Take the bus to the Transient Officers' Mess downtown."

I asked about the bus schedule. "Last bus left at 0745," he said. It was then 0750.

"Well, how do you like 'chicken' for breakfast?" I asked Lamont as we walked out to the empty street.

There was nothing to do but walk along until we could hail a passing vehicle. We had gone a good half mile before we got a lift. Knowing that the downtown mess closed at eight, I thought we'd better try the mess hall at the Military Government Detachment where the officers usually lingered till about eight-thirty. Among the laggards we found Ham Coulter and Craig. After airing our views on the subject of Third Army hospitality, we settled down to a good breakfast and a full account of our trip back from Hohenfurth. We told Craig that a couple of our French drivers were to meet us at the Collecting Point at nine. They were to bring some of the trucks around for unloading before noon. It was a Saturday and in Bavaria everything stopped at noon. Once in a great while Craig could persuade members of his civilian crew to work on Saturday afternoons, but it was a custom they didn't hold with, so he avoided it whenever possible. There were those who frowned on this kind of "coddling," as they called it, but they just didn't know their Bavarians. Craig did, and I think he got more work out of his people than if he had tried to change their habits.

We spent part of the morning with Herr Döbler, the chief packer, at the Collecting Point, helping him decipher our trucking lists, hastily prepared at Hohenfurth in longhand. Meanwhile the trucks, one after another, drew up to the unloading platform and disgorged their precious contents. The descent of the marble Muse caused a flurry of excitement. Our description of loading the statue had lost nothing in the telling and we were anxious to see how she had stood the trip. The roads had been excruciatingly rough in places, especially at Linz and on the dread detour near Rosenheim. At each chuckhole I had offered up a little prayer. But my worries had been groundless—she emerged from the truck in all her gleaming, snow-white perfection.

Just before noon, Captain Posey summoned Lamont and me to his office. He cut short our account of the Hohenfurth operation with the news that we were to leave that afternoon for the great mine at Alt Aussee. At last we were to join George—both of us. George was going to have his team after all.

A command car had already been ordered. The driver was to pick us up at one-thirty. Posey got out a map and showed us the road we were to take beyond Salzburg. As his finger ran along the red line of the route marked with the names St. Gilgen, St. Wolfgang, Bad Ischl and

Bad Aussee, our excitement grew. Untold treasures were waiting to be unearthed at the end of it.

He said that the trip would take about six hours. We could perhaps stop off at Bad Aussee for supper. Two naval officers—Lieutenants Plaut and Rousseau, both of them OSS—had set up a special interrogation center there, an establishment known simply as "House 71," and were making an intensive investigation of German art-looting activities. They lived very well, Posey said with a grin. We could do a lot worse than to sample their hospitality. I knew Jim Plaut and Ted Rousseau—in fact had seen them at Versailles not so many weeks ago—so I thought we could prevail on them to take us in.

The mention of food reminded Lamont that we ought to pick up a generous supply of rations—the kind called "ten-in-ones"— somewhere along the road. The captain gave us a written order for that, and also provided each of us with a letter stating that we were authorized to "enter art repositories in the area occupied by the Third U. S. Army." Our earlier permits had referred to specific localities. These were blanket permits—marks of signal favor, we gathered from the ceremonious manner in which they were presented to us.

There were various odds and ends to be attended to before we could get off, among them the business of our PX rations. That was Lamont's idea. He said that we might not be able to get them later. He was right; they were the last ones we were able to lay our hands on for three weeks.

LOOT UNDERGROUND: THE SALT MINE AT ALT AUSSEE

It was nearly two o'clock by the time we were ready to start. I was now so familiar with the road between Munich and Salzburg that I felt like a commuter. Just outside Salzburg, Lamont began looking for signs that would lead us to a Quartermaster depot. He finally caught sight of one and, after following a devious route which took us several miles off the main road, we found the depot. We were issued two compact and very heavy wooden boxes bound with metal strips. We dumped them on the floor of the command car and drove on into town.

Across the river, we picked up a secondary road which led out of the city in a southeasterly direction. For some miles it wound through hills so densely wooded that we could see but little of the country. Then, emerging from the tunnel of evergreens, we skirted Fuschl See, the first of the lovely Alpine lakes in that region. Somewhere along its shores, we had been told, Ribbentrop had had a castle. It was being used now as a recreation center for American soldiers.

Our road led into more rugged country. We continued to climb and with each curve of the road the scenery became more spectacular. After an hour's drive we reached St. Gilgen, its neat white houses and picturesque church spire silhouetted against the blue waters of St. Wolfgang See. Then on past the village of Strobl and finally into the crooked streets of Bad Ischl, where the old Emperor Franz Josef had spent so many summers. From Bad Ischl our road ribboned through Laufen and Goisern to St. Agatha.

Beyond St. Agatha lay the Potschen Pass. The road leading up to it was a series of hairpin turns and dangerous grades. As we ground slowly up the last steep stretch to the summit, I wondered what route George was using for his convoys from the mine. Surely not this one. Large trucks couldn't climb that interminable grade. I found out later that this was the only road to Alt Aussee.

On the other side of the pass, the road descended gradually into a rolling valley and, in another half hour, we clattered into the narrow main street of Bad Aussee. From there it was only a few miles to Alt Aussee. Midway between the two villages we hoped to find the house of our OSS friends.

We came upon it unexpectedly, around a sharp bend in the road. It was a tall, gabled villa, built in the gingerbread style of fifty years ago. Having pictured a romantic chalet tucked away in the mountains, I was disappointed by this rather commonplace suburban structure, standing behind a stout iron fence with padlocked gates, within a stone's throw of the main highway.

Jim and Ted received us hospitably and took us to an upper veranda with wicker chairs and a table immaculately set for dinner. We were joined by a wiry young lieutenant colonel, named Harold S. Davitt, who bore a pronounced resemblance to the Duke of Windsor. He was the commanding officer of a battalion of the 11th Armored Division stationed at Alt Aussee, the little village just below the mine. Colonel Davitt's men constituted the security guard at the mine. He knew and admired our friend George Stout. It was strange and pleasant to be again in an atmosphere of well-ordered domesticity. To us it seeriied rather a fine point when one of our hosts rebuked the waitress for serving the wine in the wrong kind of glasses.

During dinner we noticed a man pacing about the garden below. He was Walter Andreas Hofer, who had been Göring's agent and adviser in art matters. A shrewd and enterprising Berlin dealer before the war, Hofer had succeeded in ingratiating himself with the Reichsmarschall. He, more than any other single individual, had been responsible for shaping Göring's taste and had played the stellar role in building up his priceless collection of Old Masters.

Some of his methods had been ingenious. He was credited with having devised the system of "birthday gifts"—a scheme whereby important objects were added to the collection at no cost to the Reichsmarschall. Each year, before Göring's birthday on January twelfth, Hofer wrote letters to wealthy industrialists and businessmen suggesting that the Reichsmarschall would be gratified to receive a token of their continued regard for him. Then he would designate a specific work of art—and the price. More often than not, the piece in question had already been acquired. The prospective donor had only to foot the bill. Now and then the victim of this shakedown protested the price, but he usually came through.

In Hofer, the Reichsmarschall had had a henchman as rapacious and greedy as himself. And Hofer had possessed what his master lacked—a wide knowledge of European collections and the international art market. Göring had been a gold mine and Hofer had made the most of it.

Hofer had been arrested shortly after the close of hostilities. He had been a "guest" at House 71 for some weeks now, and was being grilled daily by our "cloak and dagger boys." They were probing into his activities of the past few years and had already extracted an amazing lot of information for incorporation into an exhaustive report on the Göring collection and "how it grew." Hofer was just one of a long procession of witnesses who were being questioned by Plaut and Rousseau in the course of their tireless investigation of the artistic depredations of the top Nazis. These OSS officers knew their business. With infinite patience, they were cross-examining their witnesses and gradually extracting information which was to lend an authentic fascination to their reports.

Hofer's wife, they told us, had ably assisted her husband. Her talents as an expert restorer had been useful. She had been charged with the technical care of the Göring collection—no small job when one stopped to consider that it numbered over a thousand pictures. Indeed, there had been more than enough work to keep one person busy all the time. We learned that Frau Hofer was living temporarily at Berchtesgaden where, until recently, she had been allowed to attend to emergency repairs on some of the Göring pictures there.

We turned back to the subject of Hofer, who had not yet finished his daily constitutional and could be seen still pacing back and forth below us. He was, they said, a voluble witness and had an extraordinary memory. He could recall minute details of complicated transactions which had taken place several years before. On one occasion Hofer had recommended an exchange of half a dozen paintings of secondary importance for two of the very first quality. As I recall, the deal involved a group of seventeenth century Dutch pictures on the one hand, and two Bouchers on the others. Hofer had been able to reel off the names of all of them and even give the price of each. It was just such feats of memory, they said with a laugh, that made his vague and indefinite answers to certain other questions seem more than merely inconsistent.

Listening to our hosts, we had forgotten the time. It was getting late and George would be wondering what had happened to us. There had been a heavy downpour while we were at dinner. The , weather had cleared now, but the evergreens were dripping as we pulled out of the drive.

The road to Alt Aussee ran along beside the swift and milky waters of an Alpine river. It was a beautiful drive in the soft evening light. The little village with its winding streets and brightly painted chalets was an odd setting for GIs and jeeps, to say nothing of our lumbering command car.

We found our way to the Command Post, which occupied a small hotel in the center of the village. There we turned sharply to the right, into a road so steep that it made the precipitous grades over which we had come earlier that afternoon seem level by comparison. We drove about a mile on this road and I was beginning to wonder if we wouldn't soon be above the timber line—perhaps even in the region of "eternal snow" to which Roger had once so poetically referred—when we came to a bleak stone building perched precariously on a narrow strip of level ground. Behind it, a thousand feet below, stretched an unbroken sea of deep pine forests. This was the control post, and the guard, a burly GI armed with a rifle, signaled us to stop. We asked for Lieutenant Stout. He motioned up the road, where, in the gathering dusk, we could distinguish the outlines of a low building facing an irregular terrace. It was a distance of about two hundred yards. We drove on up to the entrance where we found George waiting for us.

He took us into the building which he said contained the administrative offices of the salt mine—the Steinbergwerke, now a government monopoly—and his own living quarters. We entered a kind of vestibule with white plaster walls and a cement floor. A narrow track, the rails of which were not more than eighteen inches apart, led from the entrance to a pair of heavy doors in the far wall. "That," said George, "is the entrance to the mine."

He led the way to a room on the second floor. Its most conspicuous feature was a large porcelain stove. The woodwork was knotty pine. Aside from the two single beds, the only furniture was a built-in settle with a writing table which filled one corner. The table had a red and white checked cover and over it, suspended from the ceiling, was an adjustable lamp with a red and white checked shade. Opening off this room was another bedroom, also pine-paneled, which was occupied by the captain of the guard and one other officer. George apologized for the fact that the only entrance to the other room was through ours. Apparently, in the old days, the two rooms had formed a suite—ours having been the sitting room—reserved for important visitors to the mine. For the first few days there was so much coming and going that we had all the privacy of Grand Central Station, but we soon got used to the traffic. George and Steve Kovalyak shared a room just down the hall. Lamont had spoken of Steve when we had been at Hohenfurth, and I was curious to meet this newcomer to the MFA&A ranks. George said that Steve would be back before long. He had gone out with Shrady. That was Lieutenant Frederick Shrady, the third member of the trio of Monuments Officers at the mine.

While Lamont and I were getting our things unpacked, George sat and talked with us about the work at the mine and what he expected us to do. As he talked he soaked his hand in his helmet liner filled with hot water. He had skinned one of his knuckles and an infection had set in. The doctors wanted to bring the thing to a head before lancing it the next day. I had noticed earlier that one of his hands looked red and swollen. But George hadn't said anything about it. As he was not one to relish solicitous inquiries, I refrained from making any comment.

George outlined the local situation briefly. The principal bottleneck in the operation lay in the selection of the stuff which was to be brought out of the various mine chambers. There were, he said, something like ten thousand pictures stored in them, to say nothing of sculpture, furniture, tapestries, rugs and books. At the moment he was concentrating on the pictures and he wanted to get the best of them out first. The less important ones—particularly the works of the nineteenth century German painters whom Hitler admired so much—could wait for later removal.

He and Steve and Shrady had their hands full aboveground. That left only Sieber, the German restorer, who had been at the mine ever since it had been converted into an art repository, to choose the paintings down below. In addition Sieber had to supervise the other subterranean operations, which included carrying the paintings from the storage racks, dividing them into groups according to size, and padding the corners so that the canvases wouldn't rub together on the way up to the mine entrance. Where we could be of real help would be down in the mine chambers, picking out the cream of the pictures and getting them up topside. (George's vocabulary was peppered with nautical expressions.)

In the midst of his deliberate recital, we heard a door slam. The chorus of "Giannina Mia" sung in a piercingly melodic baritone echoed from the stairs. "Steve's home," said George.

A second later there was a knock on the door and the owner of the voice materialized. Steve looked a bit startled when he caught sight of two strange faces, but he grinned good-naturedly as George introduced us.

"I thought you were going out on the town with Shrady tonight," said George.

"No," said Steve, "I left him down in the village and came back to talk to Kress."

Kress was an expert photographer who had been with the Kassel Museum before the war. He had been captured when our troops took over at the mine just as the war ended. Since Steve's arrival, he had been his personal PW. Steve was an enthusiastic amateur and had acquired all kinds of photographic equipment. Kress, we gathered, was showing him how to use it. Their "conversations" were something of a mystery, because Steve knew no German, Kress no English.

"I use my High German, laddies," Steve would say with a crafty grin and a lift of the eyebrows, as he teetered on the balls of his feet.

We came to the conclusion that "High German" was so called

because it transcended all known rules of grammar and pronunciation. But, for the two of them, it worked. Steve—stocky, gruff and belligerent—and Kress—timid, beady-eyed and patient— would spend hours together. They were a comical pair. Steve was always in command and very much the captor. Kress was long-suffering and had a kind of doglike devotion to his master, whose alternating jocular and tyrannical moods he seemed to accept with equanimity and understanding. But all this we learned later.

That first evening, while George went on with his description of the work, Steve sat quietly appraising Lamont and me with his keen, gray-green eyes. He had worked with Lamont at Bemterode, so I was his main target. Now and then he would look over at George and throw in a remark. Between the two there existed an extraordinary bond. As far as Steve was concerned, George was perfect, and Steve had no use for anyone who thought otherwise. If, at the end of a hard day, he occasionally beefed about George and his merciless perfection—well, that was Steve's prerogative. For his part, George had a fatherly affection for Steve and a quiet admiration for his energy and resourcefulness and the way he handled the men under him.

Presently Steve announced that it was late and went off to bed. I wondered if he had sized me up. There was a flicker of amusement in Lamont's eyes and I guessed that he was wondering the same thing. When George got up to go, he said, "You'll find hot water down in the kitchen in the morning. Breakfast will be at seven-thirty."

Steve roused us early with a knock on the door and said he'd show us the way to the kitchen. We rolled out, painfully conscious of the cold mountain air. Below, in the warm kitchen, the sun was pouring in through the open door. There were still traces of snow on the mountaintops. The highest peak, Steve said, was Loser. Its snowy coronet glistened in the bright morning light.

When my eyes became accustomed to the glare, I noticed that there were several other people in the kitchen. One of them, a wrinkled little fellow wearing *Lederhosen* and white socks, was standing by the stove. Steve saluted them cheerfully with a wave of his towel. They acknowledged his greeting with good-natured nods and gruff monosyllables. These curious mountain people, he said, belonged to families that had worked in the mine for five hundred years. They were working for us now, as members of his evacuation crew.

We washed at a row of basins along one wall. Above them hung a sign lettered with the homely motto:

"Nach der Arbeit
Vor dem Essen
Hande waschen
Nicht vergessen"

It rang a poignant bell in my memory. That same admonition to wash before eating had hung in the little pension at near-by Gründlsee where I had spent a summer fifteen years ago.

Our mess hall was in the guardhouse down the road, the square stone building where the sentry had challenged us the night before. We lined up with our plates and, when they had been heaped with scrambled eggs, helped ourselves to toast, jam and coffee and sat down at a long wooden table in the adjoining room. George was finishing his breakfast as the three of us came in. With him was Lieutenant Shrady, who had recently been commissioned a Monuments officer at Bad Homburg. Subsequently he had been sent down to Alt Aussee by Captain Posey. He was a lean, athletic, good-looking fellow. Although he helped occasionally with the loading, his primary duties at the mine were of an administrative nature—handling the workmen's payrolls through the local Military Government Detachment, obtaining their food rations, making inspections in the area, filing reports and so on. After he and George had left, Steve told us that Shrady was a portrait painter. Right now he was working on a portrait of his civilian interpreter-secretary who, according to Steve, was something rather special in the way of Viennese beauty. This was a new slant on the work at the mine and I was curious to know more about the glamorous Maria, whom Steve described as being "beaucoup beautiful." But George was waiting to take us down into the mine. As we walked up the road, Steve explained to us that the miners worked in two shifts—one crew from four in the morning until midday, another from noon until eight in the evening. The purpose of the early morning shift was to maintain an uninterrupted flow of "stuff" from the mine, so that the daytime loading of the trucks would not bog down for lack of cargo.

At the building in which the mine entrance was located we found George with a group of the miners. It was just eight o'clock and the day's work was starting. We were introduced to two men dressed in white uniforms which gave them an odd, hybrid appearance—a cross between a street cleaner and a musical-comedy hussar. This outfit consisted of a white duck jacket and trousers. The jacket had a wide, capelike collar reaching to the shoulders. Two rows of ornamental blade buttons converging at the waistline adorned the front of the jacket, and a similar row ran up the sleeves from cuff to elbow. In place of a belt, the jacket was held in place by a tape drawstring. A black garrison cap completed the costume.

The two men were Karl Sieber, the restorer, and Max Eder, an engineer from Vienna. It was Eder's job to list the contents of each truck. Perched on a soapbox, he sat all day at the loading entrance, record book and paper before him on a makeshift desk. He wrote down the number of each object as it was carried through the door to the truck outside. The truck list was made in duplicate: the original was sent to Munich with the convoy; the copy was kept at the mine to be incorporated in the permanent records which Lieutenant Shrady was compiling in his office on the floor above.

In the early days of their occupancy, the Nazis had recorded the loot, piece by piece, as it entered the mine. The records were voluminous and filled many ledgers. But, during the closing months of the war, such quantities of loot had poured in that the system had broken down. Instead of a single accession number, an object was sometimes given a number which merely indicated with what shipment it had arrived. Occasionally there would be several numbers on a single piece. Frequently a piece would have no number at all. In spite of this confusion, Eder managed somehow to produce orderly lists. If the information they contained was not always definitive, it was invariably accurate.

George was anxious to get started. "It's cold down in the mine," he said. "You'd better put on the warmest things you brought with you."

"How cold is it?" I asked.

"Forty degrees, Fahrenheit," he said. "The temperature doesn't vary appreciably during the year. I believe it rises to forty-seven in the winter. And the humidity is equally constant, about sixty-five per cent. That's why this particular salt mine was chosen as a repository, as you probably know."

While we went up to get our jackets and mufflers, George ordered Sieber to hitch up the train. When we returned we noticed that the miners, who resembled a troop of Walt Disney dwarfs, were wearing heavy sweaters and thick woolen jackets for protection against the subterranean cold.

The train's locomotion was provided by a small gasoline engine with narrow running boards on either side which afforded foothold for the operator. Attached to it were half a dozen miniature flatcars or "dollies." The miners called them "Hünde," that is, dogs. They were about five feet long, and on them were placed heavy wooden boxes approximately two feet wide. The sides were roughly two feet high.

Following George's example, we piled a couple of blankets on the bottom of one of the boxes and squeezed ourselves in. Each box, with judicious crowding, would accommodate two people facing each other.

At a signal from Sieber, who was sardined into a boxcar with George, one of the gnomes primed the engine. After a couple of false starts, it began to chug and the train rumbled into the dim cavern ahead. For the first few yards, the irregular walls were whitewashed, but we soon entered a narrow tunnel cut through the natural rock. It varied in height and width. In some places there would be overhead clearance of seven or eight feet, and a foot or more on either side. In others the passageway was just wide enough for the train, and the jagged rocks above seemed menacingly close. There were electric lights in part of the tunnel, but these were strung at irregular intervals. They shed a dim glow on the moist walls.

George shouted that we would stop first at the Kaiser Josef mine. The track branched and a few minutes later we stopped beside a heavy iron door set in the wall of the passageway. This part of the tunnel was not illuminated, so carbide lamps were produced. By their flickering light, George found the keyhole and unlocked the door.

We followed him into the unlighted mine chamber. Flashlights supplemented the wavering flames of the miners' lamps. Ahead of us we could make out row after row of huge packing cases. Beyond them was a broad wooden platform. The rays of our flashlights revealed a bulky object resting on the center of the platform. We came closer. We could see that it was a statue, a marble statue. And then we knew—it was Michelangelo's Madonna from Bruges, one of the world's great masterpieces. The light of our lamps played over the soft folds of the Madonna's robe, the delicate modeling of the face. Her grave eyes looked down, seemed only half aware of the sturdy Child nestling close against her, one hand firmly held in hers. It is one of the earliest works of the great sculptor and one of his loveliest. The incongruous setting of the bare boards served only to enhance its gentle beauty.

The statue was carved by Michelangelo in 1501, when he was only twenty-six. It was bought from the sculptor by the Mouscron brothers of Bruges, who presented it to the Church of Notre Dame early in the sixteenth century. There it had remained until September 1944, when the Germans, using the excuse that it must be "saved" from the American barbarians, carried it off.

In the early days of the war, the statue had been removed from its traditional place in the Chapel of the Blessed Sacrament to a specially built shelter in another part of the church. The shelter was not sealed, so visitors could see the statue on request. Then one afternoon in September 1944, the Bishop of Bruges, prompted by the suggestion of a German officer that the statue was not adequately protected, ordered the shelter bricked up. That night, before his orders could be carried out, German officers arrived at the church and demanded that the dean hand over the statue. With an armed crew standing by, they removed it from the shelter, dumped it onto a mattress on the floor of a Red Cross lorry and drove away. At the same time, they perpetrated another act of vandalism. They took with them eleven paintings belonging to the church. Among them were works by Gerard David, Van Dyck and Caravaggio. The statue and the pictures were brought to the Alt Aussee mine. It was a miracle that the two lorries with their precious cargo got through safely, for the roads were being constantly strafed by Allied planes.

Now we were about to prepare the Madonna for the trip back. This time she would have more than a mattress for protection.

In the same mine chamber with the Michelangelo was another plundered masterpiece of sculpture—an ancient Greek sarcophagus from Salonika. It had been excavated only a few years ago and was believed to date from the sixth century B.C. Already the Greek government was clamoring for its return.

On our way back to the train, George said that the other cases— the ones we had seen when we first went into the Kaiser Josef mine— contained the dismantled panels of the Millionen Zimmer and the Chinesisches Kabinett from Schonbrunn. The Alt Aussee mine, he said, had been originally selected by the Viennese as a depot for Austrian works of art, which accounted for the panels being there. They had been brought to the mine in 1942. Then, a year later, the Nazis took it over as a repository for the collections of the proposed Führer Museum at Linz.

We boarded the train again and rumbled along a dark tunnel to the Mineral Kabinett, one of the smaller mine chambers. Again there was an iron door to be unlocked. We walked through a vestibule into a low-ceilinged room about twenty feet square. The walls were light partitions of unfinished lumber. Ranged about them were the panels of the great Ghent altarpiece—the *Adoration of the Mystic Lamb*—their jewel-like beauty undimmed after five hundred years. The colors were as resplendent as the day they were painted by Hubert and Jan van Eyck in 1432.

This famous altarpiece, the greatest single treasure of Belgium, had also been seized by the Germans. One of the earliest examples of oil painting, it consisted originally of twelve panels, eight of which were painted on both sides. It was planned as a giant triptych of four central panels, with four panels at either side. The matching side panels were designed to fold together like shutters over a window. Therefore they were painted on both sides. '

I knew something of the history of the altarpiece. It belonged originally to the Cathedral of St. Bavon in Ghent. Early in the nineteenth century, the wings had been purchased by Edward Solly, an Englishman living in Germany. In 1816, he had sold them to the King of Prussia and they were placed in the Berlin Museum. There they had remained until restored to Belgium by the terms of the Versailles Treaty. From 1918 on, the entire triptych was again in the Cathedral of St. Bavon. In 1933, the attention of the world was drawn to the altarpiece when the panel in the lower left-hand corner was stolen. This was one of the panels painted on both sides. The obverse represented the *Knights of Christ;* the reverse, *St. John the Baptist.*

According to the story, the thief sent the cathedral authorities an anonymous letter demanding a large sum of money and guarantee of his immunity for the return of the panels. As proof that the panels were in his possession, he is said to have returned the reverse panel with his extortion letter. The authorities agreed to these terms but sought to lay a trap for the culprit. Their attempt was unsuccessful and nothing was heard of the panel until a year or so later.

On his deathbed, the thief—one of the beadles of the cathedral-confessed his guilt. As he lay dying, he managed to gasp, "You will find the panel..but he got no further. The panel has never been found.

In May 1940, the Belgians entrusted the altarpiece to France for safekeeping. Packed in ten cases, it was stored in the Château of Pau together with many important works of art from the Louvre. The Director of the French National Museums, mindful of his grave responsibilities, obtained explicit guarantees from the Germans that these treasures would be left inviolate. By the terms of this agreement, confirmed by the Vichy Ministry of Fine Arts, the Ghent altar was not to be moved without the joint consent of the Director of the French National Museums, the Mayor of Ghent and the German organization for the protection of French monuments.

Notwithstanding this contract, the Director of the French National Museums learned quite by accident in August 1942 that the altarpiece had just been taken to Paris. Dr. Ernst Buchner, who was director of the Bavarian State Museums, in company with three other German officers had gone to Pau the day before with a truck and ordered the Director of the Museum there to hand over the retable. A telegram from M. Bonnard, Vichy Minister of Fine Arts, arriving simultaneously, reinforced Dr. Buchner's demands. Nothing was known of its destination or whereabouts, beyond the fact that it had been taken to Paris.

There the matter rested until the summer of 1944. With the arrival of Allied armies on French soil, reports of missing masterpieces were received by pur MFA&A officers. The Ghent altarpiece was among them. But there were no clues as to where it had gone. Months passed and by the time our troops had approached Germany, our Monuments officers, all similarly briefed with photographs and other pertinent data concerning stolen works of art, began to hear rumors about the *Lamb*.

It might be in the Rhine fortress of Ehrenbreitstein; perhaps it had been taken to the Berghof at Berchtesgaden or possibly to Karinhall, Göring's palatial estate near Berlin. And then again it might have been flown out of the country altogether—to one of the neutral countries, Spain or Switzerland.

Captain Posey and Private Lincoln Kirstein picked up additional rumors from museum directors in Luxembourg. They had heard that the altarpiece was in a salt mine, but they had also been told that it was in the vaults of the Berlin Reichsbank. It was impossible to reconcile these conflicting pieces of information. Finally, near Trier, Posey and Kirstein tracked down a young German scholar who had been in France during the occupation. Lincoln told me later that it was hard to believe that this unassuming fellow had been high in the confidence of Göring and other members of the Nazi inner circle. From him they learned that the altarpiece had been taken to Alt Aussee.

Then followed the rapid advance across Germany. To Posey and Kirstein it was a period of agonizing suspense. They couldn't be sure that Third Army would move into the area in which the mine lay. Just as their hopes began to fade, occupancy of the cherished area did fall to Third Army. Tactical troops were alerted to the importance of the isolated mountain region. It was of no significance as a military objective and would doubtless otherwise have been left unoccupied for the moment. They pressed forward through Bad Ischl and the wild confusion of capitulating German troops to the wilder confusion of surrendering SS units in the little village of Alt Aussee itself. From there it was but a mile to the mine.

When they reached the mine, they found it heavily guarded by men of the 80th Infantry Division, but the mine had been dynamited. It wasn't possible to go into the mine chambers. Armed with acetylene lamps, Posey and Lincoln entered the main tunnel. They groped their way along the damp passageway for a distance of a quarter of a mile or more before they reached the debris of the first block. After assessing the damage they returned to consult the Austrian mineworkers. The miners said it would take from ten days to two weeks to clear the passageway. Captain Posey thought that the Army Engineers could do it in less than a week, perhaps in two or three days. Both were wrong. They entered the first mine chamber the next day.

And now, here before us, stood the fabulous panels which they had found on that May morning a few weeks before. While we examined them, Sieber pieced out the one gap in the story of the altarpiece: the Nazis had taken it from Paris to the Castle of Neuschwanstein where a restorer from Munich worked on the blisters which had developed on some of the panels. The altarpiece remained at the castle for two years. It was brought to the mine in the summer of 1944. Pieces of waxed paper were still affixed to the surface of the panels, on the places where the blisters had been laid. The big panel representing St. John had split lengthwise with the grain of wood. This had happened at the mine. Sieber had repaired it, and George said he had done a good job. As we were leaving the Mineral Kabinett, Sieber asked me if An* drew Mellon really had offered ten million dollars for the altarpiece. People had said so in Berlin. I hated to tell him that the story was without foundation, so far as I knew.

When we came out of the mine at noon we found that Steve and Shrady had finished loading two trucks. They said· they had enough pictures left to fill two more. The afternoon crew would be coming on at four. In the meantime it was up to Lamont and me to select at least two hundred paintings, so that the loading could go on without interruption.

After lunch we returned to the mine with Sieber. This time the trip on the train was much longer. Our objective was a part of the mine called the Springerwerke. Owing to the peculiar honeycomb structure of the mine network, it had been necessary to establish guard posts at intervals along the tunnels. One of these was at the entrance to the Springerwerke. Two GIs were on duty. It was a dismal assignment as well as a cold one. They were bundled up in fleece-lined coats which had been made for German troops on the Russian front. George and Steve had obtained about two hundred of these coats and were using them for packing unframed pictures. Each time a convoy of empty trucks returned from Munich, they counted the coats carefully to make sure that none had disappeared.

The Springerwerke contained more than two thousand paintings. They were arranged in two tiers around three sides and down the center of a room fifty feet long and thirty feet wide. In one section we found thirty or forty Italian paintings of the fourteenth and fifteenth centuries from the well known Lanz Collection of Amsterdam. Next to them we came upon the group of canvases, which the Germans in their greedy haste had filched from Bruges when they had made off with the Michelangelo *Madonna*. Aside from these two lots, the pictures had been stored according to size rather than by provenance. It was a bewildering assortment. Quality was to be our guide in making this initial selection. And as a kind of corollary, we were to set aside for shipment all pictures bearing the infamous "E.R.R." stencil—the initials of the Rosenberg looting organization. We had Sieber and four of the gnomes to help. Sieber stood by with list and flashlight. Two of the gnomes hauled out the pictures for us to examine. The other two put protective pads of paper filled with excelsior across the corners of the ones chosen.

By the end of the afternoon we had picked out between a hundred and fifty and two hundred paintings. The crew which had come on at four had already gone up with one trainload. We took stock of the lot waiting to go. We hadn't done so badly: our selection included works of Hals, Breughel, Titian, Rembrandt, Tintoretto, Rubens, Van Dyck, Lancret, Nattier, Reynolds, and a raft of smaller examples of the seventeenth century Dutch school. Not a dud among them, we agreed smugly.

Before we knocked off for supper, Sieber showed us an adjoining room divided into small compartments. Each one contained a miscellaneous assortment of art objects—pictures, porcelain, bric-a-brac of various kinds. Each compartment bore a label with the name of a different family, fifteen or twenty in all. They were the pilfered possessions of Viennese Jewish families. Our feelings were of both pathos and disgust. After working with the fruits of looting on a grand scale, we found these trifles sordid evidences of greedy persecution.

Lamont and I spent the next two days in the Springerwerke. We worked nights as well. It was a molelike existence. On the third morning we transferred our base of operations to the Kammergrafen, the largest of the mine caverns and the most remote. It was three-quarters of a mile from the mine entrance. Whereas the other mine chambers were on one level, the great galleries of the Kammergrafen were on several. Beyond those in which floors had been laid, there were vast unlighted caves of echoing blackness.

The galleries were so high that those on the first level could accommodate three tiers of pictures between floor and ceiling, while those on the second had four tiers.

The records listed *six thousand* pictures. In addition there were quantities of sculpture, hundreds of examples of the very finest eighteenth century French cabinetwork, tapestries and rugs; and the books and manuscripts of the Biblioteca Herziana in Rome— one of the greatest historical libraries in the world. Kammergrafen was quality and quantity combined, for here had been stored the collections for Linz.

Among the pictures, for example, were canvases from the Rothschild, Gutmann and Mannheimer collections, the celebrated tempera panels of the fourteenth century Hohenfurth altarpiece, Rem-, brandts and other great Dutch masters from the stock of Goudstikker, who had been the Duveen of Amsterdam, a collection of French pictures known as the "Sammlung Berta," and hundreds of nineteenth century German paintings, these last the objects of Hitler's special veneration.

The sculpture ranged from ancient to modern, with notable emphasis on examples of the Gothic period.* There were Egyptian tomb figures, Roman portrait busts, Renaissance and Baroque bronzes, exquisite French marbles of the eighteenth century and delicate Tanagra figurines. A bewildering hodgepodge of the plastic arts.

There were tapestries from Cracow, furniture from the Castle at Posen, rows of inlaid tables and cabinets from the Vienna Rothschilds, shelves and cases filled with the finest porcelains, prints and drawings of the sixteenth, seventeenth and eighteenth centuries, the decorations from the Reichskanzlei in Berlin, and Hitler's own purchases from the annual exhibitions of German art in Munich. Such was the Kammergrafen treasure. And the best of it, as I have said before, was to have adorned the galleries of the unbuilt Führer Museum at Linz, the city by the Danube which Hitler aspired to raise to the dignity of Vienna.

The rarest treasure of that collection was the celebrated Vermeer *Portrait of the Artist in His Studio.* This superb work of the seventeenth Dutch master, by whom there are only some forty unquestioned examples in the world, had been for years in the collection of Count Czernin at Vienna. The collection was semipublic; I had visited it before the war. Known simply as the "Czernin Vermeer," the picture had long been coveted by the great collectors. It had remained for Hitler to succeed where others had failed: he acquired this masterpiece in 1940 for an alleged price of one million, four hundred thousand Reichsmarks—part of his earnings from the sale of *Mein Kampf*. He boasted at the time that Mr. Mellon had offered six million dollars for it. Whether the sale was made under duress is still a matter of controversy. Members of the Czernin family today contend that it was. The picture has now been returned to Vienna where the matter will be ultimately decided.

Rivaling the Vermeer in international significance were the fifteen cases of paintings and sculpture from Monte Cassino. The paintings included Titian's *Danaë*, Raphael's *Madonna of the Divine Love*, Peter Breughel's *Blind Leading the Blind*, a *Crucifixion* by Van Dyck, an *Annunciation* by Filippino Lippi, a *Sacra Conversazione* by Palma Vecchio, a *Landscape* by Claude Lorraine, and Sebastiano del Piombo's *Portrait of Pope Clement VII*. Among the sculpture were antique bronzes of the greatest rarity and importance from Herculaneum and Pompeii. All had belonged to the Naples Museum. In 1943 the Italians had placed them, together with one hundred and seventy-two other cases of objects from the Naples Museum, in the Abbey of Monte Cassino for safekeeping. The following January, arrangements were made for all of the cases to be returned to the Vatican. When they arrived, fifteen were missing. Members of the Hermann Göring Division had carried them off as a birthday gift for the Reichsmarschall. Göring was incensed, when he learned of the arrival of these treasures, and refused to accept them. There is reason to believe that such was his reaction, for he had striven to maintain a semblance of legality in his art transactions. Even this rapacious collector could not have interpreted the behavior of his loyal officers as "correct," so far as the Monte Cassino affair was concerned. After the Reichsmarschall's refusal of the cases, they were brought to Alt Aussee for storage, pending their later return to Italy.

The Springerwerke had been child's play compared with the task confronting us in the Kammergrafen. We began arbitrarily with the big pictures. Titian, Tintoretto, Veronese, Van Dyck, Rubens, Rembrandt— all were represented in profusion. Many of them were from private collections in Holland, Belgium and France, and were unknown to us save through reproduction. It was a great lesson in connoisseurship, particularly when we had exhausted the "stars" and come to the lesser masters. The Dutch school of the seventeenth century was abundantly represented. There were scores, hundreds, of still lifes and flower paintings. My predilection for them amused Lamont and Sieber. I had always admired these incredibly deft creations of the seventeenth century Dutch artists, and here was an unparalleled opportunity to study them.

There was one peculiar thing about our selections: if a picture looked good to us down in the mine, it invariably looked better when we examined it later in the light of day at the mine entrance. This happened time and again. I remember one instance in particular. The painting was a large Rembrandt, a study of two dead peacocks. Down in the mine we had looked at it without much enthusiasm, though we admired it, and had even hesitated to include it in that first selection, which was to number only the best of the best. The next morning, as it was being loaded onto the truck, we were struck by its distinction.

And I remember the next time I saw that picture: it was at the Rijksmuseum in Amsterdam. It was included in the small group of outstanding Dutch masterpieces returned to Holland by special plane as a gesture of token restitution in the name of General Eisenhower!

Lamont and I liked Sieber, the German restorer. Lamont referred to him as the "tragic Gilles in white." Not that there was anything particularly tragic about him, any more than there was about the plight in which most Nazis found themselves. He made no bones about having joined the Party in the early thirties—ironically enough at the suggestion of one of his clients, a Jewish art dealer, who had thought it would be a good thing for Sieber's business. Sieber had been a restorer of pictures in Berlin and had done a little dealing on the side. It was the half-mournful expression he perpetually wore, together with his white costume, that accounted for Lamont's appellation. George had described him as a good, run-of-the-mill restorer, perhaps a little better than average. He had sized him up as a man ninety-eight per cent preoccupied with his profession and possibly two per cent concerned with politics. And George, as I think I have observed before, was a good judge of men. Sieber was a quiet, willing worker. He was neither fawning on the one hand, nor arrogant on the other. When you asked him a question, you always got a considered answer.

One evening we drew Sieber out on the subject of the attempted destruction of the mine. We had heard several versions of this fantastic plot and, according to one, Sieber had been instrumental in foiling the conspirators. The story was as follows: On the tenth, thirteenth and thirtieth of April 1945, Glinz, the Gauinspektor of Ober-Donau, had come to the mine with eight great cases marked in black letters *"Marmor—Nicht stürzen,"* that is, "Marble—Don't drop." He was acting on explicit instructions from Eigruber, Gauleiter of the region, to place them at strategic positions in the mine tunnels. Each case contained a hundred-pound bomb. Had these bombs been detonated, the entire contents of the mine would have been destroyed. The resulting cave-ins would have blocked every means of access. It would have taken months to repair the apparatus which carried off the water seeping constantly into the mine chambers. By that time the treasures they contained would have been completely ruined. It is generally agreed that Eigruber had obtained Hitler's tacit consent to this artistic Götterdammerung, if not his actual approval of it.

I learned later that Captain Posey found a letter from Martin Bormann, Hitler's deputy, stating in the first paragraph that the contents of the mine must, at all costs, be kept from falling into the hands of the enemy. And then the second paragraph stated that the contents of the mine must not be harmed.

Members of the Austrian resistance movement got wind of this diabolical plan and took Sieber into their confidence. His intimate knowledge of the mine passageways enabled him to set off small charges of dynamite here and there along the tunnels without endangering the contents of the chambers beyond. The resulting damage was slight and served a twofold purpose: it gave the impression that the mine had been permanently walled up; and, if that ruse were discovered, immediate access to the art works themselves was denied the plotters. Eigruber did discover that his attempt had been thwarted and in his rage gave orders for the counterconspirators to be rounded up and shot. But by that time it was the seventh of May, so the tragedy was mercifully averted.

Sieber told the story in a straightforward, factual way. I don't think it mattered to him who got control of the mine, but it was simply unthinkable that any harm should come to the precious things it housed. It was very much to his credit that he never capitalized on the part he played in this affair. The only other reference he made to it was when he later showed us the places where he had set off the charges of dynamite.

During all the time we were at the mine, Sieber made only one request of us. It came at the very end of our stay and was reasonable enough: he asked if we could expedite his return to Germany. There seemed to be little prospect of regular employment for him in Austria, but that was of less concern to him than the welfare of his wife and young daughter who lived with him in a house near the mine. Some months later, one of our officers tried to get him a job in Wiesbaden, but he was not acceptable to the Military Government authorities there because of his political affiliations. The last I heard of him, he and his family were still at Alt Aussee, waiting for permission to go back to Germany. I hope they finally got it.

Our concentrated efforts underground produced the desired results. Pictures were coming out of the mine at such a prodigious rate that George called a halt. Enough of a backlog had been accumulated to make further selection down in the mine unnecessary for a couple of days. Lamont and I had better help with the actual loading.

Loading a truck was a specialized operation, and George had perfected the technique. Lamont, Steve and Shrady were his pupils. That left me the only neophyte. So far I had had experience only with the loading of cases and heavier objects such as furniture and sculpture.

Packing pictures, especially unframed ones—and -there were a great many of the latter at Alt Aussee—was an altogether different problem. The first step was to place a length of waterproof paper over the side bars of the truck and spread it smoothly on the floor to the center of the truck bed. For this we had a large supply of stout, green, clothlike paper which had been used by the Wehrmacht as protection against gas attacks. Then a strip of felt was laid over the paper. The third step was to place "sausages" in two rows, end to end, on the floor of the truck. The space between the rows would depend on the size of the pictures to be loaded, for they were intended to cushion the shock as the trucks rumbled along over bumpy roads. The "sausages" had been George's invention. Packing materials of all kinds were at a premium, and certain types just didn't exist. To make up for the lack of the usual packer's pads, George had improvised this substitute. In one of the mine chambers he had found a large supply of ordinary curtain material of machine-made ecru lace. This had been cut up into yard lengths, eighteen inches wide. When rolled around a central core of coarser cloth, or sometimes excelsior, and tied with string, they were a very satisfactory "ersatz" product. We used to refer to them augustly as the pads made from Hitler's window curtains. Their manufacture was periodically one of the major industries at the mine. George-had trained a crew of the gnomes and they loved to turn them out. It was easy work. Seated at long benches they resembled a kind of Alpine "husking bee."

Once the paper, felt and "sausages" were in place, the pictures could be brought to the truck. One after another they were placed in a stack leading from the sideboards of the truck to the center. Pads and small blankets were inserted between them to prevent rubbing. To ensure safe packing, all the pictures in a given row had to be carefully selected as to size, ranging from large to medium in one, and from medium to small in another. That was the most tedious part of the entire operation. As soon as a row had been "built," it required only a few minutes to bring first the felt and then the green paper over the top of the row, tuck both down along the sides, and then lash the whole stack firmly to the side of the truck. By this method it was possible to load as many as a hundred and fifty medium-sized canvases on a single truck, for three rows of twenty-five each could be built up on either side of our big two-and-a-half-ton trucks. A truck loaded in this way could often accommodate several pieces of sculpture as well. Carefully padded and swathed in blankets, these could be placed down the center. The final step was to adjust the tarpaulin over the bows and to close the tailboard. A truck of the size we used could normally be loaded in two hours.

We were at the mercy of the weather, as far as loading was concerned. On rainy days we could work on only one truck at a time, because there was but one doorway with a protective stoop under which a single truck could park. Taking advantage of the sunny mornings, we would divide up into two teams—George and Steve on one truck, Lamont and I on another. As soon as a truck was filled and the tarpaulin securely fastened down, it was driven to one side of the narrow terrace in front of the building. The average convoy consisted of six trucks.

We had a crew of eighteen Negro drivers. Barboza, the C.O., was a very starchy lieutenant, Jamaica born. He and his men were billeted down in the little town of Bad Aussee. They were magnificent drivers but a bit reckless. Their occasional disregard for their vehicles was a worry to George. It would have been so with any drivers, I guess. A breakdown on the steep mountain roads could be a serious matter. It meant the complete disruption of the convoy schedule, involving reloading en route. To provide for this contingency, we made a practice of loading the trucks to three-quarters of their capacity. The contents of a single truck could thus be absorbed by the others.

When a convoy was ready to start, either George or I would lead off in a jeep and escort the six trucks down the precipitous road to Alt Aussee. Two half-tracks from the 11th Armored Division, as front and rear guards, would be waiting to accompany the convoy to Munich.

At breakfast one morning George said, "This looks like a good day to load the gold-seal products." He meant the Michelangelo Madonna and the Ghent altarpiece. This was an important event, for they were unquestionably the two most precious things still at the mine. Every possible precaution would have to be taken to make this operation a success. It must go off without a hitch. If anything happened to either of these masterpieces, the repercussions would be catastrophic. They would overshadow all the accomplishments of our MFA&A officers.

For the past several days, George and Steve had been working on the Madonna. She was now heavily padded and trussed up like a ham, ready to be brought out of the mine. We all went down to the Kaiser Josef chamber where we had first seen her. George made a final inspection of the ropes and pulleys which had been set up to hoist her onto the waiting train. Then, with a satisfied smile, he said, "I think we could bounce her from Alp to Alp, all the way to Munich, without doing her any harm."

Once the statue was gently loaded on the little flat car, the train pulled slowly out of the mine chamber and switched back onto the track of the main tunnel. From there it chugged slowly— George walking alongside—to the mine entrance where the truck stood waiting. This truck and the one which was to carry the altarpiece had been put in perfect condition. And George had put the fear of God into the two drivers, both of whom he had personally chosen from our crew. A dozen of the gnomes were waiting to lift the marble onto the truck. We slid it cautiously to the fore part where boards had been laid parallel and nailed to the floor. These would prevent shifting. On either side of the statue, small packing cases about two feet square were arranged in even rows and lashed firmly to the sides of the truck. These cases had been stored in a chamber of the mine called the Kapelle. They contained the coin collection intended for the Linz Museum and were accordingly marked "Münz Kabinett" or Coin Room. Blankets were wedged in between the cases and the statue. The large case containing the Greek sarcophagus from Salonika was set in place behind the statue and similarly secured to the floor and at the sides. That done, the truck was ready to go.

As George was putting the finishing touches on the packing, he said, "Tom, will you go down and get the 'Lamb'?" To be entrusted with the removal of the great altarpiece was an exciting assignment. I wanted to share it with someone who would also get a kick out of telling his grandchildren that he had actually brought the famous panels out of their underground hiding place. I called Lamont, and the two of us, followed by eight of the gnomes, hitched four of the "dogs" to the little engine and proceeded to the Mineral Kabinett. One of the "dogs," especially designed to carry pictures of unusual height, had a lower bed than the others. We would use this one for the big central panel of the altarpiece. Otherwise it would not clear a portion of the mine tunnel where the jagged rocks hung low over the track.

The panels were now in their cases, and it was a relatively simple matter to carry them from the storage room to the train. We had to make two trips down and back in order to get all ten cases up to the mine entrance. They were much lighter than the statue, but the loading was a more exacting undertaking. Lashing them upright in parallel rows, in the truck, and stowing cases on either side for ballast, took time. We didn't finish until well after six. It had taken most of the day to load the "gold-seal products."

That night we held a conference in George's room. He was to go to Munich the next morning with the convoy to supervise the unloading of the Madonna and the "Lamb" at the depot. He expected to come back directly, but might have to go on up to Frankfurt. He mapped out the work he wanted us to do while he was away. In addition to the job at the mine, there was a special one down at Bad Ischl. A series of famous panels by Albrecht Altdorfer, one of the greatest German painters of the fifteenth century, was stored on the second floor of a highly combustible old inn. These panels were among his finest works and belonged to the monastery of St. Florian outside Linz. Fifty or sixty pieces of sculpture—mostly polychromed wood figures, fifteenth century Gothic—also the property of the monastery, were stored there too. George thought we'd better figure on two trucks. We were to pick up the stuff, bring it back to the mine and then send it to Munich with the next convoy.

We made notations of what he had told us, and then Steve produced drinks—something of an occasion, for liquor was hard to come by at the mine. Somehow he had got hold of a bottle of cognac and insisted on making "Alpine Specials." This was a drink consisting of a jigger of cognac and an equal amount of a pink syrupy liquid resembling grenadine. Steve prized the syrup. Eder, the chemical engineer at the mine, had concocted it especially for him. The mixture made a drink of dubious merit. We drank to the success of George's trip to Munich.

The convoy got off early the next morning. Lamont and I went down with George as far as the village. Two half-tracks were waiting to escort the trucks to Munich. They were equipped with radios for intercommunication, in case of delays along the way. Between Alt Aussee and Salzburg, the road led through isolated country. Conditions were as yet far from settled. Small bands of SS troops still lurked in the mountains. The half-tracks weren't just going along for the ride.

When we returned to the mine, we found Steve and Shrady in conversation. They were planning an excursion and asked us to join them. We expressed pious disapproval of letting up on the job the minute George's back was turned. Steve's answer was, "That's a crock. I haven't taken a day off in two weeks. You can do as you like, me lads; I'm off to see the wizard." The two of them climbed into the sporty Mercedes-Benz convertible which Shrady had recently acquired, and drove off down the mountain.

"I have an idea," said Lamont. "They can have their fun today. We'll have ours tomorrow, while they pick up the Altdorfer panels at Bad Ischl."

Lamont turned to the loading of trucks, while I went down to the Kammergrafen with Sieber. In the course of the morning I selected approximately two hundred pictures. We concentrated on those of small size, which were stored on the top racks, and the work went rapidly. Among the paintings we chose was one which had a typewritten label on the back. I read the words "Von dem Führer noch nicht entschieden"—not yet decided upon by the Führer. I asked Sieber what this signified. He explained that every picture intended for the Linz Museum—and this was one of them— had to be personally approved by Hitler before it could be officially included in the prospective collection. I could easily understand that the Führer would have wanted to examine the more important acquisitions, but that each canvas had to receive his personal approval struck me as preposterous. Hitler had entrusted the formation of his collections first to Dr. Hans Posse, a noted scholar, and, after his death, to Dr. Hermann Voss, director of the Dresden Gallery. This meticulous procedure, involving the submission of all pictures to the Führer in Munich, must have been trying to those two luminaries of the German art world.

When I came up from the mine for lunch I found that Lamont had completed the loading of two trucks. As the stock of pictures in the packing room at the mine entrance was almost exhausted, he said that he would join Sieber and me in making further selections. We returned to the Kammergrafen and continued with the smaller pictures.

On one of the top shelves we found a cardboard carton bearing the name of Dr. Helmut von Hummel, who had been connected with the formation of the Linz collections. The label indicated that the contents had been destined for the museum. On the carton appeared the word *"Sittenbilder."* Lamont and I knew the word *"Bilder"* meant pictures, but the other two syllables conveyed nothing. Sieber knew very little English but tried to explain. He thought perhaps the word meant "customs," or something like that. I thought that I understood him. He probably meant that they were little scenes from everyday life.

We opened the carton. On top were three small watercolors, with beautiful gray-blue mounts and carved, gilt frames. If they were not by Francois Boucher, they were by a close pupil. The workmanship was exquisite and they were highly pornographic. So these were *"Sittenbilder."* In our limited German we tried to tell Sieber that they might be called "scenes from life," but hardly everyday life.

The rest of the things in the carton were of the same order, some of them contemporary, all of them licentious. None approached the first three watercolors in sheer virtuosity of technique. We wondered just which department of the Linz Museum would have harbored them.

Later we showed them to Steve. When he looked at the three watercolors he asked, "Who did those?"

"They look very much like Boucher," I said without thinking.

"Boucher?" asked Steve incredulously. "Not the fellow who painted that 'Holy Family' I saw this afternoon?"

Lamont said quickly, "Tom means a pupil of Boucher, not Boucher himself."

"Well, that's more like it," said Steve. "I didn't see how an artist who painted anything so beautiful as that big picture could paint smutty things like these."

The Holy Family to which he referred was a sensitive and tender representation. Steve's point was well taken. The fact that he had not seen much eighteenth century French painting didn't alter the validity of his argument.

On our way up from the Kammergrafen that afternoon we stopped at the Kapelle. This was one of the mine chambers which I had visited only long enough to take out some of the cases used in packing the Bruges Madonna. In addition to the Miinz Kabinett collections, the Kapelle contained the magnificent collection of Spanish armor—casques, breastplates, full suits of armor, and a great number of firearms—which had been gathered together at Schloss Konopischt by the late Archduke Franz Ferdinand. Most of it was of sixteenth century workmanship, exquisitely inlaid with gold and silver. Formerly Austrian, it had been the property of the Czech government since the last World War. Nonetheless, the Germans had carried it off, using some flimsy nationalistic argument to justify their action. While the atmosphere of the mine was excellent for paintings, it was not satisfactory for metal objects. Consequently, every piece in the Konopischt collection had been heavily coated with grease to keep it from oxidizing.

Their storage room, the Kapelle, was—as the name indicates—a chapel, dedicated to the memory of Dollfuss, the Austrian Chancellor. It had an electrically illuminated altar, hewn from a block of translucent salt crystal, which was one of the sights of the mine.

That night when Steve and Shrady returned from their outing we all had hot chocolate and cheese and crackers in the comfortable kitchen on the ground floor of the main building. They had had a wonderful day. Maria, Shrady's interpreter-secretary, had been with them. They had gone first to St. Wolfgang. There a sentry had tried to prevent them from driving up the road leading to the little church. Leopold, the Belgian king, was living near there with his wife, and motorists were not allowed on that road. But they had got around the sentry and gone into the church to see the wonderful carved altarpiece by Michael Pacher. Steve had brought us some colored photographs of it. Afterward they had had a swim in the lake and a picnic lunch. And in the afternoon—this had been the high spot of the day—they had gone over to Bad Ischl and called on Franz Lehar. The old fellow had been delighted to see them, had played the Merry Widow waltz for them and given them autographed photographs. It sounded like fun. Our day at the mine had been very prosaic in comparison. Mention of Bad Ischl reminded Lamont of his scheme for the next day. He proposed to Steve and Shrady that they should call for the Altdorfer panels. They fell in with the suggestion at once, and before we could explain that we thought we'd take the day off,

Steve was telling us about some of the things we should see in the neighborhood.

We slept late and when we got up the sky was gray and threatening. It was no day for an outing. In fact it was so cold that we decided we'd be warmer down in the mine. There was still one series of chambers which we had not explored. This was the Mondsberg, and it took us almost three-quarters of an hour to reach it. The pictures were arranged on racks as in the Kammergrafen and the Springerwerke, only in the Mondsberg there were a great many contemporary paintings. It didn't take us long to run through them. They were all obviously German-owned and, judging from the labels, the great majority of the canvases had been included in the annual exhibitions at the Haus der Deutschen Kunst in Munich.

Ranged along one side of the main chamber was a row of old pictures. These were of high quality, and we went through them carefully. I came to a canvas which looked vaguely familiar. It was the portrait of a young woman dressed in a gown of cherry brocade. I guessed it to be sixteenth century Venetian, perhaps by Paris Bordone. I said to Lamont, "I'm sure I've seen that picture somewhere, but I can't place it."

"Let's see if there's any mark on the back that might give you a lead," said Lamont.

He found a label and started reading aloud, "California Palace of the Legion of Honor, San Francisco ."

I thought he was joking. But not at all. There was the printed label of my museum. And there too *in my own handwriting* appeared the words "Portrait of a Young Woman, by Paris Bordone"! No wonder the portrait had looked familiar. I had borrowed it from a New York art dealer for a special loan exhibition of Venetian painting in the summer of 1938. I learned from the mine records that the dealer had subsequently sold the picture to a Jewish private collector in Paris. The Nazis had confiscated it with the rest of his collection. It was a weird business finding it seven years later in an Austrian salt mine.

After supper that evening Shrady asked us to go down to Alt Aussee with him. Some Viennese friends of his were having an evening of music. The weather had cleared and the snow on the mountains was pink in the afterglow as we drove down the winding road from the mine. The house, a small chalet, stood on the outskirts of the village. Our host, his wife and their two daughters, had taken refuge there just before the Russians reached Vienna.

He introduced us to Dr. Victor Luithlen, one of the curators of the Vienna Museum, who had driven over from Laufen. Many of the finest things from the museum were stored in the salt mine there. Dr. Luithlen was the custodian.

Both he and Shrady played the piano well. Luithlen played some Brahms and Shrady followed with the music he had composed for a ballet based on Poe's "Raven." Shrady said that it had been produced by the Russian Ballet in New York. It was a very flamboyant piece and Shrady performed it with terrific virtuosity.

Afterward coffee and strudel were served. The atmosphere of the household was casual and friendly. I was reminded of what an Austrian friend of mine had once told me: "In other countries, conditions are often serious, but not desperate; in Austria they are often desperate but never serious."

Thinking that George Stout might have returned from Munich, Lamont and I went back up to the mine that night before the others.

George had just come in. He brought exciting but disturbing news.

We were to continue the work at Alt Aussee for another ten days. Then we were to transfer our base of operations to Berchtesgaden. Our job there would be the evacuation of the Göring collection! On our way through Salzburg we were to pick up the pictures and tapestries from the Vienna Museum. These were the paintings by Velásquez, Titian and Breughel which had been highjacked by the Nazis two months ago and later retrieved by our officers. The disturbing part of what George had to tell was that he was going to leave us to carry on .alone at the mine. He would try to join us at Berchtesgaden. But there was a possibility that he might not be able to make it.

Months ago George had put in a request for transfer to the Pacific. He felt that things were shaping up on the European scene and that others could carry on the work. There would be a big job protecting and salvaging works of art in Japan. He didn't think that a program had been planned. He had offered his services. He had already told us that he had asked for this assignment, but we had never considered it as a possibility of the present or even of the immediate future. Now it looked as though it might materialize at once. In any case he was going up to Frankfurt the day after tomorrow to find out.

"As senior officer, Tom," George said, "you will take over as headman of the team. I'll take you down to see Colonel Davitt before I go. He is responsible for the security guard here at the mine and has been extremely co-operative. You should go to him if you have any complaints about the arrangements after I am gone."

Back in our rooms that night Lamont said, "I have a hunch that this is the last we'll see of George. It's not like him to talk the way he did tonight if he hasn't a pretty good idea that he won't be coming back."

Together we mapped out a tentative division of the work ahead. Steve, who had come into the room in time to hear George's news, joined our discussion. It was after midnight when the first meeting of the "three powers" broke up.

While George was in Munich he had been informed of the imminent withdrawal of Third Army from the part of Austria in which we were working. No one could, or would, tell him the exact date, but it appeared likely that it would take place within two weeks. It was difficult for me to understand why the arrival of another American army—General Mark Clark's Fifth from Italy—should cause the cessation of our operations. But of course the Army had its own way of doing things. We were attached to Third Army and if they were getting out, we would have to get out with them. All along we had known that this might happen before we could empty the mine. It was quite probable that Fifth Army would want to resume the work, but it would take time. Such a delay would impede the processes of restitution, and we had therefore been giving first attention to the finest things.

Having taken stock of the paintings, sculpture and furniture on which we were going to concentrate in the time we had left, we spent George's last day working as usual. The loading went well and we finished four more trucks. Another convoy would be ready to take off in the morning.

George had his own jeep and driver and could make better time than the convoy, so after early breakfast we went down to Colonel Davitt's office. George explained the change in his own plans and said that I would be taking over at the mine. Then he thanked the colonel for his co-operation. It was a long speech for George.

When he had finished, Colonel Davitt said, "In all the time you've been here, you haven't made a single unreasonable demand. If Lieutenant Howe can come anywhere near that record, we'll get along all right."

Compliments embarrassed George, so he said good-by as quickly as possible and climbed into his jeep. He wished me luck and drove off. I waited for Lamont to come down with the convoy and give me a lift back up the mountain.

THE ROTHSCHILD JEWELS; THE GÖRING COLLECTION

We had our share of troubles during those last ten days at Alt Aussee. They began that first day of my investiture as head of the team. Lamont and I were sorting pictures in the room at the mine entrance. It was early in the afternoon and we were about to start loading our third truck. I had just said to Lamont that I thought the morning's convoy had probably passed Salzburg, when a jeep pulled up to the door. The driver called out to us that one of our trucks had broken down at Goisern. That was an hour's drive from the mine. Why hadn't we been notified earlier? I asked. He didn't know. Perhaps there hadn't been anybody around to bring back word. Maybe the driver had thought he could repair the truck.

We got hold of Steve and the three of us started for Goisern in the messenger's jeep. We'd have to transfer the load, so an empty truck followed us. We were thankful that the breakdown hadn't happened while the convoy was going over the Pötschen Pass. It would have been a tough job to shift the pictures from one truck to another on that steep and dangerous part of the road. It was bad enough as it was, because it looked as though we'd have rain. One of the trucks had a lot of very large pictures. We hoped that it wasn't the one that had broken down.

It was a little after three when we reached Goisern. The truck had been parked by the headquarters of a small detachment of troops on the edge of town. There were several houses near by but plenty of room for us to maneuver the empty truck alongside. The Negro driver of the stranded truck said that it had "thrown a rod" and would have to be taken to Ordnance for repairs. That meant that the vehicle would be laid up for two or three weeks. We'd have to see about a replacement. The main thing was to get on with the unloading before it began to rain. And it was the truck with the big pictures.

With the two trucks lined up alongside, and only a few inches apart, we could hoist the pictures over the sideboards. In this way each row of paintings was kept in the same order. Lamont and Steve boarded the empty truck, while one of the gnomes from the mine and I started unlashing the first stack of loaded pictures. Before long a crowd of women and children had collected to watch this unusual operation. There were excited "oh's" and "ah's" as we began to transfer one masterpiece after another—two large Van Dycks, a Veronese, a pair of colossal decorative canvases by Hubert Robert, a Rubens, and so on. The spectators were quiet and well behaved, whispering among themselves. They didn't pester us with questions. We rather enjoyed having an audience. We finished the job in an hour and a half.

It wasn't too soon, for as we were securing the tarpaulin at the rear of the newly loaded truck, it began to pour. We parked the truck, arranged for an overnight guard, then climbed into our jeep and started back to the mine. In a few minutes the rain turned to hail. The stones were so large that we were afraid they'd break the windshield of the jeep. We pulled over to the side of the road and waited for the storm to let up. While we waited, the gnome told us that sometimes the hailstones were large enough to kill sheep grazing in the high meadows. Only the summer before he had lost two of his own lambs during one of the heavy summer storms. He swore that the stones were the size of tennis balls.

We were thoroughly soaked and half frozeh when we got back to the mine. But we had won our race with the weather, and the truck would proceed to Munich with the next convoy.

During the next three days we were beset by a series of minor difficulties. Two of the trucks broke down on the way up to the mine to be loaded. It took half a day to get replacements, so the convoy was delayed. One night the guard on duty at the mine entrance developed an unwarranted interest in art and poked around among the pictures which Lamont and I had carefully stacked according to size for loading the next morning. No harm was done, but it caused a delay. He was under strict orders to let no one into the temporary storage room and was not to go in there himself. It was partly our fault; we shouldn't have trusted him with the key. The captain of the guard was notified and appropriate disciplinary action taken. The gnomes developed a tendency to prolong their regular rest periods beyond a point Steve considered reasonable, and we had to come to an understanding about that. On the whole, however, the work went fairly well.

Even the great chambers of the Kammergrafen were beginning to thin out. They were far from empty, but we had cleared them of a substantial part of the external loot, that is, the loot which had come from countries outside Germany. There were still quantities of things taken from Austrian collections, but they had not been our primary concern. The time had come to make a final check, to make sure that we had not overlooked anything important in the category of external loot.

Together with Sieber, we started this last inspection. We checked off the pictures first. Our work there had been pretty thorough.

After that the sculpture. This also seemed to be well weeded out. And the furniture too.

Sieber was ahead of us with his flashlight. The light fell on two cartons standing in a dark corner behind a group of Renaissance bronzes. I asked what was in them. Sieber shrugged his shoulders. They had never been opened. He had forgotten that they were there. We dragged them out and looked for an identifying label. Sieber recalled that one of the former custodians at the mine had said the things inside were *"sehr wertvoll"*—very valuable, but he knew nothing more.

We carried the boxes to a table where there was better light. They were the same size, square, and about two feet high. They were not heavy. We pried open the lid of one of them with great care. It might be Roman glass, and that stuff breaks almost when you look at it. But it wasn't Roman glass. Inside was a row of small cardboard boxes. I lifted the lid and removed a layer of cotton. On the cotton beneath lay a magnificent golden pendant studded with rubies, emeralds and pearls. The central motif, a mermaid exquisitely modeled and wrought in iridescent enamel, proclaimed the piece the work of an Italian goldsmith of the Renaissance. The surrounding framework of intricate scrolls, shells and columns blazed with jewels.

There were forty boxes filled with jewels—necklaces, pendants and brooches—all of equal splendor. The collection was worth a fortune. Each piece bore a minute tag on which appeared an identifying letter and a number. These were Rothschild jewels. And we had stumbled on them quite by accident.

Lamont and I agreed that they should be taken to Munich without delay. There they could be stored in a vault. Furthermore we decided to deliver them ourselves. It wouldn't do to risk such precious objects with the regular convoy. We admonished Sieber to say nothing about our find. In the meantime we would keep the two boxes under lock and key in our room.

That night we told Steve we had a special surprise for him. After barring the door against unexpected visitors, we emptied the boxes onto one of the beds. We told him not to look until we were ready. We arranged each piece with the greatest care, straightening out the links of the necklaces, adjusting the great baroque pearls of the pendants, balancing one piece with another, until the whole glittering collection was spread out on the white counterpane. Then we signaled to Steve to turn around.

"God Almighty, where did you find those?" he asked.

While we were telling him how we had happened onto the two cartons that afternoon, he kept shaking his head, and when we had finished, said solemnly, 'They're beyond my apprehension." The expression stuck and from that time on we invoked it whenever we were confronted with an unexpected problem.

Early the following morning we stowed the jewels in the back seat of our command car and set out for Munich. Halfway to Salzburg we encountered Captain Posey, headed in the opposite direction. He was surprised to see us, and still more surprised when we told him what we had in the car. He was on his way to the mine. There were some things he wanted to tell us about our next job—at Berchtesgaden—but if we would come to his office the next day that would be time enough. He wasn't going to stay at the mine more than a couple of hours. He should be back in Munich before midnight. He said there was one thing we could do when we reached Salzburg—call on the Property Control Officer and arrange for clearance on the removal of the Vienna Museum pictures to the Munich depot. This was an important part of the plan which

George had outlined, so we said that we'd see what we could do.

We had some difficulty finding the right office. There were two Military Government Detachments in Salzburg—one for the city, and the other for the region. They were on opposite sides of the river. We caught Lieutenant Colonel Homer K. Heller, the Property Control Officer, as he was leaving for lunch. I explained that it was our intention to call for the paintings and tapestries on our way to Berchtesgaden the following week. He said he could not authorize the removal; that we would have to see Colonel W. B. Featherstone at the headquarters across the river. If the colonel gave his O.K., it would be all right with him. He didn't think that the colonel would take kindly to the idea. This was a surprise. Who would have the temerity to question the authority of Third Army? Lamont was amused. He told me I could have the pleasure of tackling Colonel Featherstone alone.

It was after two o'clock before the colonel was free. Nothing doing on the Vienna pictures. That would require an O.K. from Verona. Why Verona, I asked? "General Clark's headquarters," was the answer. Didn't I know that the Fifth Army was taking over the area very shortly? Then the colonel, in accents tinged with sarcasm, expressed his satisfaction at finally meeting one of the Monuments officers of the Third Army. He had heard such a lot about them and the wide territory they had covered. He had been told that a group of them was working at the Alt Aussee mine, but I was the first one he had laid eyes on.

I gathered that he was mildly nettled by Third Army in general and by me in particular. As a matter of fact, the colonel's attitude about the Vienna pictures was logical: why move them out of Austria? If, as he supposed, they were to be returned to Vienna eventually, why take them all the way to Munich? I had no answer to that and took refuge in the old "I only work here" excuse. He found it rather droll that the Navy should be mixed up in this high-class van and storage business. I had too, once, but the novelty had worn off. I rejoined Lamont and the jewels. I wondered what Captain Posey would have to say to all this.

We reached Munich too late that afternoon to see Craig at the depot, so we took the jewels with us to his quarters. I had not seen him since my departure for Alt Aussee some weeks before. In the interim, there had been a tightening up on billeting facilities. As a result he and Ham Coulter were now sharing a single apartment. I was the only one adversely affected by this arrangement. Craig no longer had a spare couch for chance guests.

When Lamont and I walked in, we found them talking with a newly arrived naval lieutenant. He was Lane Faison, who had been around Harvard in my day. In recent years he had been teaching at Williams and was at present in OSS. After we had been there a little while, Lamont asked very casually, "Would you boys care to see the Rothschild jewels?"

Ham wanted to know what the hell he was talking about. "Well, we have two boxes filled with them here in the hall," Lamont said.

For the second time we displayed the treasures. Craig's enthusiasm was tempered with concern for their safety. He was relieved when we said we had come purposely to put them in one of the steel vaults at the depot. We went with him to the Königsplatz forthwith and stowed them safely for the night.

Lamont and I continued on our way to Third Army Headquarters. Lincoln was working late. When we walked in he looked up from his typewriter and said "Hello" in a flat voice. Lincoln was in one of his uncommunicative moods. We left him alone and busied ourselves with letters from home which we found on

Posey's desk. Lincoln went on with his typing. Presently he stopped and said, "George's orders came through. He's gone to the Pacific." •

"It ought to be interesting work," said Lamont.

"Oh, you knew about his orders?" asked Lincoln.

"No," said Lamont.

That broke the mood. We had a lively session for the next hour. Lincoln was always a reservoir of information, a lot of it in the realm of rumor, but all of it fascinating. That evening he was unusually full of news. He had a perfect audience in Lamont and me because we had been completely out of touch with things while at the mine.

After exhausting his stock of fact and fiction, he produced his latest box of food from home. There were brandied peaches, tins of lobster and caviar, several kinds of cheese, dried fruits and crackers. It was a combination you'd never risk at home, if you were in your right mind.

"You do very well for yourself," I said when he had the refreshments spread out on his desk.

"My wife knows the enlisted men's motto: 'Nothing is too good for our boys, and nothing is what they get.' "

We finished the box and Lincoln showed us an article he had written on Nazi sculpture. We were reading it when Captain Posey came in. He asked if we had stopped in Salzburg to see Colonel Heller. I told him what had happened there. If he was annoyed, he gave no sign of it. He rummaged in his desk and brought out a list of instructions for us in connection with the operation at Berchtesgaden. He suggested that we stop there on the way back to Alt Aussee; it wouldn't be very much out of our way. He gave us the names of the officers we should see about billeting, and so on. It would be well to have all these things settled in advance. Then he gave us some special orders for Lieutenant Shrady, who was to be transferred to Heidelberg, now that the evacuation of the mine was ending.

Captain Posey said that I was to take over the Mercedes-Benz. It had been obtained originally for the evacuation team. We were to take it with us to Berchtesgaden. I could make good use of the car, transportation facilities being what they were, but I didn't relish the prospect of taking it from Shrady. He had spent money of his own fixing it up and looked on it as his personal property. I told Captain Posey how I felt. He said he had a letter for me which would take care of the matter. It was a letter directing me to deliver Lieutenant Shrady's orders and to appropriate the car.

When we saw Faison at the depot the next morning, he asked if he might drive back with us. He was joining Plaut and Rousseau at House 71 to work with them on the investigation of Nazi art looting. I said we'd be glad to have him. The three of us started off after early lunch. We were looking forward to the Berchtesgaden detour. None of us had been there during the Nazi regime and I, for one, was curious to see what changes had taken place in the picturesque resort town since I had last seen it fifteen years before.

We took the Salzburg Autobahn past Chiemsee almost to Traunstein, and then turned off to the southwest. This was the finest secondary road I ever traveled. It led into the mountains and the scenery was worthy of Switzerland. Thanks to perfectly banked turns, we made the ninety-mile run in two hours.

The little town was as peaceful and quiet as I remembered it. In fact it was so quiet that Lamont and I had difficulty locating an Army outfit to give us directions. We learned that the 44th AAA

Brigade had just moved in and that the last remnants of the famous 101st Airborne Division were pulling out. There was no love lost between the two,'as we found out later. Consequently, when I asked an officer of the AAA Brigade where I would find Major Anderson of the 101st Airborne, he informed me curtly that that outfit was no longer at Berchtesgaden. Then I asked if he knew where the Göring collection was. He didn't seem to know what I was talking about, so I rephrased my question, inquiring about the captured pictures which had been on exhibition a short time ago. Yes, he knew vaguely that there had been some kind of a show. He thought it had been over in Unterstein, not in Berchtesgaden. Well, where was Unterstein? He said it was about four kilometers to the south, on the road to the Konigssee.

His directions weren't too explicit, but eventually we found the little back road which landed us in Unterstein ten minutes later. In a clearing on the left side of the road stood the building we were looking for. It was a low rambling structure of whitewashed stucco in the familiar Bavarian farmhouse style. It had been a rest house for the Luftwaffe. The center section, three stories high, had a gabled roof with widely overhanging eaves. On either side were long wings two stories high, similarly roofed. The casement windows were shuttered throughout.

We found Major Harry Anderson on the entrance steps. He was a husky fellow with red hair and a shy, boyish manner. He was not altogether surprised to see us because George had stopped by on his last trip to Munich and told him we'd be arriving before long. How soon could we start to work on the collection? In four or five days' time, we thought. Could he make some preliminary arrangements for us? We would need billets for three officers, that is, the two of us—and Lieutenant Kovalyak. No, there would be four, we had forgotten to include the Negro lieutenant in charge of the truck drivers. Then there would be twenty drivers. Could we say definitely what day we'd arrive? Lamont and I made some rapid calculations. It was a Tuesday. How about Friday evening? That was fine. The sooner the better as far as the major was concerned. He was slated to pull out the minute the job was done, so we couldn't start too soon to suit him.

He asked if we'd care to take a preliminary look around but we declined. It was getting late and we still had a hard three-hour drive ahead of us. As we turned to go, Jim Plaut and Ted Rousseau came out of the building. They had been expecting Faison but were surprised to find him with us. Wouldn't we all have dinner with them that night at House 71? They had come over from Bad Aussee that afternoon, bringing Hofer with them. They had been quizzing him about certain pictures in the collection and he had wanted to refresh his memory by having a look at them. They pointed to a stocky German dressed in gray tweeds who stood a little distance away talking with a tall, angular woman. We recognized him as the man we had seen pacing the garden at House 71 weeks before—the evening Lamont and I first reported to George at the mine. That was his wife, they said. Would we mind taking Hofer back with us? If we could manage that, they'd take Faison with them. There were some urgent matters they'd like to talk over with him in connection with their work. We agreed and Ted brought Hofer to the car.

As we left he called out, "Wiederschauen, liebe Mutti," and kept waving and throwing kisses to his tall wife. I was struck by the stoical expression on her face. She watched us go but made no effort to return his salutations. I wondered if she gave a damn.

Hofer was a loquacious passenger. All the way to Bad Aussee he kept up a line of incessant chatter, half in English, half in German, on all sorts of subjects. He gesticulated constantly with both hands, notwithstanding the fact that one of them was heavily bandaged. He explained that he had scalded it. The bandage had been smeared with evil-smelling ointment which had soaked through. As he gestured the air was filled with a disagreeable odor of medication. Did we know Salzburg? Ah, such a lovely city, so musical! Did we know Stokowski? He knew him well. "Then you'll probably be interested to know that he has just married one of the Vanderbilt heiresses, a girl of nineteen," I said. But I must be joking. Was it really so?

I was getting bored with this chatterbox when he suddenly began to talk about Göring and his pictures. We asked him the obvious question: What did Göring really like when it came to paintings? Well, he was fond of Cranach. Yes, we knew that. And Rubens; he had greatly admired Rubens. And many of the Dutch masters of the seventeenth century. But according to Hofer it was he who had directed the Reichsmarschall's taste. Then, to my surprise, he mentioned Vermeer. Did we know about the Vermeer which Göring had bought? After that he went into a lengthy account of the purchase, leading up to it with an involved story of the secrecy surrounding the transaction, which had many confusing details. When we pulled up before House 71, Hofer was still going strong. Lamont and I were worn out.

Shrady departed the following morning in compliance with the orders I had brought him. He left the Mercedes-Benz behind. If I could have foreseen the trouble that car was going to cause us, nothing could have tempted me to add it to our equipment. Even then Lamont eyed it with suspicion, but we were both talked out of our misgivings by Steve, who rubbed his hands with satisfaction at the prospect of the £clat it would lend our future operations.

With Shrady's going, we fell heir to his duties. During our last three days at the mine they complicated our lives considerably. There were records to be put in order, reports to be finished, pay accounts to be adjusted, ration books to be extended for the skeleton crew which would remain at the mine. In addition, I had to see Colonel Davitt about the reduction and reorganization of the guard, and make provision for different billeting and messing facilities.

In the midst of these preparations, Ted Rousseau telephoned from House 71. Were we planning to take Kress, the photographer, with us to Berchtesgaden? We certainly were. Steve would sooner have parted with his right eye. Well, they wanted to interrogate him before we left. How long would they need him? A few days. I suggested they start right away. We'd be needing him too. Steve was wild when he heard about it. I agreed that it was a nuisance but that we'd have to oblige. The OSS boys came for Kress that afternoon. Steve watched them, balefully, as they drove off down the mountain. Then he resumed the work he had been doing on his big Steyr truck. This was a cumbersome vehicle which he and Kress had been putting in order. It had belonged originally to the *Einsatzstab Rosenberg* and was part of Kress' photographic unit. He and Steve were refitting it to serve our purposes in a similar capacity. It was a fine idea, but so far they hadn't been able to get it in running order. Steve had had it painted. When he had nothing better to do, he tinkered with the dead motor. Next to Kress, the truck was his most prized possession.

I returned to Shrady's old office where I found Lamont in conversation with Dr. Hermann Michel. Michel was a shadowy figure who had been working at the mine with Sieber and Eder throughout our stay. When Posey and Lincoln Kirstein had arrived at Alt Aussee in May, he had identified himself as one of the ringleaders of the Austrian resistance movement and vociferously claimed the credit of saving the mine. Since then he had been working in the mine office. Captain Posey had given him permission to make a routine check of the books and archives stored there. He was such a talkative fellow that we kept out of his way as much as possible. And we didn't like his habit of praising himself at the expense of others. He was forever running to Plaut and Rousseau at House 71 with written and oral reports, warning them to beware of this or that man in the mine organization.   '

Lamont looked decidedly harassed when I walked in. Michel was protesting our demands for a complete set of the records. We were to leave them in Colonel Davitt's care when we closed the mine. Michel had taken the opportunity to say a few unpleasant things about Sieber. We finally made it clear to him that there would be no nonsense about the records, and also that what we did about Sieber was our business. We finally packed him off still protesting and shaking his head.

The afternoon before our departure Lamont and I had to go over to St. Agatha. The little village lay in the valley on the other side of the Potschen Pass. We were to verify the report that a small but important group of paintings was stored in an old inn there. A fine Hubert Robert *Landscape,* given to Hitler by Mussolini, was said to be among them.

We went first to the Bürgermeister who had the key. He drove with us to the inn. It was an attractive Gasthaus, built in the early eighteenth century. The walls were frescoed and a wrought-iron sign hung over the doorway. When we arrived . the proprietress was washing clothes in the arched passageway through the center of the building.

She took us to a large corner room on the second floor. There were some fifty pictures, all of them enormous and unframed. The Bürgermeister helped us shift the unwieldy canvases about, so that we could properly examine them. They were, for the most part, of indifferent quality—sentimental landscapes by obscure German painters of the nineteenth century.

But we did find five that were fine: the mammoth landscape with classical ruins by Hubert Robert, the eighteenth century French master—this was the one Mussolini had given the Führer; an excellent panel by Pannini—it too a landscape; a Van Dyck portrait; a large figure composition by Jan Siberechts, the seventeenth century Flemish painter; and a painting by Ribera, the seventeenth century Spanish artist. We set them aside and said we'd return for them in a few days.

We had hoped to leave for Berchtesgaden by midmorning the next day, but we didn't get off until three in the afternoon. At the last minute I received word from Colonel Davitt's office that the Mercedes-Benz was to be left at the mine. I said that since we had no escort vehicle, it was an indispensable part of our convoy. That being the case, the colonel's adjutant said we could take the car, but on condition that we return it within twenty-four hours. I said I'd see what I could do about that.

Steve fumed while I talked. When I hung up the receiver he said, "Don't be a damn fool. Once the car's out of his area, the colonel hasn't got a thing to say about it. Let's get going."

Sieber and Eder, together with a dozen of the gnomes, were waiting in front of the mine building when we came down the stairs. Lamont was already in the car. I gave final instructions to the captain of the guard, said good-bys all around, and got in the car myself. Everybody smiled and waved as we drove off.

The evacuation had been a success. Ninety truckloads of paintings, sculpture and furniture had been removed from the mine during the past five weeks. Although it was by no means empty, the most important treasures had been taken out. Third Army was withdrawing from the area. From now on the mine would be the responsibility of General Clark's forces.

We were a lengthy cavalcade. Lamont and I took the lead. Steve followed in the Steyr truck, in running order at last. Behind him trailed five trucks. We were to pick up eight more at Alt Aussee. It wasn't going to be easy to keep such a long convoy in line. If we could only stay together until we got over the pass, the rest of the trip wouldn't be too difficult.

We made it over the pass without mishap. From time to time Lamont looked back to make sure the trucks were still following. He couldn't count them all, they were so strung out and the road was so winding. But we had instructed the Negro lieutenant to give orders to his men to signal the truck ahead in case of trouble, so we felt reasonably sure that everything was in order. When we reached Fuschl See we stopped along the lake shore to take count. One after another eight trucks pulled up. Five were missing. Fifteen minutes passed and still no sign of the laggards. Steve said not to worry, to give them another quarter of an hour.

The blue waters of the lake were inviting. Schiller might have composed the opening lines of *Wilhelm Tell* on this very spot. "Es lächelt der See, er ladet zum Bade." Steve and Lamont decided to have a swim. I dipped my hand in the water; it was icy. While they swam I kept an eye out for the missing vehicles. Presently two officers drove by in a jeep. I hailed them and ask if they had seen our trucks. They had—about ten miles back two trucks had gone off the road. They thought there had been two or three others at the scene of the accident. Lamont and Steve dressed quickly. Steve said he'd go on with the eight trucks and meet us in Salzburg. Then Lamont and I started back toward Bad Ischl.

We hadn't gone more than five miles when we came upon three of our vehicles. We signaled them to pull over to the side of the road. At first we couldn't make out what the drivers were saying— all three talked at once. We finally got the story. A driver had taken a curve too fast and had lost control of his truck. The one behind had been following too closely and had also crashed over the side. The first driver had got pinned under his truck and they had had to amputate a finger before he could be extricated. The lieutenant in charge had stayed behind to take care of things. He had told them to try to catch up with the rest of the convoy. By the time they had given us all the details, we realized that they had been drinking. And we guessed that alcohol had also had something to do with the truck going off the road. We would have something to say to the lieutenant when he reached Berchtesgaden. He was new on the job, having replaced Lieutenant Barboza only two days ago. We were thankful that our precious packing materials had been put in two of the trucks up ahead.

Steve was waiting for us in the Mozart Platz when we reached

Salzburg an hour and a half later with our three trucks in tow. He told the drivers where they could get chow. The three of us went across the river to the Gablerbrau, the small hotel for transients, for our own supper. The Berchtesgaden operation hadn't begun auspiciously.

Our troubles weren't over. When we pulled into Berchtesgaden at eight o'clock, we couldn't find Major Anderson, so we had to fend for ourselves. We managed to put the drivers up for the one night in a barracks by the railway station before going on to Unterstein ourselves. The lieutenant in charge of the drivers hadn't turned up when we were ready to go, so I left word that he was to report to me first thing the next morning. While we three felt unhappy over the lack of billeting arrangements for us, we were too tired to think much about it that night. Bed was all that mattered. .The officer on duty at the Unterstein rest house said there was an empty room over the entrance hall which we could use until we got permanent quarters. There were three bunks, so we moved in.

By contrast, everything started off beautifully the following morning. Major Anderson appeared as we were finishing breakfast.

His apologies were profuse and he did everything he could to make amends. We declined his offer to obtain rooms for us at the elegant Berchtesgadener Hof in town. We wanted to be on the spot. There was plenty of room in the rest house where we would be working; and we could mess with the half-dozen officers billeted in the adjacent barracks. The major introduced us to Edward Peck, the sergeant, who had been working on an inventory of the collection.

Together we made a tour of the premises. The paintings alone filled forty rooms. Four rooms and a wide corridor at the end of the ground-floor hall were jammed with sculpture. Still another room was piled high with tapestries. Rugs filled two rooms adjoining the one with the tapestries. Two more rooms were given over to empty frames, hundreds of them. There was the "Gold Room" where the objects of great intrinsic value were kept under lock and key. And there were three more rooms crammed with barrels, boxes and trunks full of porcelain. One very large room was a sea of books and magazines, eleven thousand altogether. A small chapel on the premises was overflowing with fine Italian Renaissance furniture.

The preliminary survey was discouraging. Although the objects were infinitely more accessible than those at the mine had been, this advantage was largely offset by the fact that they were all loose and would have to be packed individually. Even the porcelain in barrels would have to be repacked.

Our first request was for a work party of twelve men—GIs, not PWs. We suggested to the young C.O., Major Paul Miller, that he call for volunteers. If possible, we wanted men who might prefer this, kind of job to guard duty or other routine work. They could start in on the books while we mapped out our plan of attack on the rest of the things. Steve went off with Major Miller to select the crew, and Lamont and I settled down to discuss other problems with Major Anderson and Sergeant Peck.

It was the sergeant's idea that the collection could be packed up one room at a time. He had compiled his inventory with that thought in mind. Unfortunately we couldn't carry out the evacuation in that order. We explained why his system wouldn't work: paintings, for example, had to be arranged according to size. Otherwise we couldn't build loads that would travel safely. Even if we could have packed the pictures as he suggested—one room at a time—it would have meant the loss of valuable truck space. We assured him that, in the long run, our plan was the practical one. It did, however, involve considerable preliminary work. The first job would be to assemble all of the pictures—and there were a thousand of them—in a series of rooms on one floor of the building. As the sergeant had not quite finished his lists, we agreed to devote our energies to the books for the rest of the day. By morning he would have his inventory completed. Then the pictures could be shifted.

Lamont and I wanted to know more about the collection. How did it get to Berchtesgaden in the first place? Major Anderson was the man who could answer our questions.

As the war ended, the French reached the town ahead of the Americans. They had it to themselves for about three days and had raised hell generally. Göring's special train bearing the collection had reached Berchtesgaden just ahead of the French. The collection, having been removed from the Reichsmarschall's place, Karinhall, outside Berlin, was to have been stored in an enormous bunker by his hunting lodge up the road. But there hadn't been time. The men in charge of the train got only a part of the things unloaded. Some of them were put in the bunker, others in a villa near by. Most of the collection was left in the nine cars of the train. The men had been more interested in unloading a stock of champagne and whisky which had been brought along in two of the compartments.

When the French entered the town, the train was standing on a siding not far from the bunker. They may have made off with a few of the things, but there were no apparent depredations. They peppered it along one side with machine-gun fire. However, the damage had been relatively slight.

Then the French had cleared out and the train was, so to speak, dumped in Major Anderson's lap, since he was the Military Government Officer with the 101st Airborne Division. Under his supervision, the collection had been transferred from the train, from the bunker and from the villa, to the rest house. Later he had been instrumental in having it set up as an exhibition. The exhibition had been a great success—perhaps too great a success. He meant that it had attracted so much attention that some of the higher-ups began to worry about the security of the things. Finally he had received orders that the show was to close and of course he had complied at once.

He said that General Arnold had come to see the exhibition the day after that. We asked if he had let him in. Well, what did we think? But he had turned down a three-star general who had come along after hearing that General Arnold had been admitted. The general, he said, was hopping mad.

The major's most interesting experience in connection with the collection was his visit with Frau Göring. He heard that some of the best pictures were in her possession, so he took a run down to Zell am See where she was staying in a Schloss belonging to a South American. He found the castle; he found Emmy; and he found the pictures. There were indeed some of the best pictures— fifteen priceless gems of the fifteenth century Flemish school, from the celebrated Renders collection of Brussels. Göring had bought the entire collection of about thirty paintings. We knew that M. Renders was already pressing for the return of his treasures, claiming that he had been forced to sell them to the Reichsmarschall. But that was another story.

Frau Göring wept bitterly when the major took the pictures, protesting that they were her personal property and not that of her husband. On the same visit he had recovered another painting in the collection. Frau Göring's nurse handed over a canvas measuring about thirty inches square. She said Göring had given it to her the last time she saw him. As he placed the package in her hands he had said, "Guard this carefully. It is of great value. If you should ever be in need, you can sell it, and you will not want for anything the rest of your life." The package contained Göring's Vermeer.

Major Anderson stayed for lunch. As we walked back from the mess, a command car pulled up in front of the rest house. Bancel La Farge and a man in civilian clothes climbed out. I hadn't seen Bancel for two months. He was a major now. The civilian with him was an old friend of mine, John Walker, Chief Curator of the National Gallery at Washington and a special adviser to the Roberts Commission. John had flown over to make a brief inspection tour of MFA&A activities. Bancel was serving as his guide. They were on their way to Salzburg and Alt Aussee.

Major Anderson proposed a trip to the Eagle's Nest, Hitler's mountain hide-out, suggesting that the visitors could look at the Göring pictures that evening. Lamont and I said we had work to do, but we were easily talked out of that.

You could see the Eagle's Nest from the rest house. It was perched on top of the highest peak of the great mountain range which rose sharply from the pine forests across the valley. We crossed to the western side and began a steep ascent. About a thousand feet above the floor of the valley we came to Obersalzberg, once a select community of houses belonging to the most exalted members of the Nazi hierarchy. In addition to the Berghof, Hitler's massive chalet, it included a luxurious hotel—the Platter Hof—SS barracks, and week-end "cottages" for Göring and Martin Bormann. The British bombed Obersalzberg in April 1945. The place was now in ruins. The Berghof was still standing but gutted by fire and stripped of all removable ornamentation by souvenir hunters.

We continued up the winding road carved from the solid rock, through three tunnels, at length emerging onto a terraced turnaround, five thousand feet above Berchtesgaden. The major told us that the road had been built by slave labor. Three thousand men had worked on it for almost three years.

The Eagle's Nest was still four hundred feet above. From the turnaround there were two means of access: an elevator and a footpath. The elevator shaft, hewn out of the mountain itself, was another feat of engineering skill. A broad archway of carved stone marked the entrance. Beside the elevator stood a sign which read, "For Field Grade Officers Only"—that is, majors and above.

"A sentiment worthy of the builder," Lamont observed as we took to the footpath.

On our steep climb we wondered what Steve would say to such discrimination. We hadn't long to wait. He made a trip to the Eagle's Nest a few days later. When stopped by the guard, he looked at him defiantly and asked, "What do you take me for, a Nazi?" Steve rode up in the elevator.

The Eagle's Nest was devoid of architectural distinction. Built of cut stone, it resembled a small fort, two stories high. From the huge, octagonal room on the second floor—a room forty feet across, with windows on five sides—one could look eastward into Austria, southward to Italy. A mile below lay the green valleys and blue lakes of Bavaria. They used to say that every time Hitler opened a window a cloud blew in. The severity of the furnishings matched the bleakness of the exterior. An enormous conference table occupied the center of the room. Before the stone fireplace stood a mammoth sofa and two chairs. A smaller room adjoined the main octagon at a lower level. The heavy carpet was frayed along one side. The caretaker, pointing to the damage, said that in his frequent frenzies Hitler used to gnaw the carpet, a habit which had earned him the nickname of "Der Teppich-Beisser," the rug-biter. Considering the labor expended on this mountain eyrie, the place had been little used. The same caretaker told us that Hitler had never stayed there overnight. Daytime conferences had been held there occasionally, but that was all.

It was late when we got back to the rest house, so our guests postponed their inspection of the Göring collection until the following morning. That evening Lamont and I made a second and more thorough survey of the rooms in which the paintings were stacked. We began with a room which contained works of the Dutch, Flemish, German and French schools. The inventory listed five Rembrandt portraits. One was the *Artist's Sister;* another was his son *Titus;* the third was his wife,

Saskia; the fourth was the portrait of a *Bearded Old Man;* and the fifth was the likeness of a *Man with a Turban.*

We examined the backs of the pictures for markings which might give us clues to previous ownership. Two of the portraits— those of Saskia and of the artist's sister—had belonged to Katz, one of the best known Dutch dealers. I had been surprised to learn in Paris that Katz, a Jew, had done business with the Nazis. But I was also told that only through acceding to their demands for pictures had he been able to obtain permits for his relatives to leave Holland. According to the information I received, he had succeeded thereby in smuggling twenty-seven members of his family into Switzerland. A revealing commentary on the extent and quality of his paintings.

The portrait of Titus had been in the Van Pannwitz collection. Mme. Catalina van Pannwitz, South American born, but a resident of the Netherlands, I believe, had sold a large part of her collection to Göring. Whether it had been a bona fide or a forced sale was said to be a moot question.

Another important Dutch private collection, that of Ten Cate at Almelo, had "contributed" the *Man with a Turban.* And the *Bearded Old Man* had been bought from the Swiss dealer, Wendland, who had agents in Paris. He had allegedly discovered the painting in Marseilles.

These five pictures posed an interesting problem in restitution. To whom should they be returned? Who were the rightful owners—as of the summer of 1945?

At the time we were beginning our work on the Göring collection, definite plans for the restitution of works of art were being formulated by the American Military Government. They were an important part of the general restitution program then being planned by the Reparations, Deliveries and Restitution Division of the U. S. Group Control Council. Pending the implementation of the program, the Monuments, Fine Arts and Archives Section of U. S. Forces, European Theater, was the technical custodian of all art works eventually to be restituted.

Bancel La Farge, who became Chief of the Section when SHAEF dissolved, had outlined the plans to us on our way back from the Eagle's Nest that afternoon. There were two main categories of works of art slated for prompt restitution to the overrun countries from which they had been taken. The first included all art objects *easily identifiable as* loot—the great Jewish collections and the property of other "enemies of the state" which had been seized by the Nazis. The second embraced all art works *not* readily identifiable as loot, but for which some compensation was known or believed to have been paid by the Nazis.

The actual restitution was to be made on a wholesale scale. Works of art were to be returned *en bloc* to the claimant nations, *not* to individual claimants of those nations. To expedite this "mass evacuation" country by country, properly qualified art representatives would be invited to the American Occupied Zone, specifically to the Central Collecting Point at Munich, where they could present their claims. Once their claims were substantiated—either by documents in their possession or by records at the Collecting Point—the representatives would be responsible for the actual removal.

We asked Bancel how the various representatives were to be selected. He explained that several of the overrun countries had set up special Fine Arts Commissions. The one in France was called the *Commission de Récupération Artistique.* The one in Holland had an unpronounceable name, so it was known simply as "C.G.R."—the intials stood for the name translated into French, *Commission de Récupération Générale.* And the one in Belgium had such a long name that he couldn't remember it offhand. Czechoslovakia, Poland and Greece would probably establish similar committees before long. Each commission would choose a representative and submit his name to the MFA&A Section for approval. Once the names were approved and the necessary military clearances obtained, the representatives could enter the American Zone, proceed to Munich and start to work.

Bancel said that each representative would have to sign a receipt in the name of his country before he could remove any works of art from the Collecting Point. The receipt would release our government from'all further responsibility for the objects concerned— as of the time they left the Collecting Point. Furthermore, it would contain a clause binding the receiving nation to rectify any mistakes in restitution. For example, if the Dutch representative inadvertently included a painting which later turned out to be the property of a Belgian, then, by the provisions of the receipt,

Holland would be obligated to return that painting to Belgium. The chief merit of this system of fine arts restitution lay in the fact that it relieved American personnel of the heavy burden of settling individual claims. From the point of view of our government, this was an extremely important consideration because of the limited number of men available for so formidable an undertaking. And from the point of view of the receiving nations, the system had the advantage of accelerating the recovery of their looted treasures.

In the room where Lamont and I had seen the Rembrandts, we found a pair of panels by Boucher, the great French master of the eighteenth century. Each represented an ardent youth making amorous advances to a coy and but half-protesting maiden in a rustic setting. They were appropriately entitled *Seduction* and were said to have been painted for the boudoir of Madame de Pompadour. According to the inventory, the panels had been bought from Wendland, the dealer of Paris and Lucerne.

These slightly prurient canvases flanked one of the most beautiful fifteenth century Flemish paintings I had ever seen, *The Mystic Marriage of St. Catherine* by Gerard David. The Madonna with the Child on her lap was portrayed against a landscape background, St. Catherine kneeling at her right, dressed in russet velvet Round about were grouped five other female saints, each richly gowned in a different color. It was not a large composition, measuring only about twenty-five inches square, but it possessed the dignity and monumentality of a great altarpiece. The authenticity of its sentiment put to shame the facile virtuosity of the two Bouchers which stood on either side.

The second room we visited that evening contained an equally miscellaneous assortment of pictures. Here the canvases were even more varied in size. A Dutch Interior by Pieter de Hooch, a *View of the Piazza San Marco* by Canaletto, and two Courbet landscapes were lined up along one wall. The de Hooch, an exceptionally fine example of the work of this seventeenth century master, was listed in the inventory as having belonged to Baron Edouard de Rothschild of Paris. The Courbets were something of a rarity, as Göring had few French paintings of the nineteenth century. One of the landscapes, a winter scene, was an important work, signed and dated 1869. The inventory did not indicate from whom it had been acquired. In one corner stood a full-length portrait of the Duke of Richmond by Van Dyck. Our list stated that it had come from the Katz collection. Beside it was a brilliant landscape by Rubens. There were perhaps ten other pictures in the room, among them several nondescript panels which appeared to be by an artist of the fifteenth century Florentine school, a portrait by the sixteenth century German master, Bernhard Strigel, a "fête champêtre" by Lancret, and two or three seascapes of the seventeenth century Dutch school.

Lamont and I had been looking at this assemblage for some little time before we noticed an unframed canvas standing on the washbasin by the window. The upper edge of the picture leaned against the wall mirror at an angle which made it difficult to get a good look at the composition from where we stood. Closer inspection revealed the subject to be *Christ and the Woman Taken in Adultery*.

I studied it for a few minutes and was still puzzled. Turning to Lamont I asked, "What do you make of this? I can't even place it as to school, let alone guess the artist."

"Unless I am very much mistaken," he said slowly, "that is the famous Göring 'Vermeer.' "

"You're crazy," I said. "Why, I could paint something which would look more like a Vermeer than that."

We consulted the inventory. Lamont was right. A few lines below the listing of the Rubens landscape—a picture I had just been admiring in another part of the room—appeared the entry "Vermeer, Jan . . .. 'The Adulteress'... Canvas, 90 cm. x 96 cm." The subject coincided with that of the picture on the washbasin. The measurements were identical.

I tried to visualize the picture properly framed, properly lighted and hanging in a richly furnished room. But still I couldn't conceive how such trappings could blind one to the flat greens and blues, the lack of subtlety in the modeling of the flesh tones, the absence of that convincing rendering of the "total visual effect" which Vermeer had so completely mastered.

"Who attributed this painting to Vermeer?" I asked.

"I don't know," said Lamont, "but it is related stylistically to the 'Vermeer,' in the Boymans Museum at Rotterdam, the *Christ at Emmaus*."

So this was the painting Hofer was talking about; this was the painting Göring had given the nurse. One of the notorious Van Meegeren fakes.

Lamont's reference to the Boymans' "Vermeer" called to mind the great furor in the art world nearly a decade ago when that picture had turned up in the art market.

Dr. Bredius, the famous connoisseur of Dutch painting, discovered the picture in Paris in 1936. He was convinced that it was a hitherto unknown work by Vermeer, the rarest of all Dutch masters. The subject matter was of special interest to Dr. Bredius, for the *only* other Vermeer which dealt with a religious theme was the one in the National Gallery at Edinburgh.

Hie past history of the picture was as reassuring as that of many another accepted "old master." Dr. Bredius learned that it had belonged to a Dutch family. One of the daughters had married a

Frenchman in the middle eighties. The picture had been a wedding present and she had taken it with her to Paris. But their house had been too small for such a large painting—it was four feet high and nearly square—so the canvas had been relegated to the attic. According to the story, they hadn't known that it was particularly valuable or they might have sold it. In any case, the picture remained in the attic until the couple died. It had come to light again when the house was being dismantled.

Through Dr. Bredius, the Boymans Museum had become interested in the picture. Other experts were called in. A few questioned it, but the majority accepted it as a Vermeer. In 1937, the directors of the Boymans Museum purchased the *Christ at Emmaus* for the staggering price of three hundred and seventy-five thousand dollars.

Unknown to the outside world, several more Vermeers were "discovered" during the war years. All were of religious subjects. One was bought at a fantastic price by Van Beuningen, the great private collector of Rotterdam; another by the Nazi-controlled Dutch Government for an exorbitant sum; and a third by Hermann Göring. Though the Reichsmarschall did not pay cash for his Vermeer, the price was high; he traded one hundred and thirty-seven pictures from his collection. According to Hofer, his adviser and agent, the paintings he gave in exchange were all of high quality.

The final chapter in the story of these newly found Vermeers is one of the most interesting in the annals of the art world. At the close of the war, Dr. van Gelder, the director of the Mauritshuis— the museum at

The Hague—and other Dutch art authorities began an official investigation. It was curious that so many lost Vermeers had come to light in such a short space of time. It was recalled that in 1942 an artist named Van Meegeren had delivered a million guilders to a Dutch bank for credit to his account. The money was in thousand-guilder notes, which the Germans had ordered withdrawn from circulation at that time. The artist was not known to be a man of means and his mediocre talents as a painter could not have enabled him to amass such a fortune.

Van Meegeren was questioned and finally admitted that he had painted the *Christ at Emmaus* and the other lately discovered "Vermeers." Even after he had made a full confession, there were certain Dutch critics who doubted the truth of his statements. This nettled Van Meegeren, and he promptly offered to demonstrate his prowess. His choice of a subject might have been symbolic: Jesus Confounding the Doctors. It took him two months to finish the picture. The work was done in the presence of several witnesses. He painted entirely from memory, using no models.

In the course of the demonstration, he explained the ingenious methods he had used to defraud the experts. In the first place his compositions were original but painted *in the style* of Vermeer. In the second, he used old canvas and only the pigments known to the Dutch masters of the seventeenth century. It had not been difficult to pick up at auctions old paintings of little value. It was not always necessary to remove the existing pictures. He frequently adapted portions of them to his own compositions, or, conversely, rearranged his to take advantage of part of an old picture. He was scrupulously careful to avoid modern zinc white and used only lead white which had been employed by the artists of the seventeenth century. He took equal precautions with his other colors, using ground lapis lazuli and cochineal for his blues and reds. He had obtained these, at great expense, from abroad.

At the time I was evacuating the Göring pictures, the Dutch government was completing its investigation of Van Meegeren's activities. Subsequently, the Ministry of Education, Arts and Sciences publicly announced its findings, confirming the fact that Henrik van Meegeren was the author of the celebrated picture in the Boymans Museum and also of "other forgeries done so marvelously that the best art experts pronounced them genuine."

Bancel La Farge and John Walker returned the following morning. Although it was Sunday, our crew of GIs had reported for work at seven-thirty and, under Steve's supervision, continued to pack books. Some eight thousand volumes remained to be placed in cases before they could be loaded onto the trucks. While this work was in progress Lamont and I made a tour of the pictures with our guests. We looked again at the rooms we had visited the night before, singling out the paintings we thought would be of greatest interest to them, such as the best of the Dutch and Flemish masters, the Cranachs, the eighteenth century French pictures and the finest sculptures. We concluded the tour at noon. Our visitors had to get started on their way to the mine at Alt Aussee.

After lunch Lamont joined the crew at work on the books, while I went in search of Sergeant Peck. We had explained to him that all of the paintings would have to be numbered before we could prepare them for loading. The sergeant had agreed, but I was not certain that he altogether understood why we were so insistent on this point. I found Peck in his room at the end of the south wing of the rest house. As usual, he was working on the inventory. He was a serious, scholarly fellow. Before entering the Army, he had been an art teacher at an Ohio college, so his present assignment was very much to his liking. He had done a remarkably fine job on the inventory. It was a detailed seventy-page document giving the title of each picture, the name of the artist, the dimensions of the canvas and, where known, the name of the collection from which it had been acquired.

I told him that we hoped to get started on the pictures the next morning. We would arrange them in rooms on the second floor of the center section of the building. Those rooms were the ones most accessible to the door leading to our loading platform. We would want him to be responsible for checking off each picture as it was carried onto the truck. Since there were more than a thousand paintings in the inventory, there was only one practical way this checking could be done: by going through all the rooms and numbering each picture, setting down the corresponding number on the correct entry in the inventory.

I asked if he could spare the time to help me with the numbering that afternoon. He agreed; so, armed with the inventory and some chalk, we began with the rooms on the second floor. By midafternoon we had finished marking two hundred pictures. Lamont could start with these the next forenoon. They would keep him busy until we had numbered an additional batch.

At three Steve and I drove over to Brigade Headquarters to make arrangements for escort vehicles. We expected to have our first convoy ready to leave for Munich the following afternoon. It was only a ninety-mile run, Autobahn all the way, so two jeeps would suffice.

The 44th AAA Brigade was established in General Keitel's old headquarters, about two miles northwest of Berchtesgaden. With its smooth gravel driveways and well-tended lawns, the place had the air of a luxurious country club. The administrative offices were located in an L-shaped building, a modern adaptation of the familiar Bavarian provincial style. The surrounding buildings— barracks and small houses—had been designed in the same style.

We were received by Captain Putman, the Chief of Staff s adjutant, a brisk young man, who promised to provide us with the necessary escort vehicles.

"Cocky fellow, wasn't he?" said Steve as we left the office.

"Yes, but I have a feeling we'll get our jeeps on schedule," I said.

My hunch was right. Only once during the entire Berchtesgaden operation did the escort vehicles fail to report for duty at the appointed hour. That one time was when Captain Putman had a day off.

By noon the next day our first convoy of four trucks was ready for the road. Two of the trucks were filled with books, twenty-seven cases of them. The other two contained twenty-five cases, but not cases of books: four were filled with glassware (308 pieces) ; seven contained porcelain (1135 pieces) ; eight contained gold and silver plate (415 pieces); and the remaining six were packed with rugs. These were from Karinhall, near Berlin, the largest of Göring's seven households.

As soon as we had dispatched the convoy, Lamont and four members of the work party resumed the sorting and stacking of the numbered paintings. Sergeant Peck and I, with two helpers to shift the larger canvases, proceeded with the numbering. Steve took off for Alt Aussee to pick up Kress, the photographer, and his paraphernalia.

That night Lamont decided we should improve our quarters. This involved moving from the room we occupied at the front of the building to a much larger one at the back. The new room had several advantages which the old one lacked. It had been the reading room of the rest house in the days of the Luftwaffe occupancy and was attractively paneled in natural oak with built-in bookshelves. It was thirty feet long and fifteen wide, nearly twice the size of our former room, and opened onto a broad porch. There were French doors and two large windows which afforded a spectacular view of the mountain range to the east. The Eagle's Nest crowned the highest of the peaks. At one end of the room was an alcove, with a built-in desk and couch. With a little fixing up, it could be turned into a comfortable sitting room.

Before we could transfer our belongings to this spacious apartment, we had to clear out a few of the Reichsmarschall's—half a dozen pieces of sculpture and three large altarpieces. The outstanding piece of sculpture was a life-size statue of the Magdalene which Göring had acquired from the Louvre. Similarly, the most important of the three altarpieces was a big triptych which also had come from the Louvre. Göring did not remove these objects by force. He obtained them by exchange after prolonged negotiations with the officials of the museum. According to the information given me, both parties were well pleased with the trade. As I recall, the Louvre received six objects from the Reichsmarschall's collection in return for the triptych and the statue. I was told that one of the six pieces was a painting by Coypel, the eighteenth century French artist, which had belonged to one of the Paris Rothschilds. It was because they were of German workmanship that Göring particularly coveted the pieces which he obtained from the Louvre. It is presumed that this did not prejudice the Louvre in their favor.

The statue, portraying the Magdalene clothed only in her long blonde tresses, was known as "la belle allemande," the beautiful German. It was an exceptionally fine example, in polychromed wood, of the work of Gregor Erhardt, a Swabian sculptor of the first quarter of the sixteenth century. I fancied that Göring detected a resemblance between the statue and his wife. Lamont and I carried the statue down to the first floor of the rest house and placed it at the foot of the stairs.

It was one of the last objects we packed for shipment and, during our stay at Berchtesgaden, I had the uncomfortable feeling that I had caught Frau Göring on her way to the bath, I was not the only one with that idea. One evening I found the GI guard draping a raincoat about the Magdalene's shoulders. I had given strict orders that the guards were to touch nothing in the collection, so I stopped to have a word with him on the subject. He said with a sheepish look, "I didn't mean to break the rules, sir, but I thought Emmy looked cold."

The altarpiece which Göring acquired from the Louvre was a sumptuous affair consisting of three panels painted with nearly life-size figures against a gold background. It was by the Master of the Holy Kinship, an artist of the Cologne School of the fifteenth century. The large center panel represented the *Presentation in the Temple;* the right-hand panel, the *Adoration of the Magi;* the left-hand panel, *Christ Appearing to Mary.* During its recent peregrinations the central panel had cracked from top to bottom. But fortunately the cleavage, which ran through the center of the middle panel, fell in an area devoid of figures. An adroit restorer could easily repair the damage. We shifted the altarpiece to an adjoining room.

The two remaining altarpieces were works of the fifteenth century French school. One represented the *Crucifixion;* the other, the *Passion of Christ.* The *Crucifixion* had belonged to the Paris dealer Seligmann, whose collection had been confiscated by the Nazis. The inventory did not show the name of the former owner of the other panel. A highly imaginative composition with nocturnal illumination, it was attributed to the rare French master,

Jean Bellegambe. As we carried the altarpieces into the room in which we had placed the one from the Louvre, I remarked to Lamont that for a godless fellow Göring seemed to have had a nice taste for religious subjects. The pieces of sculpture, which we added to the collection in the lower hallway, were also of devotional character: two Gothic statues of St. George and the Dragon, one of St. Barbara, and two of the Madonna and Child.

We brought three large wardrobes from our old room, placed two of them at right angles to the walls to form a partition, and set the third in a corner of the new room. The beds came next. In another hour we had the furniture arranged to our satisfaction. By the time we had added a silver lamp, borrowed temporarily from the Göring collection, and tacked up a few of our photographs, the place looked as though we had been living there for weeks.

Without Steve the loading went more slowly, but we managed to finish three trucks by two o'clock the next day. The driver of one of the escort jeeps had brought us a message from Munich that it would simplify the work at the Central Collecting Point if we dispatched the trucks in groups of three or four instead of waiting until we had six loaded. At the Alt Aussee mine we hadn't been able to work on such a schedule because we lacked sufficient escort vehicles. We didn't have that problem at Berchtesgaden because the shorter distance made possible a one day turnaround. The jeeps could easily make the round trip in half a day. Accordingly, we sent off our second convoy that afternoon. The trucks contained the rest of the books—forty-three cases in all—sixty-five paintings and fifteen of the larger pieces of sculpture.

In anticipation of Kress' arrival, we spent the next morning assembling all the paintings that appeared to have suffered recent damage of any kind. His first job would be to make a photographic record which we would include in our final report on the evacuation of the collection. We found thirty-four pictures in this category. Only two had sustained serious injury. These were the side panels of a large triptych by the sixteenth century Italian artist, Raffaellino del Garbo. They had been badly splintered by machine-gun fire while the collection was still aboard the special train which had brought it to Berchtesgaden. Three other panels bore the marks of stray bullets, but the harm done was relatively slight. In general, the damage consisted of minor nicks and scratches and water spots. Considering the hazards to which the collection had been exposed, the pictures had come through remarkably well. I was reminded of what George Stout had said, "There's a lot of nonsense talked about the fragility of the 'old masters.' By and large, they are a hardy lot. Otherwise they wouldn't have lasted this long."

We had worked our crew all day Sunday, so we told them to knock off as soon as we had finished selecting and segregating the damaged pictures. With the afternoon to ourselves, we turned our attention to the miscellaneous assortment of objects in the "Gold Room." This was the name given the small room on the ground floor in which Sergeant Peck had stored the things of great intrinsic value. There were seventy-five pieces in all: gold chalices studded with precious stones; silver tankards; reliquaries of gold and enamel work; boxes of jade and malachite; candelabra, clocks and lamps of marble and gold; precious plaques of carved ivory; and sets of gold table ornaments. They presented a specialized packing job which Lamont and I could handle better alone than with inexperienced helpers.

Our first problem was to find some small packing cases. We searched the rest house without success. Then Lamont remembered seeing a pile of individual wooden file cabinets in the little chapel where most of the furniture was stored. These were admirably suited to our purpose. They were rectangular boxes about six feet long and two feet high. Each was divided into three compartments. There were thirty of them—more than enough for the job. We had a supply of flannel cloths which we had borrowed from a packing firm in Munich. After wrapping each piece, we placed it in one of the compartments of the file cabinet. We stuffed the compartments with excelsior so that the objects could not move about.

A few of the items were equipped with special leather cases. Among these were two swords: one, with a beautifully etched blade of Toledo steel, had been presented to Göring by the Spanish air force; the other, with a jewel-studded gold handle, had been a gift from Mussolini. There was also a gold baton encrusted with precious stones, a present from the Reichsmarschall's own air force.

Of all these objects, perhaps twenty were of modern workmanship. In contrast to the older things, they were ornate without being beautiful. Ugliest of the lot was a standing lamp. The stalk, eight inches in diameter, was a shaft of beaten gold. The shade, with a filigree design, was also of gold, as were the pull cords. Rivaling it in costly vulgarity was a set of gold table ornaments. The large centerpiece consisted of an elliptical framework. At each end and in the center of the two sides stood Egyptian maidens, fashioned of gold, four feet high. The German slang word for such stuff is "kitsch." I think the closest English equivalent is "corny."

Toward the end of the afternoon we were waited on by a delegation of three officers from the 101st Airborne Division. They had come to inquire if we would consider turning over to them the gold sword which Mussolini had given to Göring. They wanted it as a trophy for a dub of 101st Airborne officers which they were organizing. They planned to set up a clubroom when they got back home and have annual reunions. The sword, they said, would be such an appropriate souvenir. I told them that I had been directed to ship everything to

Munich and did not have authority to make any other disposition of objects in the collection. But, since the sword could not be regarded as a "cultural object"—a fact which I called to their attention—I suggested that they take the matter up with Third Army Headquarters in Munich. I refrained from informing them that, for all of me, they could have their pick of the modern objects in the "Gold Room."

We made an interesting discovery that afternoon. Rummaging in a closet off the "Gold Room" we found a stack of photograph albums. At the bottom of the heap lay an enormous portfolio. It contained architect's drawings for the proposed expansion of Karinhall. The estate, greatly enlarged, was to have become a public museum. We had heard that Göring intended to present his art collection to the Reich on his sixtieth birthday. Here was concrete proof of those intentions. Each drawing bore the date "January 1945."

Steve returned in triumph at noon the next day. With him in the command car was Kress, looking more timid than ever. Steve said that Kress had had a bad time after we left Alt Aussee; the boys at House 71 had clapped him in jail and left him there for two days before interrogating him. Steve had been "burned up" about it and had given them a piece of his mind. He said contemptuously that he had known all along they didn't have anything on Kress. But he was content to let bygones be bygones. Steve had his man Friday back again.

He pointed happily to the six-by-six which had pulled up behind the command car. All of Kress' photographic equipment was packed up inside it. There was a tremendous lot of stuff: three large cameras, a metal table for drying prints, reflectors, a sink, pipes of various sizes, boxes of film and paper, and a couple of large cabinets. Steve planned to get everything installed at once. Kress was to sleep in one of the rooms of the rest house. An adjoining room was to be set up as a darkroom.

We showed Steve our new quarters and suggested that Kress take over our old room. The one next door would make a good darkroom. I asked Steve how he was going to get all the stuff installed. He'd have to have a plumber. That didn't bother Steve. He asked me to tell the mess sergeant that Kress was to have his meals with the civilian help in the kitchen. He'd take care of everything else. Steve was as good as his word. He found a plumber and by the end of the day Kress was ready to start work.

Notwithstanding these interruptions, Lamont and I managed to load and dispatch a convoy of three trucks. This third convoy contained two hundred paintings, thirty tapestries, fifteen more pieces of large sculpture and a dozen pieces of Italian Renaissance furniture.

At odd moments during our first days at Berchtesgaden, we had worried about the sculpture. In the first three convoys we had disposed of only thirty of the two hundred and fifty pieces. Most of those remaining were just under life size. We had no materials with which to build crates. And even if we had had the lumber, the labor of building them would have greatly delayed the evacuation. That evening we found the solution of the problem. The three of us were standing on the open porch outside our room after supper. Two of the trucks were parked by the loading platform directly below. Why not make a checkerboard pattern of ropes, strung waist high across the truck bed? The floor of the truck could be padded with excelsior. We could set a statue in each of the squares. The ropes would hold eaqh piece in place. If we stuffed quantities of excelsior between the statues, they wouldn't rub. Perhaps it was a crazy idea. On the other hand, it might work.

The following morning Steve and two of the men prepared the truck while Lamont and I selected the statues for the trial load. We chose thirty of the largest pieces. We figured on seven or eight rows, with four statues in each row.. Kress set up his camera on the porch and photographed the progress of the operation. One by one the long row of madonnas, saints and angels was set in place. We hadn't been far off in our calculations. There were twenty-nine in all. The truck looked like a tumbrel of the French Revolution filled with victims for the guillotine. It was a new technique in the packing of sculpture. Steve said we'd have to send George Stout a photograph. "And we'll have to .send for more excelsior, too," Lamont said. He was quite right. We had used up the last shred.

That afternoon Steve combed the countryside for a fresh supply of excelsior, returning just before supper with three new bales. In the meantime, Lamont went over, with Kress, the paintings to be photographed. Sergeant Peck and I completed numbering the last of the pictures.

The next day we loaded three more trucks. With Steve on hand to crack the whip over the men, the loading went fast, so fast in fact that Sergeant Peck had a hard time checking off the paintings as they were hoisted onto the trucks. We packed four hundred pictures, the cases containing the gold and silver objects which Lamont and I had finished the day before, and another dozen pieces of furniture. The convoy—our fourth—got off in the early afternoon.

We placed a special guard on the truck with the sculpture to make sure that the driver didn't smoke on the way.

We finished one more truck and stopped for a cigarette. It was a hot day and we didn't feel like doing any more work. Steve had gone up to the darkroom to see Kress. Lamont said, "Let's go up to Munich."

"That suits me, but what excuse have we got?" I asked.

"If we must have an excuse, I can think of at least four," he said thoughtfully. "We're out of cigarettes and candy. We ought to be on hand when they unpack the sculpture at the Collecting Point. We've worked for a week without taking a day off. And perhaps there'll be some mail for us at Posey's office."

"What about the little brown bear? Do you think he'll mind our taking off?" I asked. This was Lamont's name for Steve, but it was never used when he was within earshot.

"Steve's had his trip for this week," said Lamont, meaning Steve's trip to Alt Aussee. -

Sergeant Peck, who had overheard part of our conversation, asked if he might join us. We told him to be ready in ten minutes and went off to notify Steve of our plans and to pack up our musette bags. Steve was so busy helping Kress with his developing that he scarcely paid any attention to us. After leaving him a final injunction to have at least three trucks loaded before we got back the next evening, we called for the command car. The driver, a restless redhead named Freedberg, who hated the monotonous routine at Berchtesgaden, was delighted with the idea of going to Munich. Sergeant Peck appeared and we set off.

We chose the shorter road through the mountains and overtook the convoy on the Autobahn, halfway to Munich. The front escort jeep was holding the speed down to thirty-five miles an hour, in accordance with my instructions. The driver waved envyingly as we passed them doing fifty. Twenty miles from Munich, Freedberg turned west off the Autobahn and took the back road from Bad Tolz, a short cut which brought us directly to Third Army Headquarters.

We arrived at Captain Posey's office just as Lincoln Kirstein was leaving for chow. He told us that the captain had gone to Pilsen the middle of the week but was due back that evening. "There's quite a lot of mail for both of you," Lincoln said. He handed us each a thick batch of letters. It was the first mail I had received from home in six weeks. There were forty-two letters!

"I told you there'd be mail for us," said Lamont with a satisfied smile.

We had supper with Craig Smyth and Ham Coulter at the Detachment that evening. Craig said that the convoy had not arrived before he left the Collecting Point, but two of his German workmen were to be on duty the next morning, even though it was Sunday. We arranged to meet him at his office and supervise the unloading. Lincoln had said that Posey would not be back before ten, so we spent the evening with Craig and Ham at their apartment.

Just before we returned to Third Army Headquarters, Ham gave us a small paper-bound volume. It was entitled *The Ludwigs of Bavaria*. The author was Henry Channon.

"This is one of the most fascinating books I've ever read," Ham said. "You might take it along with you."

I thanked him, and stuck it in my musette bag. Before our operations in Bavaria ended two months later, that little book had come to mean a great deal to the members of the evacuation team. We called it our "Bavarian bible." So alluring were Channon's descriptions of the "Seven Wonders of Bavaria" that whenever we had a free day—or even a few hours to ourselves—we made excursions to these architectural fantasies: the swirling, baroque churches of Wies, Weltenburg, Ottobeuren and Vierzehnheiligen; the Amalienburg and the palace of Herrenchiemsee. The Residenz at Würzburg, which we had seen, was one of the seven. Unofficially we added an eighth to the list: Schloss Linderhof, Ludwig II's opulent little palace \$ear Oberammergau—ornate and vulgar, yet fascinating in its lonely mountain setting.' But these were extracurricular activities, falling outside the orbit of our official work.

We found Captain Posey at his office when we got there a few minutes before ten that evening. He asked us for a complete account of our operations at Berchtesgaden. We reported that we had sent a total of fourteen truckloads up to Munich the first week; that we had cleaned out half the pictures, but that we had just begun on the sculpture. We estimated that it would take us another ten days to finish; we would probably fill seventeen or eighteen more trucks.

We asked him what plans he would have for us when we completed the job. He said he might send us to the Castle of Neuschwanstein. The place was full of things looted from Paris. In fact, it was one of the major repositories of the *Einsatzstab Rosenberg*. The French were clamoring to have it evacuated. Then there was another big repository in a Carthusian monastery at Buxheim. That too contained loot from Paris. Perhaps we could take a run down to both places and size up the jobs after we had finished with the Göring things. The captain was tired after his long trip, so we didn't go into details about either of the two prospective assignments. He offered us a billet for the night and the three of us turned in shortly after eleven. It was none too soon for me: I still had forty-two unopened letters from home in the pocket of my jacket.

When we arrived at the Collecting Point the next morning, the two German workmen who had been with me at Hohenfurth were starting to unpack the truck with the sculpture. Lamont and I examined each statue as it was lifted from its nest of excelsior. All twenty-nine had come through without a scratch. Our experiment was a success. We would be able to use the same technique with the rest of the sculpture. I instructed the workmen to leave all of the excelsior in the truck, as we had none to spare.

I persuaded Craig to drive back to Berchtesgaden with us for the night. He looked tired and I thought the change would do him good. His responsibilities at the Collecting Point the "Bau," as we called it (our abbreviation for Verwaltungsbau)—were heavy; and he never took a day off.

On the return trip he told us his latest troubles. Only three days ago a small bomb had exploded in the basement of the "Bau." It had blown one of the young German workmen to bits. Craig gave all the grisly details, which included discovering one of the poor fellow's arms in a heap of debris fifty feet from the scene of the explosion. The tragedy had had one beneficial result. For weeks Craig had been harping on the subject of additional guards for the Collecting Point. His words had fallen on deaf ears—until the bomb episode. He said that a general and three colonels arrived at the building within half an hour. Since then everyone had been so "security-conscious" that he had had no further difficulty in obtaining the desired number of guards. The Bomb Disposal Unit inspected the premises and some pointed comments were made about the thoroughness of the original survey.

In our absence Steve had loaded three trucks. As a reward for his labors, I suggested that he take Craig up to the Eagle's Nest the following morning. While they were gone, Lamont and I finished three more loads. We had the convoy of six lined up by noon. Craig returned to Munich in one of the escort jeeps. This fifth convoy contained one hundred and sixty-seven paintings, one hundred and six pieces of sculpture, twenty-five tapestries, sixty-eight cases filled with bibelots, and fifty-three pieces of furniture. It was our largest convoy out of Berchtesgaden thus far.

It was also the first one to break down. Late in the afternoon, the rear escort jeep arrived at the rest house with word that two of the trucks had broken down fifteen miles out of Berchtesgaden. Steve and I drove to Berchtesgaden to arrange to have them towed in for reloading. I also wanted to do a little investigating. There could be little excuse for breakdowns on the Munich road if the trucks had been in good mechanical condition when they started out.

On the way into town, Steve said, "Tom, I think I know what caused the trouble. I didn't think of it till just now. But the other day on the road back from Alt Aussee, two six-by-sixes passed me at a hell of a clip. I thought I recognized the drivers as two of ours."

I questioned the lieutenant in charge of the drivers. He professed ignorance of any unauthorized junkets back to Alt Aussee.

"I am going to have a word with Tiny," said Steve as we left the lieutenant's room. Tiny was the head mechanic and the only one of the entire crew who was always on the job. Steve wanted to talk to him alone, so I waited in the car.

A few minutes later he came back with a satisfied grin on his face. "I got the whole story," he said. "The drivers have been racing back and forth to Alt Aussee all the time we've been here.

They were crazy about it up at the mine. Tiny says they hate it here at Berchtesgaden."

"Well, we'll fix that," I said. I went back to see the lieutenant. "How many drivers have you got and how many trucks?" I asked. "Sixteen drivers and thirteen trucks," he said.

"Send eight of the drivers and five of the trucks up to Munich first thing in the morning and have them report to the trucking company. We can finish the job here without them."

Steve always sang when he was in a particularly happy frame of mind. That evening, on the way back to the rest house, he was in exceptionally good voice.

Five days later we completed the evacuation of the Göring collection. The last two convoys, of four and seven trucks respectively, contained the larger pictures, one hundred and seventy-seven of them; sixty pieces of sculpture, twenty miscellaneous cases, sixty-seven pieces of furniture and two hundred empty picture frames. We had heavy rain that last week and the mud was ankle-deep around the loading platform. Although it was early August, the nights were cold and the rest house, emptied of its treasures, was a cheerless place. We were glad to see the last of the trucks pull out of the drive. It had been a strenuous operation—thirty-one truckloads in thirteen days. In the early afternoon we would collect our personal belongings and return to Munich.

~ 8 ~

LOOTERS' CASTLE: SCHLOSS NEUSCHWANSTEIN

A telephonb call from Brigade Headquarters changed our plans. It was Major Luther Miller of G-2. He had just made an inspection of a house belonging to one of Göring's henchmen and there was a lot of "art stuff" in it. He had reported the find to Third Army Headquarters and Captain Posey had told him to get in touch with me. Could I go up to the house with him that afternoon? *

Major Miller picked me up after lunch. He was a handsome fellow, tall and sparely built. He had an easy, pleasant manner. As we drove along he gave me further details about the house to which we were going. It had been occupied until the day before by Fritz Görnnert and his wife. Görnnert had been the social secretary and close confidant of Göring. The Görnnerts had been living on the second and third floors. They shared the house with a man named Angerer, who had the first floor. Both Görnnert and Angerer had been apprehended and were now in jail. Major Miller had found a suspiciously large number of tapestries and other art objects on the premises. He thought they might be loot.

The house was an unpretentious villa hidden among pine trees high up in the hills above the town. The place was under guard. On the ground floor we examined the contents of a small storeroom. There were several cases bearing Angerer's name and three or four large crates containing Italian furniture. A similar storeroom on the second floor contained a dozen tapestries, a pile of Oriental rugs, a large collection of church vestments and nearly a hundred rare textiles mounted on cardboard. I noticed that the tapestries, vestments and textiles were individually tagged and that the markings were in French. Concealed beneath the tapestries were ten cases, each one about two feet square and a foot high. Major Miller hadn't seen these before. On each one was stenciled in Gothic letters: "Reichsmarschall Hermann Göring." They contained a magnificent collection of Oriental weapons.

In a room which Görnnert had apparently used for a study we found six handsome leather portfolios filled with Old Master drawings. The drawings were by Dutch and French artists of the seventeenth and eighteenth centuries.

There was a possibility that all of these things, with the exception of the weapon collection, which Göring had probably entrusted to Görnnert, were the legitimate property of the tenants. It was equally possible that they had been illegally acquired. In the circumstances, Major Miller wished me to take charge of them. I said that I could take them to the Central Collecting Point at Munich where they would be held in safekeeping until ownership had been determined.

The house had been thoroughly ransacked. Drawers had been pulled out and their contents disarranged. Closet doors stood open and the clothing on the hangers had been gone over. The beds were rumpled, for even the mattresses had been searched. Despite the topsy-turvy look of things, there was no evidence of wanton destruction. The search had been thorough and methodical. I asked the major what his men had been looking for, but his answer was noncommittal. He did say, though, that the discovery of documents hidden in a false partition in the living room had prompted the search.

The following morning Steve, Lamont and I went to the Gomnert house in the command car. It would have been difficult to take a large truck up the narrow winding road. In any case, I thought we could probably load all of the stuff in the command car. Major Miller had sent one of his officers ahead with the key. The house had been searched again. This time it looked as though a cyclone had struck it. Pillows had been ripped open; drawers had been emptied on the floor; clothes were scattered all over the bedrooms. I was relieved to find that the things which we had come to take away had not been tampered with. I asked the lieutenant with the key what had been going on in the house, and he muttered something about "those CIC boys." I seemed to have touched on a sore subject, so I didn't pursue the matter. Lamont, who knew the ways of the Army far better than I, said that probably there had been a "jurisdictional dispute" over who had the right to search the place and that perhaps two different outfits had taken a crack at it, I was glad that Major Miller's emissary was there to bear witness to *our* behavior.

We bundled up the rugs, tapestries and textiles and got out as quickly as possible. They completely filled the command car. Lamont and Steve sat in front with the driver. I wedged myself in between the top of the pile and the canvas top of the car. There was no room for the ten cases of weapons, so I sent a message to Major Miller to have one of his men deliver them to us later in the day.

When we got back to the rest house, Kress had dismantled his darkroom and after lunch we loaded the photographic equipment onto the one truck we had held over for that purpose. There was ample space for the things from the Görnnert house. Before packing them we had to make a complete list of the items. There were two hundred and thirteen church vestments, eighty-one mounted textiles, twenty rugs and eleven tapestries. It was suppertime when we finished. As the ten cases of weapons hadn't arrived, we decided to wait till morning and load everything at once.

That evening Major Anderson of the 101st Airborne came over with the official receipt which I was to sign. It was an elaborate document comprising Sergeant Peck's seventy-page inventory and a covering letter from the C.O. of the 101st Airborne Division to the Commanding General of the Third Army stating that I had received from Major Anderson the entire Göring collection for delivery to the Central Collecting Point at Munich. Having discharged his responsibility, the major was free to go home to the U.S.A. That called for a celebration and he had brought a bottle of cognac. It was sixty years old. He said that it came from Hitler's private stock at the Berghof. Even Steve, who had harbored a slight grudge toward Anderson since the night of our arrival in Berchtesgaden, relented and the four of us toasted the successful evacuation of the Göring treasures.

The major had another surprise for us: he had engaged a room at the Berchtesgadener Hof. He insisted that the three of us move over from the rest house. The next day was Sunday. What would be the point of going up to Munich? We had been working hard for two weeks. Why not take life easy for a day or two?

The Berchtesgadener Hof was a luxurious resort hotel. Its appointments were modem and lavish. In the days of the Nazi regime, it had been patronized by all visiting dignitaries, save the chosen few who had been invited to stay at the Berghof or the small hotel at Obersalzberg. It was now being used by the Army as a "leave hotel." We had an enormous double room with twin beds and a couch. We had our own private terrace. The room faced south with a wonderful view of the mountains. We even had a telephone which worked. I hadn't seen such magnificence since the Royal Monceau in Paris. There was a room for our driver on the top floor. The final de luxe touch was the schedule of meal hours; breakfast wasn't even served until eight-thirty. It was hard to believe that we were in Germany.

We were awakened early by a call from Major Miller. He had another job for me—two, in fact. They had been interrogating Görnnert and he had told them that several pieces of valuable sculpture had been buried in the grounds of his house. The major had located the spot and the things were to be excavated before noon. Also he wanted me to go with him to inspect a cache of pictures reported hidden in a forester's house not far from Berchtesgaden. I said I'd be ready in an hour.

The phone rang again. This time it was Captain Posey. Had we remembered to pick up the pictures at St. Agatha? The ones Mussolini had given to Hider? No, we hadn't. We were to be sure to attend to that before we returned to Munich. Steve was cursing these early callers and Lamont was shaking his head sadly. Our life of ease was getting off to a hell of a poor start.

When Major Miller and I reached the Görnnert place, the Sergeant of the Guard and one of his men were standing beside a hole in the ground some twenty yards behind the house. The hole was about six feet square and four feet deep. Four bundles wrapped in discolored newspaper lay on the ground at the edge of the excavation. The first bundle I opened contained a wood statue of the Madonna and Child, about eighteen inches high. It had been an attractive example of the fifteenth century French school, but moisture had seriously damaged the original polychromy and the wood beneath was soft and pulpy. The next two bundles contained pieces of similar workmanship, but they were not polychromed. One was a Madonna and Child; the other a figure of St. Barbara. Although they were damp, the wood had not disintegrated. The fourth package contained the prize of the lot, an ivory figure of the Madonna and Child. It was a fine piece from the hand of a French sculptor of the late fourteenth century. The ivory was discolored but otherwise in good condition. I wrapped the statues in fresh paper and put them in the car.

Our next objective was the little village of Hintersee, a few kilometers west of Berchtesgaden. The forester's house, a large chalet with overhanging eaves, stood at the edge of a meadow several hundred yards from the road. I explained the purpose of our visit to the young woman in peasant dress who answered our knock. She took us to a room on the second floor which was filled with unframed canvases stacked in neat rows along the walls. They were the work of contemporary German painters and, according to the young woman, had been the property of the local Nazi organization. From my point of view, the trip had been a waste of time. There wasn't a looted picture in the lot. While I looked at the paintings, Major Miller thumbed through a pile of books on a big table in one corner of the room. Among them he found a volume called *Die Polnische Grausamkeit—The Polish Atrocity*. A characteristic sample of German propaganda, it was a compilation of "horror photographs" illustrating the alleged inhuman treatment of Germans by the Poles. It added a gruesome touch to our visit.

When I got back to the hotel at noon I found mesages from Steve and Lamont. Steve had gone over to Unterstein to see about the repairs on his Steyr truck, the one he and Kress had spent so much time on—fitting it up as a mobile photographic unit. There was also some work to be done on the Mercedes-Benz, which had been standing idle, concealed behind a clump of bushes by the rest house, during our evacuation of the Göring collection. Steve had been right about the car; Colonel Davitt at Alt Aussee had not pressed his claim to it.

Lamont had taken off for St. Agatha in a truck borrowed from Brigade Headquarters to pick up the Hitler-Mussolini pictures.

There was also a message brought down by courier from Captain

Posey's office. It contained a list of three places in the vicinity of Berchtesgaden which should be inspected on the chance that they contained items from the Göring collection. One of them was the forester's hut at Hintersee which I had just seen. The other two were castles in the neighborhood: Schloss Stauffeneck-Tiereck and Schloss Marzoll. I asked Major Anderson at lunch what he knew about them. He had nothing to contribute on the subject and said I'd probably draw a blank on all three. After removing the Göring things from the train, he had taken the precaution of publishing a notice to all residents of the area instructing them to declare all art works in their possession. He had done this as a means of recovering objects which might have been sequestered by Göring's agents and objects which might have been surreptitiously removed from the train while it stood on the siding. The results had been disappointing. Only about thirty pictures had been turned in and none of them was in any way connected with Göring.

The major's prediction was correct. Lamont, Steve and I visited the two castles the next day. In addition to their own furnishings, Schloss Stauffeneck-Tiereck and Schloss Marzoll contained only books from the University of Munich. These fruitless researches took all day. It was after five when we left Berchtesgaden.

It was raining when we reached Munich three hours later. Kress had no place to stay and it took us an hour to locate a civilian agency which provided billets for transients. The only thing they had to offer was a room for one night in a ruined nunnery on the Mathilde-Strasse. It was a gloomy place. There was no light and the windows were without glass. One of the Sisters, candle in hand, led us along a dark corridor to a small single room at the back. We followed with our flashlights. We gave Kress a box of K rations and told him we'd come back for him in the morning. Steve was of two minds about the place: on the one hand it wasn't good enough for Kress; on the other he was impressed by the compassion of the Sisters in offering refuge to strangers. He wanted me to point out to Kress the anomaly of his being given sanctuary by the Church. I convinced him that my German wasn't fluent enough. We thanked the Sister and went off to find ourselves a billet. We decided on the Excelsior, the hotel for transient officers. We were several miles from Third Army Headquarters, whereas the hotel was only a few blocks away.

I didn't like driving the Mercedes-Benz around Munich, even though I had got away with it so far. The Third Army regulation forbidding officers to drive was strictly enforced. Perhaps my uniform baffled the MPs. It consisted of a Navy cap with blue cover, a British battle jacket with Navy shoulder boards, khaki trousers and black riding boots. It was my personal opinion that the MPs mistook the shoulder bars for the insignia of a Polish officer. The Poles, and the other liaison officers as well, were allowed to drive their own cars. Steve used to pooh-pooh my apprehensions about the MPs. "They're a bunch of dumbheads," he would say. "I ought to know. I used to be one." All the same, he didn't do much daytime driving around town.

Captain Posey had our next job lined up for us. We were to evacuate the records of the *Einsatzstab Rosenberg*—the German art-looting organization—from Neuschwanstein Castle. The job would include the removal of part of the stolen art treasures also. The captain told us that the castle contained a great quantity of uncrated objects, mostly gold and silver. They presented a serious security problem and it wasn't safe to leave them there indefinitely. Even though the French were anxious to get everything back from Neuschwanstein, for the present they would have to be content with the gold and the silver objects and as many of the smaller cases as we could handle. It would be more practicable to ship the larger things—furniture, sculpture and pictures—direct to France by rail. This possibility was being investigated. It would save moving the things twice—first from Neuschwanstein to Munich, and then from Munich to Paris. But the records were badly needed at the Collecting Point in connection with the identification of the plunder stored there. So we were to concentrate on them and on the objects of great intrinsic value.

It was going to take three or four days to line up the trucks necessary for this operation. There was a critical shortage of transportation at the moment because all available vehicles were being used to haul firewood. This was popularly known as "Patton's pet project." For some weeks it had first priority after foodstuffs.

We welcomed the delay, for it gave us time to make a trip to Frankfurt. All three of us had urgent business to attend to there. Lamont's and Steve's records had to be straightened out. Both of them had been working in the field for so long that the headquarters to which they were technically assigned had lost track of them. And I wanted to find out what had happened to the personal belongings I had left in Frankfurt months ago. When I left I had expected to be gone ten days.

In the back of our minds, too, lurked the hope of becoming "incorporated" as a Special Evacuation Team. That's what we were in fact, but we wanted to be recognized as such in name. The three of us worked well together and did not want to be separated. The decision would rest with Major La Farge and Lieutenant Kuhn.

We wheedled a command car out of the sergeant at the motor pool and took off late in the afternoon. Lamont, Steve and I rode in the Mercedes-Benz, the command car following. I had little confidence in our rakish convertible. The car had been behaving well enough mechanically, but the tires were paper-thin. They were an odd size and we had not been able to get any replacements. It was reassuring to know that the sturdy command car was trailing along behind.

We arrived at Ulm in time for supper. Long before we reached the city, we could see the soaring single spire of the cathedral silhouetted against the sky. There was literally nothing left of the old city. All the medieval houses which, with the cathedral, had made it one of the most picturesque cities in Germany, lay in ruins. But the cathedral was undamaged.

We stopped for gas just outside Ulm. To our surprise, the Army attendant filled our tanks. This was Seventh Army territory. In Third Army area the maximum was five gallons. I mentioned this to the attendant. He said, "There's no gas shortage here. General Patton must be building up one hell of a big stockpile."

We spent the night in Stuttgart. As the main transient hotel was full, we were assigned rooms at a small inn on the outskirts of the battered city. It took us an hour to find the place, so it was past midnight when we turned in.

The next morning we detoured a few kilometers in order to visit the castle at Ludwigsburg. The little town was laid out in the French manner, and its atmosphere was that of a miniature Versailles. The caretaker told us that the kings of Wurttemberg had lived at the castle until 1918. Our visit to it was the one pleasant experience of the day, which happened to be my birthday. We had our first flat tire in the castle courtyard, a second one an hour later, and a third between Mannheim and Darmstadt. It was Sunday and we had a devilish time finding places where we could get the inner tubes repaired. It was ten p.m. when we pulled into Frankfurt. The trip from Stuttgart had taken eleven hours instead of the usual four. We had spent seven hours on tire repairs.

My old room with the pink brocaded furniture was vacant, so I moved in for the night. In my absence it had been successively occupied by three lieutenant colonels. All of my belongings had been boxed and stored away in the closet, Lamont and Steve put up at the house next door.

We called on Bancel La Farge and Charlie Kuhn at USFET Headquarters the next morning. We were lucky to find them together. Their office at that time was a kind of house divided against itself. Thanks to the organizational whim of a colonel, Bancel and Charlie had to spend part of the day in the office at the big Farben building—where we found them—and part at their office in Hochst. Hochst was about six miles away. The remnant of the U. S. Group Control Council, which had not yet moved up to Berlin, was located there—in another vast complex of I. G. Farben buildings. It was an exhausting arrangement.

Bancel and Charlie looked tired—and worried too. They seemed glad to see us, but they were preoccupied and upset about something. Presently Charlie showed us a document which had just reached his desk a few days earlier. It was unsigned and undated.

It bore the letterhead "Headquarters U. S. Group Control Council." The subject was "Art Objects in the U. S. Zone."* In the first paragraph reference was made to the great number and value of the art objects stored in emergency repositories throughout the U. S. Zone. Farther on, the art objects were divided into three classes, according to ownership.

Those in "Class C" were defined as "works of art, placed in the U. S. Zone by Germany for safekeeping, which are the bona fide property of the German nation."

Concerning the disposition of the works of art thus described, the letter had this to say: "It is not believed that the U. S. would desire the works of art in Class C to be made available for reparations and to be

---

* See article "German Paintings in the National Gallery: A Protest," by Charles L, Kuhn, in *College Art Journal*, January 1946. This and subsequent references printed by permission.

divided among a number of nations. Even if this is to be done, these works of art might well be returned to the U. S. to be inventoried, and cared for by our leading museums."

The next, and last, sentence contained this extraordinary proposal: "They could be held in trusteeship for return, many years from now, to the German people if and when the German nation had earned the right to their return."

Clipped to the document was a notation, dated July 29, 1945, bearing the signature of the Chief of Staff of General Lucius D. Clay, Deputy Military Governor. It read, in part, "General Clay states that this paper has been approved by the President for implementation after the close of the current Big 3 Conference."

We were dumbfounded. No wonder Bancel and Charlie were worried. It had never occurred to any of us that German national art treasures would be removed to the United States. After speculating on the possible consequences attendant on an implementation of the document, we dropped the subject. Momentarily there was nothing to do but wait—and hope that the whole matter would be dropped.

By comparison, our personal problems seemed insignificant. But Charlie and Bancel heard us out. They approved our idea of remaining together as a team working out of USFET. I was already permanently assigned to USFET and there were two vacancies on their T.O. (Table of Organization) to which Lamont and Steve could be appointed. The necessary "paper work" took up most of the day and involved a trip to ECAD headquarters at Bad Homburg. At five o'clock we had our new orders.

Steve suggested that we drive up to Marburg to see Captain Hancock, the Monuments officer in charge of the two great art repositories which had been established there. They were the prototype of the Central Collecting Point at Munich. However, they differed in an important respect from the one at Munich: they contained practically no loot. Virtually everything in them belonged to German museums and had been recovered by our Monuments officers from the mines in which the Germans had placed them for safekeeping during the war.

Marburg, some fifty miles north of Frankfurt, lay in the Regierungsbezirk, or government district, of Kassel, which was in turn a subdivision of the Province of Hesse. It was a two-hour drive, but we stopped en route for supper with a Quartermaster outfit at Giessen, so it was nearly eight o'clock when we arrived.

We found Walker Hancock in his office in the Staatsarchiv building. He was a man in the middle forties, and of medium height. His face broke into a smile and his fine dark eyes lighted up with an expression of genuine pleasure at the sight of Lamont and Steve. This was the first time they had seen one another since the close of the war when they had been working together in Weimar. I had never met Walker Hancock, but I had heard more about him than about any other American Monuments officer. I knew that he had had a distinguished career as a sculptor before the war and that he had been the first of our Monuments officers to reach France. He had been attached to the First Army until the end of hostilities. Lamont was devoted to Walker, and Steve's regard for him bordered on worship. While the three of them reminisced, I found myself responding to his warmth and sincerity.

He wouldn't hear of our returning to Frankfurt that night. He wanted to show us the things in his two depots and we wouldn't be able to see more than a fraction of them before morning. The few that we did see whetted our appetite for more. In the galleries on the second floor we saw some of the finest pictures from the museums of the Rhineland: there were three wonderful Van Goghs. One was the portrait of Armand Rollin, the young man with a mustache and slouch hat. It belonged to the Volkwang Museum at Essen. Color reproductions of this portrait had, in recent years, rivaled those of Whistler's *Mother* in popularity. Walker said that it had been covered with mold when he found it in the Siegen mine with the rest of the Essen pictures. His assistant, Sheldon Keck, formerly the restorer of the Brooklyn Museum, had successfully removed the mold before it had done any serious damage.

The second Van Gogh was the famous large still life entitled *White Roses*. The third was a brilliant late landscape. There were other magnificent nineteenth century canvases: the bewitching portrait of M. and Mme. Sisley by Renoir, a full-length Manet, and a great Daumier. Walker climaxed the display with the celebrated Rembrandt *Self-Portrait* from the Wallraf-Richartz Museum of Cologne. This was the last and most famous of the portraits the artist painted of himself.

We spent the night at the Gasthaus Sonne, a seventeenth century inn facing the old market place. The proprietor reluctantly assigned us two rooms on the second floor. They were normally reserved for the top brass. Judging from the austerity of the furnishings and the simplicity of the plumbing, I thought it unlikely that we would be routed from our beds by any late-arriving generals.

Walker met us for breakfast the next morning with word that the war with Japan had ended. Announcements in German had already been posted in several of the shop windows. Though thrilling to us, the news seemed to make very little impression on the citizens of the sleepy university town. The people in the streets were as unsmiling as ever. If anything, some of them looked a little grimmer than usual.

We drove to the Staatsarchiv building with Walker. He took us to a room containing a fabulous collection of medieval art objects. There were crosses and croziers, coffers and chalices, wrought in precious metals and studded with jewels—masterpieces of the tenth, eleventh and twelfth centuries. The most arresting individual piece was the golden Madonna, an archaic seated figure two feet high, dating from the tenth century. These marvelous relics of the Middle Ages belonged to the Cathedral of Metz. It was one of the greatest collections of its kind in the entire world. Its intrinsic value was enormous; its historic value incalculable. Walker said that arrangements were being made for its early return to the cathedral. The French were planning an elaborate ceremony in honor of the event.

It was a five-minute drive to the other depot under Captain Hancock's direction. This was the Jubiläumsbau, or Jubilee Building, a handsome structure of pre-Nazi, modern design. It was the headquarters of the archaeological institute headed by Professor Richard Hamann, the internationally famous medieval scholar. It also housed the archives of "Photo Marburg," the stupendous library of art photographs founded and directed by the professor. Walker was putting the resources of Photo Marburg to good use, compiling a complete photographic record of the objects in his care.

Among the treasures stored in the Jubilaumsbau were some of the choicest masterpieces from the Berlin state museums. Perhaps the most famous were the twin canvases by Watteau entitled *Gersaint's Signboard*. Regarded by many as the supreme work of the greatest painter of the French Rococo period, the two pictures had been the prized possessions of Frederick the Great. Painted to hang side by side forming a continuous composition, they represented the shop of M. Gersaint, dealer in works of art. It is said that the paintings were finished in eight days. They were painted in the year 1732 when the artist was at the height of his career. I was told that, during the early years of the war, Göring made overtures to the Louvre for one of its finest Watteaus. According to the story, the negotiations ended abruptly when the museum signified its willingness to part with the painting in exchange for *Gersaint's Signboard.*

The brilliant French school of the eighteenth century was further represented at the Jubilaumsbau by a superb Boucher—the subject, *Mercury and Venus*—and two exquisite Chardins: *The Cook,* one of his most enchanting scenes of everyday life, and the *Portrait of a Lady Sealing a Letter,* an unusually large composition for this unpretentious painter whose canvases are today worth a king's ransom.

There were masterpieces of the German school; the great series of Cranachs which had belonged to the Hohenzollerns filled one entire room. Excellent examples of Rubens and Van Dyck represented the Flemish school; Ruysdael and Van Goyen, the Dutch. The high quality of every picture attested to the taste and connoisseurship of German collectors.

Walker said that he hoped to arrange a public exhibition of the pictures. Marburg had been neglected by our bombers. Only one or two bombs had fallen in the city and the resulting damage had been slight. Concussion had blasted the windows of the Staats-archiv, but the Jubiläumsbau was untouched. Perhaps he would put on a series of small exhibitions, say fifty pictures at a time. The members of his local German committee were enthusiastic about the project. It would be an important first step in the rehabilitation of German cultural institutions which was an avowed part of the American Fine Arts program. Thanks to the hesitancy of an officer at higher headquarters who was exasperatingly "security-conscious" Walker did not realize his ambition until three months later, on the eve of his departure for the United States.

We celebrated VJ-Day on our return to Frankfurt that evening. The big Casino, behind USFET headquarters, was the scene of the principal festivities. Drinks were on the house until the bar closed at ten. It was a warm summer night and the broad terrace over the main entrance was crowded. An Army band blared noisily inside. Civilian attendants skulked in the background, avidly collecting cigarette butts from the ash trays and the terrace floor. They reaped a rich harvest that night.

The Mercedes-Benz presented a problem. Its status was a dubious one. Since it was still registered with an MG Detachment in Austria, I felt uncomfortable about driving it around Germany. At Charlie Kuhn's suggestion we filed a request with the Naval headquarters in Frankfurt for assignment of the vehicle to our Special Evacuation Team. The request was couched in impressive legal language which Charlie thought would do the trick. Armed with a copy of this request, I felt confident that we would not be molested by inquisitive MPs on our trip back to Munich.

We didn't get started until late afternoon, having wasted two hours dickering with the Transportation Officer at the Frankfurt MG Detachment for a spare tire. We returned by way of Würzburg and Niirnberg. It was dark when we reached Nürnberg, but the light of the full moon was sufficient to reveal the ruined walls and towers of the old, inner city. As we struck south of the city to the Autobahn, we could see the outlines of the vast unfinished stadium, designed to seat one hundred and forty thousand people. We had to proceed cautiously since many of the bridges had been destroyed and detours were frequent. As a result it was midnight when we reached Munich. The transient hotel was full, so we had to be content with makeshift quarters at the Central Collecting Point.

In our absence the transportation situation had eased up a little. Captain Posey told us the next morning that six trucks would be available in the early afternoon. We decided to keep the command car for the trip to Neuschwanstein and leave the Mercedes-Benz in Munich to be painted. In anticipation of registration papers from the Navy, we thought it would be appropriate to have the car painted battleship gray and stenciled with white letters reading "U. S. Navy." One of the mechanics in the garage at the Central Collecting Point agreed to do this for us in exchange for a bottle of rum and half a bottle of Scotch. Officers at Third Army Headquarters had bar privileges plus a liquor ration, but the enlisted men didn't fare so well.

Our base of operations for the evacuation of the Castle of

Neuschwanstein was the picturesque little town of Füssen, some eighty miles south of Munich, in the heart of the "Swan country." This region of southern Bavaria, celebrated for its association with the name of Richard Wagner, is one of the most beautiful in all Germany. The mountains rise sharply from the floor of the level green valley. The turreted castle, perched on top of one of the lower peaks, at an elevation of a thousand feet, is visible for miles. Built in the eighteen-seventies by Ludwig II, the "Mad King" of Bavaria, it was the most fantastic creation of that exotic monarch whose passion for building nearly bankrupted his kingdom. When we saw the castle rising majestically from its pine-covered mountain top, we were struck by the incongruity of our six-truck convoy lumbering through the romantic countryside.

We presented our credentials to a swarthy major who was the commanding officer of the small MG Detachment at Füssen. He arranged for our billets at the Alte Post, the hotel where officers of the Detachment were quartered, and, after we had deposited our gear in a room on the fourth floor, conducted us to the Schloss,

The steep road to the lower courtyard of the castle wound for more than a mile up the side of the mountain. At the castle entrance, the major identified us to the guard and our six trucks filed into the courtyard. In the upper courtyard, reached by a broad flight of stone steps, we found the caretaker who had the keys to the main section of the castle. He did not, however, have access to the wing in which the records of the *Einsatzstab Rosenberg* were stored. The only door to that part of the building had been locked and sealed by Lieutenant James Rorimer, the Monuments officer of the Seventh Army, when the castle had first fallen into American hands. We had brought the key with us from Third Army Headquarters.

Before examining those rooms, we made a tour of the four main floors of the castle. The hallways and vaulted kitchens on the first floor were filled to overflowing with enormous packing cases and uncrated furniture, all taken from French collections. Three smaller storage rooms resembling the stock rooms of Tiffany's and a porcelain factory combined, were jammed with gold and silver and rare china. Most of the loot had been concentrated on the first floor, but the unfinished rooms of the second had been fitted with racks for the storage of paintings. In addition to the looted pictures, there were several galleries of stacked paintings from the museums of Munich. The living apartments on the third floor, divested of their furnishings, were filled with stolen furniture, Louis Quinze chairs, table and sofas and ornate Italian cabinets lined the walls of rooms and corridors. They contrasted strangely with scenes from the Wagner operas which King Ludwig had chosen as the theme for the mural decorations. Only the gold-walled Throne Room and, on the floor above, the lofty Fest-Saal, were devoid of loot.

We proceeded to the wing of the castle which contained the records. Having broken the seals and unlocked the door, we entered a hallway about thirty feet long. The doors opening onto this hallway were also locked and sealed. Behind them lay the offices of the *Einsatzstab Rosenberg*. They were crowded with bookshelves and filing cabinets. In one room stood a huge showcase filled with fragile Roman glass. The rooms of the second floor were full of French furniture and dozens of small packing cases. These cases were made of carefully finished quarter-sawed oak. We had seen similar ones in the Göring collection. They had been the traveling cases for precious objects belonging to the Rothschilds. These too contained Rothschild treasures—exquisite bibelots of jade, agate, onyx and jasper, and innumerable pieces of Oriental and European porcelain.

At one end of the hallway were two rooms which had been used as a photographic laboratory. We had brought Kress with us. Steve went off to make arrangements to install his equipment, while Lamont and I calculated the number of men we would need for the evacuation work the next morning. We asked the major for twenty—two shifts of ten.

The Neuschwanstein operation lasted eight days. We worked nights as well, because there were thousands of small objects— many of them fragile and extremely valuable—which we could not trust to the inexpert hands of our work party. There was no electricity in the small storage rooms, so we had to work by candlelight. It took us one evening to pack the Roman glass and the four succeeding evenings, working till midnight, to pack the two thousand pieces of gold and silver in the David-Weill collection. The Nazi looters had thoughtfully saved the well-made cases in which they had carted off this magnificent collection from M. David-Weill's house in Paris. There were candelabra, dishes, knives, forks, spoons, snuffboxes—the rarest examples of the art of the

French goldsmiths of the seventeenth and eighteenth centuries. This unique collection had created a sensation when it was exhibited in Paris a few years before the war. The fact that the incomparable assemblage would probably one day be left to the Louvre by the eminent connoisseur, who had spent a lifetime collecting it, had not deterred the Nazi robbers. He was a Jew. That justified its confiscation. Aside from the pleasure it gave me to handle the beautiful objects, I relished the idea of helping to recover the property of a fellow Californian: M. David-Weill had been born in San Francisco. The Nazis had been methodical as usual. Every piece was to have been systematically recatalogued while the collection was at Neuschwanstein. On some of the shelves we found slips of paper stating that this or that object had not yet been photographed—"*noch nicht fotografiert.*"

The tedious manual labor involved in packing small objects and the great distance which the packed cases had to be carried when ready for loading were the chief difficulties at Neuschwanstein. Not only did the cases have to be carried several hundred feet from the storage rooms to the door of the castle; but from the door to the trucks was a long trek, down two flights of steps and across a wide courtyard. In this respect the operation resembled the evacuation of the monastery at Hohenfurth.

Three months after our partial evacuation of the castle, a team composed of Captain Edward Adams, Lieutenant (jg) Charles Parkhurst, USNR, and Captain Hubert de Brye, a French officer, completed the removal of the loot. This gigantic undertaking required eight weeks. If I remember the figures correctly, more than twelve thousand objects were boxed and carted away. The cases were built in a carpenter shop set up in the castle kitchens. One hundred and fifty truckloads were delivered to the railroad siding at Füssen and thence transported to Paris. It was an extraordinary achievement, carried out despite heavy snowfall. The only operation which rivaled it was the evacuation of the salt mine at Alt Aussee.

The last morning of our stay at Füssen, Lamont and I had a special mission to perform. A German art dealer named Gustav Rochlitz was living at Gipsmühle, a five-minute drive from Hohenschwangau, the small village below the castle. For a number of years Rochlitz had had a gallery in Paris. His dealings with the Nazis, in particular his trafficking in confiscated pictures, had been the subject of special investigation by Lieutenants Plaut and Rousseau, our OSS friends. They were the two American naval officers who were preparing an exhaustive report on the activities of the infamous *Einsatzstab Rosenberg*. They had interrogated Rochlitz and placed him under house arrest. In his possession were twenty-two modern French paintings, including works by Dérain, Matisse and Picasso, formerly belonging to well known Jewish collections. He had obtained them from Göring and other leading Nazis in exchange for old master paintings. We were to relieve Herr Rochlitz of these canvases.

At the farmhouse in which Rochlitz and his wife were living, the maid of all work who answered our knock said that no one was at home. Herr Rochlitz would not be back before noon. Lamont and I returned to our jeep and started back across the fields to the highway. We had driven about a hundred yards when we saw a heavy-set sullen-faced man of about fifty walking toward us.

'Til bet that's Rochlitz," I said to Lamont. Stopping the car, I called out to him, "Herr Rochlitz?"

After a moment's hesitation, he nodded.

"Hop in, we want to have a talk with you," I said.

We returned to the farmhouse and followed our truculent host up the stairs to a sitting room on the second floor. There we were joined by his wife, a timid young woman who, like her husband, spoke fluent English.

I said that we had come for the pictures. Rochlitz made no protest. He brusquely directed his wife to bring them in. As she left the room, I thought it odd that he hadn't gone along to help her. But she returned almost immediately with the paintings in her arms. All twenty-two were rolled around a long mailing tube. Together they spread the canvases about the room, on the table, on the chairs and on the floor. They were, without exception, works of excellent quality. One large early Picasso, the portrait of a woman and child, was alone worth a small fortune.

I was wondering what Rochlitz had given in exchange for the lot, when he began to explain how the pictures had come into his possession. He must have taken us for credulous fools, because the story he told made him out a victim of tragic circumstance. He said that Göring had made an offer on several of his pictures. Rochlitz had accepted but insisted on being paid in cash. Göring had-agreed to the terms and the pictures were delivered. Then, instead of paying in cash, Göring had forced him to accept these modern paintings. He had protested, but to no avail. Of course these pictures were all right in their way, he said deprecatingly, but he was not a dealer in modern art. Naturally he did not know that they had been confiscated. It was all a dreadful mistake, but what could he do? I said that I realized how badly he must have felt and that I knew he would be relieved to learn that the pictures were now going back to their rightful owners.

The pictures were carefully rerolled and we got up to leave. At the door, Rochlitz told us that he had lost his entire stock. He had stored all of his paintings at Baden-Baden, in the French Zone. Did we think he would be able to recover them? We assured him that justice would be done and, leaving him to interpret that remark as he saw fit, drove off with the twenty-two pictures.

~ 9 ~

HIDDEN TREASURES AT NÜRNBERG

On our return to Munich that evening, Craig told us that preparations were being made for the immediate restitution of several important masterpieces recovered in the American Zone. General Eisenhower had approved a proposal to return at once to each of the countries overrun by the Germans at least one outstanding work of art. This was to be done in his name, as a gesture of "token restitution" symbolizing American policy with regard to ultimate restitution of all stolen art treasures to the rightful owner nations. It was felt that the gracious gesture on the part of the Commanding General of United States Forces in Europe would serve to reaffirm our intentions to right the wrongs of Nazi oppression. In view of the vast amount of art which had thus far been recovered, it would be months before it could all be restored to the plundered countries. Meanwhile these "token restitutions" would be an earnest of American good will. They would be sent back from Germany at the expense of the United States Government. Thereafter, representatives of the various countries would be invited to come to our Collecting Points to select, assemble and, in transportation of their own providing, remove those objects which the Germans had stolen.

Belgium was to receive the first token restitution. The great van Eyck altarpiece—*The Adoration of the Mystic Lamb*—was the obvious choice among the stolen Belgian treasures.

The famous panels had been reposing in the Central Collecting Point at Munich since we had removed them from the salt mine at Alt Aussee. A special plane had been chartered to fly them to Brussels. The Belgian Government had signified approval of air transportation. Direct rail communication between Munich and Brussels had not been resumed, and the highways were not in the best of condition. By truck, it would be a rough two-day trip; by air, a matter of three hours.

Bancel La Farge had already flown from Frankfurt to Brussels, where plans had been made for an appropriate ceremony on the arrival of the altarpiece. The American Ambassador was to present the panels to the Prince Regent on behalf of General Eisenhower. It was to be an historic occasion.

I went out to the airport to confirm the arrangements for the C-54. It was only a fifteen-minute drive from the Königsplatz to the field. I was also to check on the condition of the streets: they were in good shape all the way.

The plane was to take off at noon. Lamont, Steve and I supervised the loading of the ten precious cases. We led off in a jeep. The truck followed with the panels. Four of the civilian packers went along to load the cases onto the plane. Captain Posey was to escort the altarpiece to Brussels.

When we got to the airport we learned that the plane had not arrived. There would be a two-hour delay. At the end of two hours, we were informed that there was bad weather south of Brussels. All flights had been canceled for the day. We drove back to the Collecting Point at the Königsplatz and had just finished unloading the panels when a message came from the field. The weather had cleared. The plane would be taking off in half an hour. I caught Captain Posey as he was leaving the building for his office at Third Army Headquarters. The cases were reloaded and we were on our way to the field in fifteen minutes.

The truck was driven onto the field where the big 054 stood waiting. In another quarter of an hour the panels were aboard and lashed securely to metal supports in the forepart of the passenger compartment. Captain Posey, the only passenger, waved jauntily as the doors swung shut. Enviously we watched the giant plane roll down the field, lift waveringly from the airstrip and swing off to the northwest.

The altarpiece was on the last lap of an extraordinary journey. We wished George Stout could have been in on this.

The plane reached Brussels without mishap. The return of the great national treasure was celebrated throughout the country. Encouraged by the success of this first "token restitution," Major La Farge directed that a similar gesture be made to France. At the Collecting Point Craig selected seventy-one masterpieces looted from French private collections. The group included Fragonard, Chardin, Lancret, Rubens, Van Dyck, Hals, and a large number of seventeenth century Dutch masters. Only examples of the highest quality were chosen.

Ham Coulter, the naval officer who worked with Craig at the "Bau," was the emissary appointed to accompany the paintings to Paris. It was decided to return them by truck, inasmuch as it would have been impracticable to attempt shipping uncrated pictures by air. The convoy consisted of two trucks—one for the pictures, the other for extra gasoline. It was a hard two-day trip from Munich to Paris. Ham got through safely, but reported on his return that the roads had been extremely rough a good part of the way. He had delivered the pictures in Paris to the Musée du Jeu de Paume, the little museum which the Germans had used during the Occupation as the clearinghouse for their methodical plundering of the Jewish collections. His expedition had been marred by only one minor incident. When the paintings were being unloaded at the museum, one of the women attendants watching the operation noticed that some of the canvases were unframed. She had asked, "And where are the frames?" This was too much for Coulter. In perfect French, the courteous lieutenant told her precisely what she could do about the frames.

Shortly after the return of the Ghent altarpiece, Captain Posey was demobilized. His duties as MFA&A Officer at Third Army Headquarters in Munich were assumed by Captain Edwin Rae. I had not seen Rae since the early summer when he and Lieutenant Edith Standen had been assigned to assist me in inventorying the collections of the Berlin museums in the vaults of the Reichsbank at Frankfurt. Edwin was a meticulous fellow, gentle but determined. Although by no means lacking in a sense of humor, he resented joking references to a fancied resemblance to Houdon's well known portrait of Voltaire, and I didn't blame him.

He took on his new responsibilities with quiet assurance and in a short time won the complete confidence of his superiors at Third Army Headquarters. Throughout his long tenure of office, he maintained an unruffled calm in the face of obstacles which would have exhausted a less patient man. He was responsible for all matters pertaining to the Fine Arts in the Eastern Military District of the American Zone—that is, Bavaria—an area more than twice the size of the two provinces Greater Hesse and Wiirttemberg-Baden comprising the Western Military District of our Zone.

During the early days of Captain Rae's regime, Charlie Kuhn paid a brief visit to Munich. He had just completed the transfer of the Berlin Museum collections from Frankfurt to the Landesmuseum at Wiesbaden. The university buildings in Frankfurt— which I had requisitioned for a Collecting Point—had proved unsuitable. The repairs, he said, would have taken months. On the other hand, the Wiesbaden Museum, though damaged, was ideal for the purpose. Of course there hadn't been a glass left in any of the windows, and the roof had had to be repaired. But thanks to the energy and ingenuity of Walter Farmer, the building had been rehabilitated in two months. Captain Farmer was the director of the new Collecting Point. When I asked where Farmer had got the glass, Charlie was evasive. All he would say was that Captain Farmer was "wise in the ways of the Army."

Charlie was headed for Vienna to confer with Lieutenant Colonel Ernest Dewald, Chief of the MFA&A Section at USFA Headquarters (United States Forces, Austria). Colonel Dewald wanted to complete the evacuation of the mine at Alt Aussee, which was now under his jurisdiction. For this project he hoped to obtain the services of the officers who had worked there when the mine had been Third Army's responsibility. Captain Rae was reluctant to lend the Special Evacuation Team, because there was still so much work to be done in Bavaria. But he agreed, provided that Charlie could sell the idea to the Chief of Staff at Third Army. This Charlie succeeded in doing, and departed for Vienna a day later. Steve was crazy to see Vienna—I think his parents had been born there—so Charlie took him along.

After they had left, Captain Rae requested Lamont and me to make an inspection trip to northern Bavaria. Our first stop was Bamberg. There we examined the *Neue Residenz,* which Rae contemplated establishing as an auxiliary Collecting Point to house the contents of various repositories in Upper Franconia. Reports reaching his office indicated that storage conditions in that area were unsatisfactory. Either the repositories were not weatherproof, or they were not being adequately guarded.

It was also rumored that UNRRA was planning to fill the *Neue Residenz* with DPs—Displaced Persons. Captain Rae was determined to put a stop to that, because the building, a fine example of late seventeenth century architecture, was on the SHAEF List of Protected Monuments. This fact should have guaranteed its immunity from such a hazard. Even during combat, the SHAEF list had been a great protection to monuments of historic and artistic importance. Now that no "doctrine of military necessity" could be invoked to justify improper use of the building, Rae did not propose to countenance its occupancy by DPs.

The *Neue Residenz* contained dozens of empty, brocaded rooms—but no plumbing. We decided that it would do for a Collecting Point and agreed with Rae that the DPs should be housed elsewhere if possible. The officer from the local MG Detachment, who was showing us around, confirmed the report that UNRRA intended to move in. He didn't think they would relinquish the building without a protest. The influx of refugees from the Russian Zone had doubled the town's normal population of sixty thousand.

It was a disappointment to find that the superb sculpture in the cathedral across the square was still bricked up. The shelters had proved a needless precaution, for Bamberg had not been bombed. Only the bridge over the Regnitz had been blown up, and the Germans had done that themselves.

From Bamberg we drove north to Coburg, where we had a twofold mission. First we were to obtain specific information about ten cases which contained a collection of art objects belonging to a prince of Hesse. The cases were said to be stored in Feste Coburg, the walled castle above the town. If they were the property of Philip of Hesse, then they would probably be taken into custody by the American authorities. We had been told that he was in prison. His art dealings during the past few years were being reviewed by the OSS officers charged with the special investigation of Nazi art-looting activities. Philip was the son of the Landgrafin of Hesse. It was in the flower-filled Waffenraum of her castle near Frankfurt that I had seen the family tombs months before.

If, on the other hand, the cases belonged to a different prince of Hesse—one whose political record was clean—and storage conditions were satisfactory, we would simply leave them where they were for the time being.

Our second objective was Schloss Tambach, a few kilometers from Coburg. Paintings stolen by Frank, the Nazi Governor of Poland, from the palace at Warsaw were stored there. Schloss Tambach also contained pictures from the Stettin Museum. Stettin was now in the Russian Zone of Occupied Germany.

On our arrival in Coburg, Lamont and I drove to the headquarters of the local MG Detachment, which were located in the Palais Edinburgh. This unpretentious building was once the residence of Queen Victoria's son, the Duke of Edinburgh. There we arranged with Lieutenant Milton A. Pelz, the Monuments officer of the Coburg Detachment, to inspect the storage rooms at the castle.

Pelz was a big fellow who spoke German fluently. He welcomed us hospitably and took us up to the castle where we met Dr. Grundmann, who had the keys to the storage rooms. This silent, sour-faced German was curator of the Prince's collections. He said that his employer was Prince Ludwig of Hesse, a cousin of Philip. The cases contained paintings and *objets d'art* which had been in the possession of the family for years. Grundmann had personally removed them from Ludwig's estate in Silesia the day before the Russians occupied the area.

Ludwig's most important treasure was the world-famous painting by Holbein known as the *Madonna of Bürgermeister Meyer*. Painted in 1526, it had hung for years in the palace at Darmstadt. The Dresden Gallery owned a seventeenth century replica. Early in the war, Prince Ludwig had sent the original to his Silesian castle for safekeeping. Grundmann had brought it back to Bavaria along with the ten cases now at Coburg. From Coburg he had taken the Holbein to Schloss Banz, a castle not far from Bamberg.

He said that the Prince was living at Wolfsgarten, a small country place near Darmstadt. Ludwig was eager to regain possession of the painting. Did we think that could be arranged? We told him he would have to obtain an authorization from Captain Rae at Munich.

Schloss Tambach was a ten-minute drive from Coburg. This great country house, built around three sides of a courtyard, belonged to the Countess of Ortenburg. She occupied the center section. A detachment of troops was bilFeted in one wing. The other was filled with the Stettin and Warsaw pictures. There were over two hundred from the Stettin Museum. Nineteenth century German paintings predominated, but I noticed two fine Hals portraits and a Van Gogh landscape among them.

The civilian custodian, answerable to the MG authorities at Coburg, was Dr. Wilhelm Eggebrecht. He had been curator of the Stettin Museum until thrown out by the Nazis because his wife was one-quarter Jewish. He was a mousy little fellow with a bald head and gold-rimmed spectacles. He asked apprehensively if we intended to send the paintings back to Russian-held Stettin. We said that we had come only to check on the physical security of the present storage place. So far as we knew, the paintings would remain where they were for the present. This inconclusive piece of information seemed to reassure him.

The paintings looted from Warsaw were the *pièces de resistance* of the treasures at Schloss Tambach—especially the nine great canvases by Bellotto, the eighteenth century Venetian master Governor Frank had ruthlessly removed the pictures from their stretchers and rolled them up for shipment. As a result of this rough handling, the paint had flaked off in places, but the damage was not serious. When we examined the pictures, they were spread out on the floor. They filled two rooms, forty feet square. Later they were taken to the Munich Collecting Point and mounted on new stretchers, in preparation for their return to Warsaw.

When we got back to Munich, Steve had returned from Vienna. He had news for us. Charlie Kuhn had already left for Frankfurt. Colonel Dewald was coming to Munich in a few days to talk to Colonel Roy Dalferes, Rae's Chief of Staff at Third Army, about reopening the Alt Aussee mine. Either Charlie or Bancel would come down from USFET Headquarters when Dewald arrived. A new man had joined the MFA&A Section at USFA—Andrew Ritchie, director of the Buffalo Museum. He had come over as a civilian. Steve thought that Ritchie would be the USFA representative at Munich. There was a lot of stuff at the Collecting Point which would eventually go back to Austria. It would have to be checked with the records there. That would be Ritchie's job. Steve told us also that Lincoln Kirstein had gone home. His mother was seriously ill and Lincoln had left on emergency orders.

The three of us went to Captain Rae's office. Lamont and I had to make a report on our trip to Coburg. Rae had a new assignment for us. He had just received orders from USFET Headquarters to prepare the Cracow altarpiece for shipment. It was to be sent back to Poland as a token restitution. This was the colossal carved altarpiece by Veit Stoss which the Nazis had stolen from the Church of St. Mary at Cracow. Veit Stoss had been commissioned by the King of Poland in 1477 to carve the great work. It had taken him ten years. After the invasion of Poland in 1939, the Nazis had carted it off, lock, stock and barrel, to Nürnberg. They contended that, since Veit Stoss had been a native of Nürnberg, it belonged in the city of his birth.

The missing altarpiece was the first of her looted treasures for which Poland had registered a claim with the American authorities at the close of the war. After months of diligent investigation, it was found by American officers in an underground bunker across the street from the Albrecht Diirer house in Nürnberg. In addition to the dismantled figures of the central panel—painted and gilded figures of hollow wood ten feet high—the twelve ornate side panels, together with the statues and pinnacles surmounting the framework, had been crowded into the bunker.

The same bunker contained another priceless looted treasure— the coronation regalia of the Holy Roman Empire. Among these venerable objects were the jeweled crown of the Emperor Conrad—commonly called the "Crown of Charlemagne"—dating from the eleventh century, a shield, two swords and the orb. Since 1804 they had been preserved in the Schatzkammer, the Imperial Treasure Room, at Vienna. In 1938, the Nazis removed them to Nürnberg, basing their claim to possession on a fifteenth century decree of the Emperor Sigismund that they were to be kept in that city.

On the eve of the German collapse, two high officials of the dty had spirited away these five pieces. The credit for recovering the treasures goes to an American officer of German birth, Lieutenant Walter Horn, professor of art at the University of California. The two officials at first disclaimed any knowledge of their whereabouts. After hours of relentless grilling by Lieutenant Horn, the men finally admitted their guilt. They were promptly tried, heavily fined and sent to prison. Three months later, at the request of the Austrian Government, the imperial treasures were flown back to Vienna. This historic shipment contained other relics which the Nazis had taken from the Schatzkammer—relics of the greatest religious significance. They included an alleged fragment of the True Cross, a section of the tablecloth said to have been used at the Last Supper, a lance venerated as the one which had touched the wounds of Christ, and links from the chains traditionally believed to have bound St. Peter, St. Paul and St. John.

On Captain Rae's instructions, Steve and I went to Nürnberg to pack the Stoss altarpiece. (At that time the coronation regalia was still in the bunker, where, on the afternoon of our arrival, we had an opportunity to examine it.) We found that the heavy framework which supported the altar panels was not stored in the bunker. Because of its size—the upright pieces were thirty feet high—it had been taken to Schloss Wiesenthau an old castle outside Forchheim, thirty miles away.

Leaving Steve to start packing the smaller figures and pinnacles, I got hold of a semitrailer, the only vehicle long enough to accommodate a load of such length. It was an hour's drive to the castle. With a crew of twenty PWs, I finished loading the framework in two hours and returned to Nürnberg in time for supper.

That evening Steve and I figured out the number of trucks we would need for the altarpiece. Lamont had remained in Munich to make tentative arrangements, pending word from us. He was going to ask for ten trucks and we came to the conclusion that this would be about the right number—in addition, of course, to the semitrailer for the supporting framework. We got out our maps and studied our probable route to Cracow. One road would take us through Dresden and Breslau; another by way of Pilsen and Prague. Perhaps we could go one way and return the other. In either case we would have to pass through Russian-occupied territory. It would probably take some time to obtain the necessary clearances. We figured on taking enough gas for the round trip, since we doubted if there would be any to spare in Poland. Altogether it promised to be a complicated expedition, but already we had visions of a triumphal entry into Cracow.

Our ambitious plans collapsed the following morning. While Steve and I were at breakfast, I was called to the telephone. The corporal in Captain Rae's office was on the wire. I was to return to Munich at once.

Major La Farge was arriving from Frankfurt and wanted to see me that night. Plans for the trip to Cracow were indefinitely postponed. Internal conditions in Poland were too unsettled to risk returning the altarpiece.

Our plans had miscarried before, but this was our first major disappointment. We had begun to look on the Polish venture as the fitting climax of our work as a Special Evacuation Team. On the way back to Munich, Steve said he had a feeling that the team was going to be split up.

Steve's misgivings were prophetic. At Craig's apartment after dinner, Bancel La Farge outlined the plans he had for us. Colonel Dalferes had acceded to Colonel Dewald's request. Lamont, Steve and a third officer—new to MFA&A work—were to resume the evacuation of the salt mine at Alt Aussee. If the snows held off, it would be possible to carry on operations there for another month or six weeks.

I was to return to USFET Headquarters at Frankfurt as Deputy Chief of the MFA&A Section, replacing Charlie Kuhn who had just received his orders to go home. I knew that Charlie would soon be eligible for release from active duty, but had no idea that his departure was so imminent.

We didn't have much to say to one another on the way to our quarters that night. Steve had already made up his mind that he wasn't going to like the new man. Lamont said that he thought it was going to be an awful anticlimax to reopen the mine. And for me, the prospect of routine administrative work at USFET was uninviting. After three months of strenuous and exiting field work, it wouldn't be easy to settle down in an office. All three of us felt that the great days were over.

During our last week together in Munich we had little time to feel sorry for ourselves. Everyone was preoccupied with the restitution program. We had our full share of the work. Another important shipment was to be made to Belgium. It was to include the Michelangelo Madonna, the eleven paintings stolen from the church in Bruges when the statue was taken, and the four panels by Dirk Bouts from the famous altarpiece in the church of St. Pierre at Louvain. These panels, which formed the wings of the altarpiece, had been removed by the Germans in August 1942. Before the first World War one wing had been in the Berlin Gallery, the other in the Alte Pinakothek at Munich. As in the case of the Ghent altarpiece, they had been restored—unjusdy, according to the Germans—to Belgium by the Versailles Treaty.

This shipment to Belgium represented the first practical application of the "come and get it" theory of restitution, evolved by Major La Farge. Belgium had already received the Ghent altarpiece as token restitution. Now it was up to the Belgians to carry on at their own expense. The special representatives who came down from Brussels to supervise this initial shipment were Dr. Paul Coremans, a great technical expert, and Lieutenant Pierre Longuy of the Ministry of Fine Arts. They had their own truck but had been unable to bring suitable packing materials. We had an ample supply of pads and blankets which we had stored at the Collecting Point after our evacuation of the Göring collection. We placed them at the disposal of the Belgians. But it was Saturday and no civilian packers were available. Dr. Coremans gratefully accepted the offer of our services. Steve, Lamont and I loaded the truck. It was the last operation of the Special Evacuation Team.

The Belgians had no sooner departed than the French and Dutch representatives arrived. Captain Hubert de Brye for France looked more like a sportsman than a scholar; but he was a man of wide cultivation and had a sense of humor which endeared him to his associates in Munich. He and Ham Coulter were kindred spirits and became great friends.

Ham, who had been responsible for the rehabilitation of both the Collecting Point and the Führerbau, now had two assistants— Captain George Lacy and Dietrich Sattler, the latter a German architect. Through this division of the work, Ham found time for new duties: he took the foreign representatives in tow, arranged for their billets, their mess cards, their PX rations and so on. It was an irritating but not a thankless job, for the recipients of his attentions were devoted to their "wet nurse."

The Dutch representative was Lieutenant Colonel Alphonse Vorenkamp. He was a little man with gray hair, shrewd gray eyes and steel-rimmed spectacles. An eminent authority on Dutch painting, he had been for several years a member of the faculty at Smith College. He enjoyed the unusual distinction of having served in both the American and Dutch Armies during the present war.

I had met him in San Francisco in 1944, shortly after his discharge from the service. He had been a buck private; and I gathered from the story of his experiences that our Army had released him in self-defense.

He told me that he often had difficulty in understanding the drill sergeant. Once, without thinking he had stepped out of formation and asked politely, "Sergeant, would you mind repeating that last order!" Vorenkamp said that he had paid dearly for his indiscretion, so dearly in fact that he had seriously considered changing his name from Alphonse to Latrinus. Alphonse, he said, was a ridiculous name for a Dutchman anyway. He preferred to be called Phonse.

Released from the Army, he had gone back to his teaching. Then, only a few months ago, the Dutch Government had requested his services in connection with the restitution of looted art. They had offered him a lieutenant-colonelcy and he had accepted.

The Dutch, as well as the British and French, had made a practice of conferring upon qualified civilians ranks consistent with the responsibilities of given jobs. Our government's failure to do likewise— so far as the art program was concerned—resulted in a disparity in rank which frequently placed American MFA&A personnel at a great disadvantage.

Of all the foreign representatives, none served his country more zealously than Phonse Vorenkamp. Throughout the fall and winter months, his convoys shuttled back and forth between Munich and Amsterdam. When I last heard from him—in the late spring—he had restored to Holland more than nine hundred paintings, up* ward of two thousand pieces of sculpture, porcelain and glass, along with truckloads of tapestries, rugs and furniture.

I left Munich on a rainy morning at the end of September. Lamont and Steve were planning to depart for Alt Aussee at the same time. The three of us had agreed to meet in front of the Collecting Point at eight-thirty. I was a few minutes late and when I got there the guard at the entrance said they had already gone. I hadn't felt so forlorn since the day Craig and I had parted in Bad Homburg months before. As I started down the steps to the command car, Phonse Vorenkamp called from the doorway. He had come to work a little earlier than usual, just to see me off. He was full of waspish good humor, joked about the magnificence of my new job in Frankfurt, and promised to look me up when he came through with his first convoy. The driver stepped on the starter and, as we rounded the corner into the Brienner-Strasse, Phonse waved us on our way.

∽ IO ∽

MISSION TO AMSTERDAM; THE WIESBADEN MANIFESTO

I reported to Major La Farge upon arrival. Since my visit to Frankfurt with Lamont and Steve six weeks before, there had been several changes in the MFA&A Section. With the removal to Berlin of the Monuments officers attached to the U. S. Group Control Council, our office at USFET Headquarters in Frankfurt had been transferred to Hochst. The move was logical enough because we were part of the Restitution Control Branch of the Economics Division, which was located there. For all practical purposes, however, we would have been better off in Frank-' furt, since our work involved daily contacts with other divisions— all located at the main headquarters.

The Hochst office was a barnlike room, some thirty feet square, on the second floor of the Exposition Building. It required considerable ingenuity to And the room, for it was tucked in behind a row of laboratories occupied by white-coated German civilians, former employees of I. G. Farben, who were now working for the American Military Government. At one end of the room were desks for the Chief and Deputy Chief. The rest of the furniture consisted of four long work tables and two small file cabinets. The staff was equally meager—Major La Farge, Lieutenant Edith Standen Corporal James Reeds and a German civilian stenographer.

The first few days were a period of intensive indoctrination. The morning I arrived, Bancel defined the relationship between our office and the one at Berlin; and between us and the two districts of the American Zone—the Eastern District, which was under Third Army, and the Western District, under Seventh Army. He described the Berlin office as the final authority in determining policy. In theory, if not always in fact, a given policy was adopted only after an exchange of views between the Frankfurt-Hochst office and the one in Berlin. The activation of policy was our function. USFET—that is, our office—was an operational headquarters. Berlin was not.

And how did we activate policy? By means of directives. Directives to whom? To Third Army at Munich and Seventh Army at Heidelberg. That sounded simple enough, until Bancel explained that a directive was not exactly an imperial decree. Just as it was our prerogative to activate policies approved by Berlin, so it was the prerogative of the Armies to implement our directives as they deemed expedient. He reminded me that the two Armies were independent and autonomous within their respective areas. In other words, we could tell them *what* to do, but not *how* to do it. Bancel was an old hand at writing directives, knowing how to give each phrase just the right emphasis. At first the longer ones seemed stilted and occasionally ambiguous. But I was not accustomed to military jargon. Later I came to realize that Army communications always sounded stilted; and what I had mistaken for ambiguity was often deliberate circumlocution, calculated to soften the force of an unpalatable order.

Bancel said there were more important things to worry about than the composition of directives. One was the problem of token restitutions. He was sorry to postpone the one to Poland, but that couldn't be helped. Now that France and Belgium had received theirs, Holland was next on the listThe ceremony in Brussels had made a great hit. He thought a similar affair might be arranged at The Hague. Vorenkamp was selecting a group of pictures at the Collecting Point. We would provide a plane to fly them to Amsterdam. Captain Rae was to notify our office as soon as Vorenkamp was ready to leave—probably within the next two days. In the meantime Bancel was having orders cut for me to go to Holland. I was to see the American ambassador, explain the idea of these token restitutions, and sound him out on the subject of planning a ceremony similar to the one our ambassador had arranged in Brussels. Colonel Anthony Biddle, Chief of the Allied Contacts Section at USFET Headquarters, had promised Bancel to write a letter of introduction for me to take to The Hague. Bancel suggested that I make tentative arrangements with the motor pool for a car and driver.

It was almost noon and Bancel had an appointment in Frankfurt at twelve-thirty. He just had time to catch the bus. After he left, Reeds and the stenographer went out to lunch, so Edith Standen and I had the office to ourselves. We had a lot to talk over, as I had not seen her since June when we worked together on the inventory of the Berlin Museum collections at the Reichsbank.

In the meantime, she had been stationed at Höchst. When the Group CC outfit—to which she was officially attached—moved to Berlin, she had preferred to remain with the USFET office. On the Organizational Chart of the MFA&A Section, Edith was listed as the "Officer in Charge of Technical Files." Actually she was in charge of a great many other things as well. When the Chief and Deputy Chief were away from headquarters at the same time—and they often were—Edith took over the affairs of the Section. She must have been born with these remarkable administrative gifts, for she could have had little opportunity to develop them as the cloistered curator of the Widener Collection where, as she said herself, she was "accustomed to the silent padding of butlers and the spontaneous appearance of orchids and gardenias among the Rembrandts and the Raphaels."

I asked her if there had been any new developments regarding the proposed removal of German-owned art to the United States. Yes, there had been. But nothing conclusive. There was a cable from General Gay to the War Department early in September.* The cable spoke of "holding German objects of art in trust for eventual return to the German people." But it didn't contain the clause "if and when the German nation had earned the right to their return" which had appeared in the original document. Besides the cable, there had been a communication from Berlin asking for an estimate of the cubic footage

---

* See article "German Paintings in the National Gallery: A Protest," by Charles L. Kuhn, io College Art Journal, January 1946.

in art repositories of the American Zone. It was a question impossible to answer accurately. But Bancel and Charlie had figured out a reply, citing the approximate size of one of the repositories and leaving it up to Berlin to multiply the figures by the total number in the entire zone. Now that John Nicholas Brown and Charlie Kuhn were back in the United States, they might be able to discourage the projected removal. I had only one piece of information to contribute on the subject: a letter from George Stout saying that he had been asked by the Roberts Commission to give an opinion, based on purely technical grounds, of the risk involved in sending paintings to America. He did so, stating that to remove them would *cube* the risk of leaving them in Germany.

When Corporal Reeds returned to the office, Edith and I went across the street to the Officers' Mess. While we were at lunch, she told me that Jim Reeds had been a discovery of George's. He had been with George and Bancel at their office in Wiesbaden.

Jim was a tall, serious fellow with sandy hair and a turned-up nose. Edith said that he had been a medical student before the war and that he came from Missouri. There was so much paper work to do in the office that he never got caught up. The German typist was slow and inaccurate. Jim had to do over nearly half the letters he gave her to copy. But his patience was inexhaustible and he never complained.

Bancel didn't get back from Frankfurt until late in the afternoon. The return of the Veit Stoss altarpiece had come up again and he had had a long talk about it with the Polish liaison officer at USFET, who was a nephew of the Archbishop of Cracow. After that he had had a session with Colonel A. J. de la Bretesdie, the French liaison officer. And, for good measure, he had to take up the problem of clearance for the two Czech representatives who would be arriving in a few days. He said wearily that practically all of his days were like that, now that restitution was going full speed ahead. I told him that I had had an uneventful but profitable afternoon, going through the correspondence which had accumulated on his desk. There had been several telephone calls, among them one from Colonel Walter Kluss. Bancel said he would answer that one in person, as he wanted to introduce me to the colonel, who was chief of the Restitution Control Branch. Restitution involved settling the claims of the occupied countries for everything the Germans had taken from them. These claims covered every conceivable kind of property—factory equipment, vehicles, barges, machinery, racehorses, livestock, household furniture, etc.

The colonel's office was at the end of the corridor. On our way down the hall, Bancel said that the Army could do with a few more officers like Colonel Kluss. This observation didn't give me a very clear picture of the colonel, but when I met him I knew what Bancel meant. There was an unassuming friendliness and simplicity about him that I didn't usually associate with full colonels. His interest in the activities of the MFA&A Section was genuine and personal. He was particularly fond of Bancel and Edith and, during our visit with him that afternoon, spoke admiringly of the work which they and Charlie Kuhn had done. While other sections of the Restitution Control Branch were still generalizing about restitution, the MFA&A Section had tackled the problem realistically. It wasn't a question of mapping out a program which might work. The program *did* work. The wisdom and foresight of Bancel's planning appealed to the practical side of Colonel Kluss' nature and, throughout the months of our association with him, he was never too busy to help us when we went to him with our troubles.

Bancel and I took the seven o'clock bus over to Frankfurt that evening. We had dinner at the Officers' Mess in the Casino behind USFET Headquarters. We were joined there by Lieutenant William Lovegrove, the officer whom Bancel had selected as our representative at Paris in connection with the restitution of looted art works to the French. With the arrival of the French representative in Munich, regular shipments would soon be departing for France. Their destination in Paris was to be the Musée du Jeu de Paume, which was now the headquarters of the *Commission de Récupération Artistique,* the commission composed of officials from the French museums charged with the task of sorting and distributing the plundered treasures. Among the officials selected to assist in this work was Captain Rose Valland, the courageous Frenchwoman who, as I mentioned earlier, had spied on the Nazi thieves in that same museum during the Occupation.

We had roughly estimated that it would require from three to six months to send back the main bulk of the French loot from Germany. Mass evacuation, as I have mentioned before, had the advantage of accelerating restitution. It had the disadvantage of rendering difficult our procedure of evaluating and photographing objects before they were returned. It was our intention that Lieutenant Lovegrove should obtain the desired photographs and appraisals. American military establishments in France were being drastically reduced, but we planned to attach him to the USFET Mission to France. We had been told that the Mission would be withdrawn in the early spring. If Lovegrove's work weren't finished by that time, Bancel thought it might be possible to attach him to our Paris Embassy when the Mission folded.

When Bancel introduced me to Lovegrove that evening at the Casino, I thought he would be very much at home in an embassy. He was of medium height, bald, had a pink and white complexion and wore a small mustache. He was self-possessed without being blasé. Lovegrove was a sculptor and had lived in Paris for many years before the war. Bancel said that he spoke a more perfect French than most Frenchmen.

Subsequent developments proved the wisdom of Bancel's choice. Lovegrove was exceedingly popular with his French associates at the Musée du Jeu de Paume. His extraordinary tact and his capacity for hard work were equally remarkable.

I particularly remember our last meeting. It was in February, when I was stopping briefly in Paris on my way home from Germany. By that time hundreds of carloads of stolen art had been received at the Jeu de Paume. There were one or two final matters which I wished to take up with M. Henraux and M. Dreyfus, members of the *Commission de Récupération Artistique.* When Lovegrove and I arrived at the museum, we found these two charming, elderly gentlemen in their office. With them was M. David-Weill. He was examining a fine gold snuffbox. The office was littered with gold and silver objects. They were part of the fabulous collection which Lamont, Steve and I had packed by candlelight in the Castle of Neuschwanstein six months before.

During the second week of October, I left for Amsterdam. It was a three-hundred-mile drive from Frankfurt. Cassidy, the driver of the jeep, was a New Jersey farm boy who, unlike most drivers, preferred long trips to short local runs. The foothills of the Taunus Mountains were bright with fall coloring along the bade road to Limburg. From there we turned west to the Rhine. Then, skirting the east bank of the river, we crossed over into the British Zone at Cologne. From Cologne—where we lunched at a British mess— our road led through Duisburg, Wesel and the skeleton of Emerich.

We crossed the Dutch frontier at five and continued through battered Arnhem to Utrecht Utrecht was full of exuberant Canadians. I stopped at the headquarters of the local Town Major to inquire about a mess for transient officers. A friendly lieutenant, a blonde Dutch girl on his arm, was on his way to supper and suggested that I join them. He said that Cassidy could eat at a Red Cross Club.

The dining room in the officers' hotel was noisy and crowded. Most of the officers, the lieutenant explained, were going home in a few days. It was good to be in a city which, superfidally at least, showed no scars of battle.

We reached Amsterdam about nine-thirty. At night the canals were confusing. Cassidy and I looked in vain for the Town Major. Finally we found a Canadian "leave hotel." The enlisted man on duty at the desk dispensed with the formality of the billet permit I should have obtained from the Town Major, and assigned us rooms on the same floor. Cassidy decided that the Canadians were a democratic outfit.

Bancel had instructed me to inform the Dutch Restitution Commission, known as the "C.G.R.," that Lieutenant Colonel Vorenkamp was scheduled to reach Amsterdam at noon on the day following my arrival, so the next morning I went to the headquarters of the commission to deliver Major La Farge's message. The commission occupied the stately old Goudstikker house on the Heerengracht Before the war, Goudstikker had been a great Dutch art dealer. In the galleries of this house had been held many fine exhibitions of Dutch painting. During the German Occupation of the Netherlands, an unscrupulous Nazi named Miedl had "acquired" the entire Goudstikker stock from the dealer's widow. We had found many of the Goudstikker pictures at Alt Aussee and in the Göring collection.

Bancel had told me to ask for Captain Robert de Vries. I was informed that the captain was in London. In his stead Nicolaes Vroom, his scholarly young deputy, received me. He had had no word of Colonel Vorenkamp's impending arrival. Vroom transmitted the message immediately to Jonkheer Roel, director of the Rijksmuseum. Twenty minutes later, this distinguished gentleman appeared in Vroom's office. With him were Lieutenant Colonel H. Polis and Captain ter Meer, both of whom were attached to the C.G.R. They were delighted to know about the plane which I told them was due at Schiphol Airport.

Telephonic connections with Munich had not yet been re-established. They had to depend on the USFET Mission at The Hague for transmission of all messages from the American Zone. It often took days for a telegram to get through.

There was barely time enough to telephone for a truck to meet the plane. Also Mr. van Haagen, Permanent Secretary of Education and Science, must be notified at once. I was told that he would accompany us to the airport. In another hour we were all on our way to Schiphol.

We waited two hours at the field and still no sign of the plane from Munich. The weather was fine at the airport, but there were reports of heavy fog to the south. At two o'clock we returned to Amsterdam and lunched at the Dutch officers' mess. My hosts apologized for the food. They said that they no longer received British Army rations. The menu was prepared from civilian supplies. It was a Spartan diet—cheese, bread and jam, and weak coffee. But they shared it so hospitably that only a graceless guest would have complained of the lack of variety. Captain ter Meer said that it was more palatable than the tulip bulbs he had lived on the winter before.

After lunch, Cassidy and I drove to the USFET Mission at The Hague. Colonel Ira W. Black, Chief of the Mission, arranged for me to see the American ambassador. The temporary offices of our embassy were located in a tall brick building on the edge of the city.

I presented Colonel Biddle's letter to Mr. Stanley Hornbeck, the ambassador, who looked more like a successful businessman than a diplomat. He frowned as he read, and when he had finished, said gruffly, "Commander, Tony Biddle is a charming fellow and I am very fond of him. I'd like to be obliging, but we've had too damn many celebrations and ceremonies in this country already. We need more hard work instead of more holidays. It's very nice about the pictures coming back, but steel mills and machinery would be a lot more welcome."

I hadn't expected this reaction and, having had little experience with ambassadors—irascible or otherwise—I hardly knew what to say. After an embarrassing pause, I ventured the remark that a very simple ceremony would be enough.

After his first outburst, the ambassador relented to the extent of saying he'd think it over. As I left his office, he called after me, "My bark's worse than my bite."

On my way back to Amsterdam, I concluded unhappily that as a diplomatic errand boy I was a washout. I'd better go back to loading trucks.

When I reached the hotel I found a message that the plane with Vorenkamp and the pictures had arrived. I met Phonse the following morning at the Goudstikker house. He introduced me to Lieutenant Hans Jaffé, a Dutch Monuments officer, who bore a striking resemblance to Robert Louis Stevenson. Several weeks later Jaffé was chosen as the Dutch representative for the Western District of the American Zone. His work at Seventh Army Headquarters in Heidelberg was comparable to that of Vorenkamp's in Munich. He was intelligent and industrious. During the next few months he was as successful in his investigations of looted Dutch art works as Phonse was in Bavaria. Jaffé didn't reap so rich a harvest, but that was only because there was less loot in his territory.

He and Phonse took me to the Rijksmuseum where the twenty-six paintings from Munich were being unpacked. They were a hand-picked group consisting mainly of seventeenth century Dutch masters, which included four Rembrandts. One of the Rembrandts was the *Still Life with Dead Peacocks* which Lamont and I had taken out of the mine at Alt Aussee. There was a twenty-seventh picture: it was the fraudulent Vermeer of the Göring collection. Phonse had brought it back to be used as evidence against its author, the notorious Van Meegeren.

The Rijksmuseum was holding a magnificent exhibition, appropriately entitled "The Return of the Old Masters." Among the one hundred and forty masterpieces, which had been stored in underground shelters for the past five years, were six Vermeers, nine paintings by Frans Hals, and seventeen Rembrandts, including the famous *Night Watch.*

That evening Phonse took Cassidy and me to the country place occupied by the officers of the C.G.R. It was called "Oud Bussum" and was near Naarden, about fifteen miles from Amsterdam. The luxurious house had been the property of a well known Dutch collaborator. Many high-ranking Nazis had been entertained there. As a mark of special favor I was given the suite which had been used by Göring.

At dinner I sat between Colonel W. G Posthumus-Meyjes, Chief of the Restitution Commission, and Phonse Vorenkamp. The colonel, to the regret of his associates, was soon to relinquish his duties in order to accept an important diplomatic post in Canada. Toward the end of the meal, Phonse asked me how I had made out with the ambassador. I gave a noncommittal reply. He looked at me shrewdly through his steel-rimmed spectacles and said, "We would not expect your ambassador to arrange a ceremony. That is for us to do. It is for us to express our gratitude to General Eisenhower."

(Phonse was as good as his word. A few weeks later, officials of the Netherlands Government arranged a luncheon in one of the rooms of the Rijksmuseum. It was the first affair of its kind in the history of the museum. Only the simplest food was served, but the table was set with rare old silver, porcelain and glass. Colonel Kluss and Bancel represented USFET Headquarters. I was told that no one enjoyed himself more than the American ambassador.)

The next morning Phonse suggested that I return with him in the plane. He had it entirely to himself except for the empty packing cases which he was taking back to Munich. He said that the slight detour to Frankfurt could be easily arranged. So I sent Cassidy back in the jeep and at noon Phonse and I—sole occupants of the C-47 which had been chartered in the name of General Eisenhower—took off from Schiphol Airport. An hour and twenty minutes later we landed at Frankfurt.

Before the end of October, a token restitution was made to Czechoslovakia. The objects chosen were the famous fourteenth century Hohenfurth altarpiece and the collections of the Army Museum at Prague. Both had been stolen by the Nazis. The altarpiece, evacuated from the Alt Aussee mine, was now at the Central Collecting Point in Munich. The Army Museum collections were stored at Schloss Banz, near Bamberg. Lieutenant Colonel František Vrecko and Captain Egon Suk, as representatives of the Czech Government, were invited to USFET Headquarters. We arranged for them to proceed from there to Schloss Banz, where they were met by Lieutenant Walter Horn. I have mentioned Horn before as the Monuments officer whose remarkable sleuthing resulted in recovery of the five pieces of the coronation regalia at Nürnberg. While the Czech officers were en route, we directed Captain Rae at Third Army to arrange for the delivery of the Hohenfurth panels to Schloss Banz. Captain Rae, in turn, designated Lieutenant Commander Coulter to transport them from Munich. (Both

Ham Coulter and I had received our additional half-stripe earlier in the month.) This joint operation was carried out successfully and, in succeeding months, restitution to Czechoslovakia became a matter of routine shipments at regular intervals.

Also before the end of October, we became involved again in the complicated problem of the Veit Stoss altarpiece. Major Charles Estreicher was selected as the Polish representative. The major spent several days at our office in Hochst studying our files for additional data on Polish loot in the American Zone before continuing to Munich and Niirnberg. Because of the condition of the roads, the actual return of the altarpiece as a token restitution to Poland was delayed until the early spring.

While we were in the midst of these negotiations Bancel conferred with Colonel Hayden Smith at USFET headquarters in Frankfurt on the subject of the proposed removal of German-owned works of art to the United States. Colonel Smith was Chief of Staff to Major General C. L. Adcock, Deputy Director of the office of military government, U. S. Zone. Bancel impressed upon the colonel the practical difficulties involved and stressed the *technical,* not the moral objections to shipping valuable works of art to America, As a result of this conference the colonel asked Bancel to prepare a memorandum on the subject for submission to his chief.

The finished memorandum which Edith and I helped Bancel prepare followed the general pattern of a staff study—a statement of the "problem" with specific suggestions relating to its solution. It contained an eloquent plea for the importation of additional MFA&A personnel to assume responsibility for the project and called attention to acute shortages in packing materials and transportation facilities. It also pointed out that the advisability of moving fragile objects across the ocean would be balanced against the advantages of leaving them in the Central Collecting Points, all three of which had been made weatherproof months before and were now provided with sufficient coal to prevent deterioration of the objects during the winter months.

Nothing came of our recommendations. Within two weeks, Colonel Harry McBride, administrator of the National Gallery in Washington, arrived in Berlin to expedite the first shipment. He flew down to Frankfurt two days later to discuss ways and means with Major La Farge.

We learned from him that General Clay's recommendation for immediate removal had been approved by the highest national authority. The General was now in Washington. The futility of protest was obvious. Bancel told the colonel that our Monuments officers were strongly opposed to the project. He said that some of them might request transfer rather than comply with the order. The colonel replied that such requests would, in all probability, be refused. The only other alternative—open defiance of the order—could have but one consequence, a courtmartial. And, assuming that our officers elected to face courtmartial, what would be gained? Nothing, according to the colonel; the order would still be carried out. If trained MFA&A personnel were not available, then the work would have to be done by such officers and men as might be obtainable, experienced or not. Bancel realized that his primary duty was the "protection and salvage" of art works. If he deliberately left them at the mercy of whatever troops might be available to do the packing, then he would be guilty of dereliction of duty. This interpretation afforded him some consolation.

As Bancel had predicted, our Monuments officers lost no time in registering their disapproval. They expressed their sentiments as follows:

U. S. FORCES, EUROPEAN THEATER, GERMANY*

7 November 1945

1.   We, the undersigned Monuments, Fine Arts and Archives Specialist Officers of the Armed Forces of the United States, wish to make known our convictions regarding the transportation to the United States of works of art, the property of German institutions or nationals, for purposes of protective custody.

2.   a. We are unanimously agreed that the transportation of those works of art, undertaken by the United States Army, upon direction from the highest national authority, establishes a precedent which is neither morally tenable nor trustworthy.

b.   Since the beginning of United States participation in the war,

---

* As printed by Kuhn in College Art Journal, January 1946, p. 81; also in Magazine of Art, February 1946, and New York Times, February 7, 1946.

it has been the declared policy of the Allied Forces, so far as military necessity would permit, to protect and preserve from deterioration consequent upon the processes of war, all monuments, documents, or other objects of historic, artistic, cultural, or archaeological value. The war is at an end and no doctrine of "military necessity" can now be invoked for the further protection of the objects to be moved, for the reason that depots and personnel, both fully competent for their protection, have been inaugurated and are functioning.

 c. The Allied nations are at present preparing to prosecute individuals for the crime of sequestering, under pretext of "protective custody," the cultural treasures of German-occupied countries. A major part of the indictment follows upon the reasoning that even though these individuals were acting under military orders, the dictates of a higher ethical law made it incumbent upon them to refuse to take part in, or countenance, the fulfillment of these orders. We, the undersigned, feel it our duty to point out that, though as members of the armed forces, we will carry out the orders we receive, we are thus put before any candid eyes as no less culpable than those whose prosecution we affect to sanction.

 3. We wish to state that from our own knowledge, no historical grievance will rankle so long, or be the cause of so much justified bitterness, as the removal, for any reason, of a part of the heritage of any nation, even if that heritage be interpreted as a prize of war. And though this removal may be done with every intention of altruism, we are none the less convinced that it is our duty, individually and collectively, to protest against it, and that though our obligations are to the nation to which we owe allegiance, there are yet further obligations to common justice, decency, and the establishment of the power of right, not might, among civilized nations.

This document was drafted and signed by a small group of Monuments officers at the Central Collecting Point in Wiesbaden. Before being submitted to Major La Farge for whatever action he deemed appropriate, it was signed by twenty-four of the thirty-two Monuments officers in the American Zone. The remaining eight chose either to submit individual letters expressing similar views, or orally to express like sentiments. The document came to be known as the

"Wiesbaden Manifesto." Army regulations forbade the publication of such a statement; hence its submission to Major La Farge as Chief of the MFA&A Section.

Further protests against the policy which prompted the Wiesbaden Manifesto appeared in the United States a few months later. The action of our Government was sharply criticized and vigorously defended in the press. Letters to and from the State Department and a petition submitted to the President concerning the issue appear in the Appendix to this book.

Preparations for the shipment—appropriately nicknamed "Westward Ho"—took precedence over all other activities of the MFA&A office during the next three weeks. Its size was determined soon after Colonel McBride's arrival. General Clay cabled from Washington requesting this information and the shipping date. After hastily consulting us, our Berlin office replied that two hundred paintings could be made ready for removal within ten days.

The next problem was to decide how the selection was to be made. Should the pictures be chosen from the three Central Collecting Points—Munich, Wiesbaden and Marburg? Time was short. It would be preferable to take them from one depot. Wiesbaden was decided upon. Quality had been stressed. The best of the Kaiser Friedrich Museum pictures were at Wiesbaden.

The decision to confine the selection to the one Central Collecting Point had the additional advantage of avoiding the disruption of MFA&A work at the other two depots, Munich and Marburg. Craig Smyth had long been apprehensive about "Westward Ho," feeling that any incursion on the Bavarian State Collections would be disastrous to his organization at the Munich Collecting Point. He said that his entire staff of non-Nazi museum specialists would walk out. This would seriously imoede the restitution program in the Eastern Military District.

So far as Marburg was concerned, I had been in the office the day Bancel told Walker Hancock of the decision to take German-owned works of art to America. Walker looked at Bancel as though he hadn't understood him. Then he said simply, "In that case I can't go back to Marburg. Everything that we were able to accomplish was possible because I had the confidence of certain people. I can't go back and tell them that I have betrayed them."

And he hadn't gone back to Marburg. Instead he went to Heidelberg for two days without telling anyone where he was going. When he finally returned, it was only to close up his work at Marburg, in the course of which he undertook to explain as best he could to Professor Hamann, the distinguished old German scholar with whom he had been associated, the decision concerning the removal of the pictures. "I quoted the official statement," Walker said, "about the paintings being held in trust for the German people and added that there was no reason to doubt it. Very slowly he said, *If they take our old art, we must try to create a fine new art/ Then, after a long pause, he added, T never thought they would take them.' "

Once it had been decided to limit selection of the paintings to the Wiesbaden Collecting Point, there arose the question of appointing an officer properly qualified to handle the job. It called for speed, discrimination and an expert knowledge of packing. There was a ten-day deadline to be met. Two hundred pictures had to be chosen. And the packing would have to be done with meticulous care. We considered the possibilities. Captain Walter Farmer couldn't be spared from his duties as director of the Collecting Point. Lieutenant Samuel Ratensky, Monuments officer for Greater Hesse, was an architect, not a museum man. Captain Joseph Kelleher was one of our ablest officers; but he was just out of the hospital where he had been laid up for three months with a broken hip. The doctor had released him on condition that he be given easy assignments for the next few weeks.

At this critical juncture, Lamont Moore telephoned from Munich. He and Steve had just completed the evacuation of the mine at Alt Aussee. Lamont said that they were coming up to Frankfurt. Steve had enough points to go home—enough and to spare. Lamont thought he'd take some leave. Bancel signaled from the opposite desk. I told Lamont to forget about the leave; that we had a job for him. Bancel sighed with relief. Lamont's was a different kind of sigh.

Lamont's arrival was providential. Aside from his obvious qualifications for the Wiesbaden assignment, he and Colonel McBride were old friends from the National Gallery where, as I have mentioned before, Lamont had been director of the educational program. The colonel was content to leave everything in his hands. Lamont and I spent an evening together studying a list of the pictures stored at Wiesbaden. He typed out a tentative selection. The next day he and the colonel went over to the Collecting Point for a preliminary inspection.

Steve was momentarily tempted by the prospect of having a part in the undertaking. But when I told him there was a chance of his being included in a draft of officers scheduled for immediate re* deployment, he decided that he'd had his share of packing. Maybe he'd come back in the spring, if there was work still to be done. His parting gift was the Mercedes-Benz, a temporary legacy, as it turned out: two weeks later the car was stolen from the motor pool where I had left it for minor repairs. Steve didn't like the idea of having to wait at a processing center before proceeding to his port of embarkation. He cheered up when he learned that he was headed for one near Marburg. He went off in high spirits at the prospect of seeing his old friend Walker Hancock again.

Under Lamont's skillful supervision, preparations for the shipment proceeded according to schedule. Lamont chose Captain Kelleher as his assistant Together they located the cases from Captain Farmer's records. Only a few of the Kaiser Friedrich pictures had been taken out of the cases in which they had been originally packed for removal from Berlin to the Merkers mine. The larger cases contained as many as a dozen pictures. It was slow work opening the cases and withdrawing a particular canvas for repacking. Seldom were any two of the specified two hundred paintings in a single case. When they were all finally assembled, each one was photographed. In the midst of the proceedings, the supply of film and paper ran out. The nearest replacements were at Mannheim. A day was lost in obtaining the necessary authorization to requisition fresh supplies. It took the better part of another day to make the trip to Mannheim and back. Thanks to Lamont's careful calculations, maximum use was made of the original cases in repacking the two hundred paintings after' a photographic record had been made of their condition.

While these operations were in progress, detailed plans for the actual shipment of the paintings had to be worked out. Colonel McBride and Bancel took up the matter of shipping space with General Ross, Chief of Transportation. Sailing schedules were consulted. An Army transport, the fames Parker, was selected. As an alternative, temporary consideration was given to the idea of trucking the pictures to Bremen and sending diem by a Naval vessel from there. But the Bremen sailing schedules were unsatisfactory. A special metal car was requisitioned to transport* the cases from Frankfurt, by way of Paris, to Le Havre. A twenty-four-hour guard detail was appointed to accompany the car from Frankfurt to the ship. Trucks and escort vehicles were procured for the twenty-five-mile trip from Wiesbaden to the Frankfurt rail yards.

It was decided that Lamont should be responsible for delivering the pictures to the National Gallery in Washington where they were to be placed in storage. Bancel drafted the orders. He worked on them a full day. It took two more days to have them cut They were unique in one respect: Lamont, a second lieutenant, was appointed officer-in-charge. His designated assistant was a commander in the Navy. This was Commander Keith Merrill, an old friend of Colonel McBride's, who happened to be in Frankfurt. He offered his services to the colonel and subsequently crossed on the fames Parker with Lamont and the pictures.

Lamont and Joe Kelleher finished the packing one Hay ahead of schedule. The forty-five cases, lined with waterproof paper, were delivered to the Frankfurt rail yards and loaded onto the car. From there the car was switched to the station and attached to the night train for Paris.

Bancel and I returned to the office to take up where we had left off. As usual, Edith Standen had taken care of everything while we had been preoccupied with the "Westward Ho" shipment. There had been no major crises. Judging from the weekly field reports, restitution to the Dutch and the French was proceeding without interruption. Edith produced a stack of miscellaneous notations: The Belgian representative had arrived in Munich. The Stockholm Museum had offered a supply of lumber to be used in repairing war-damaged German buildings of cultural importance. There had been two inquiries concerning a modification of Law 52 (the Military Government regulation which forbadc trafficking in works of art). A report from Würzburg indicated that emergency repairs to the roof of the Residenz were nearing completion. Lieutenant Rorimer had called from Heidelberg about the books at Offenbach.

Of all the problems which confronted the MFA&A Section, none was more baffling than that of the books at Offenbach. There were more than two million of them. They had been assembled from Jewish libraries throughout Europe by the *Institut zur Erforschung det Judenfrage*—Institute for the Investigation of the Jewish Question—at Frankfurt. At the close of the war, a small part of the collection was found in a large private house in Frankfurt. The rest was discovered in a repository to the north of the city, at Hungen. The house in Frankfurt had been bombed, leaving undamaged only the books stored in the cellar. One hundred and twenty thousand volumes were removed from the damp cellar to the Rothschild Library, which, though damaged, was still intact. Examination of this portion of the collection revealed that it contained more than sixty libraries looted from occupied countries. Subsequently, the rest of the collection was transferred from Hungen to an enormous warehouse at Offenbach, across the river from Frankfurt. The ultimate disposition of this library—probably the greatest of its kind in the world—was the subject of heated discussions, both written and oral. Several leading Jewish scholars had expressed the hope that it could be kept together and eventually established in some center of international study. Our immediate responsibility was the care of the books in their two present locations. That alone was exceedingly difficult. It would take months, perhaps years, to make an inventory.

Judge Samuel Rifkind, General Clay's Adviser on Jewish Affairs, had requested that twenty-five thousand volumes be made available for distribution among the DP camps. I. ref erred the request to the two archivists who had recently joined our staff, Paul Vanderbilt and Edgar Breitenbach. While I sympathized with the tragic plight of the Jewish DPs, there were the unidentified legal owners of the books to be taken into account. One of our archivists felt that we should accede to the judge's request; the other disagreed. The matter was referred to Berlin for a decision. After several weeks, we received word from Berlin that no books were to be released. The judge persisted. Ten days later, Berlin reconsidered. The books could be released—that is, twenty-five thousand of them—on condition that no rare or irreplaceable volumes were included in the selection. Also, the volumes chosen were to be listed on a custody receipt. Up to the time of my departure from Frankfurt, no books had been released.

During the latter part of November, we concentrated on future personnel requirements for the MFA&A program in the American Zone. Current directives indicated that drastic reductions in Military

Government installations throughout the Zone could be expected in the course of the next six or eight months. Already we had begun to feel the impact of the Army's accelerated redeployment program. Bancel and I took stock of our present resources. We had lost four officers and three enlisted men since the first of the month. To offset them, we had gained two civilians; but they were archivists, urgently needed in a specialized field of our work. We couldn't count on them as replacements.

We drew up a chart showing the principal MFA&A offices and depots in each of the three *Länder*. In Bavaria, for example, there were at Munich the *Land* office and the Central Collecting Point; a newly-established Archival Collecting Point at Oberammergau and the auxiliary collecting point at Bamberg; and two secondary offices, one in Upper Bavaria, another in Lower Bavaria. In Greater Hesse, there were the *Land* office and the Central Collecting Point at Wiesbaden; the offices at Frankfurt and Kassel; and the Collecting Points at Offenbach and Marburg. In Wiirttemberg-Baden, the smallest of the three *Länder*, the *Land* office was at Stuttgart. There was a secondary one at Karlsruhe. The principal repositories, requiring MFA&A supervision, were the great mines at Heilbronn and Kochendorf.

We hoped that certain of these establishments could be closed out in a few months; others would continue to operate for an indefinite period. We regarded the *Land* offices as permanent; likewise the Collecting Points, with the exception of Marburg. And Marburg would have to be maintained until it had been thoroughly sifted for loot, or until we received authorization to effect interzonal transfers. Most of the Rhineland museums were in the British Zone, but the collections were at Marburg. The British had requested their return. Until our Berlin office approved the request, we could do nothing.

It was impossible to make an accurate forecast of our personnel needs. Nevertheless we entered on the chart tentative reductions with accompanying dates. The chart would serve as a basic guide in the allocation of civilian positions when the conversion program got seriously under way. A number of our officers had already signified their intentions of converting to civilian status, if the promised program ever materialized.

Early in December, Bancel went home on thirty-days' leave.

Allowing two weeks for transportation each way, he would be gone about two months. In his absence, I was Acting Chief of the Section. Under the Navy's new point system, I had been eligible for release on the first of November, but had requested an extension of active duty in anticipation of Bancel's departure. I was not looking forward with enthusiasm to the period of his absence, because of the personnel problems which lay ahead.

My apprehensions were justified. Our chart, based on a realistic concept of the work yet to be done, was rejected by the Personnel Section. I was told that each *Land* would draw up its own T.O. (Table of Organization). Perhaps there could be some co-ordination at a later date. Even the T.O. of our own office at USFET was thrown back at us with the discouraging comment that the proposed civil service ratings would have to be downgraded. During the next eight weeks there must have been a dozen personnel conferences between the top brass of USFET and the Military Governors of the three *Länder,* and between them and the moguls of the Group Control Council. Not once, to my knowledge, was the MFA&A Section consulted. For a while I exhorted applicants for civilian MFA&A jobs to be patient; but as the weeks went by and the job allocations failed to materialize, applications were withdrawn. *Stars and Stripes* contributed to my discomfort with glittering forecasts of Military Government jobs paying from seven to ten thousand dollars a year. There were positions which paid such salaries, but *Stars and Stripes* might have stressed the fact that there were many more which paid less. I remember one mousy little sergeant who applied for a job with us. In civilian life he had received a salary of twelve hundred dollars a year. On his application blank he stipulated, as the minimum he would accept, the sum of six thousand dollars.

Fortunately there were diversions from these endless personnel problems. Edith and I fell into the habit of going over to Wiesbaden on Saturday afternoons. It was a relief to escape from the impersonal life at our headquarters to the friendly country atmosphere of the *Land* and City Detachments. We were particularly fond of our Monuments officers there.

They were a dissimilar trio—Captain Farmer, Lieutenant Ratensky and Captain Kelleher. Walter Farmer presided over the Collecting Point. Walter seldom relaxed. He was an intense fellow, jumpy in his movements, and unconsciously brusque in conversation. He was an excellent host, loved showing us about the Collecting Point—particularly his "Treasure Room" with its wonderful medieval objects—and, at the end of a tour, invariably produced a bottle of Tokay in his office.

Sam Ratensky, MFA&A officer for the *Land,* was short, slender and had red hair. In civilian life he had been associated with Frank Lloyd Wright and was deeply interested in city-planning. Sam usually looked harassed, but his patience and understanding were inexhaustible. He was accurate in his appraisals of people and had a quiet sense of humor.

Joe Kelleher, Sam's deputy, was a "black Irishman." The war had temporarily interrupted his brilliant career in the Fine Arts department at Princeton. At twenty-eight, Joe had the poise, balance and tolerance of a man twice that age. With wit and charm added to these soberer qualities, he was a dangerously persuasive character. On one occasion, during Bancel's absence, he all but succeeded in hypnotizing our office into assigning a disproportionate number of our best officers to the MFA&A activities of Greater Hesse. When Sam Ratensky went home in February, Joe succeeded him as MFA&A officer for the *Land.* He held this post until his own release several months later. His intelligent supervision of the work was a significant contribution to the success of the American fine arts program in Germany.

Another Monuments officer whose visits to Wiesbaden rivaled Edith's and mine in frequency was Captain Everett Parker Lesley, Jr. He disliked his given name and preferred to be called "Bill." Lesley had been in Europe since the invasion. He was known as the "stormy petrel" of MFA&A. And with good reason. He was brilliant and unpredictable. A master of oral and written invective, he was terrible in his denunciation of stupidity and incompetence. During the fall months, Bill was attached to the Fifteenth Army with headquarters at Bad Nauheim. This was the "paper" army, so called because its function was the compilation of a history of the war. Bill was writing a report of MFA&A activities during combat. He was a virtuoso of the limerick. I was proud of my own repertoire, but Bill knew all of mine and fifty more of his own composing. He usually telephoned me at the office when he had turned out a particularly good one.

Upon the completion of his report for Fifteenth Army, Lesley was appointed MFA&A Officer at Frankfurt. As a part of his duties, he assumed responsibility for the two million books at Offenbach and the Rothschild Library. Within a week he had submitted a report on the two depots and drafted practical plans for their effective reorganization.

While Walter Farmer was on leave in England before Christmas, Joe Kelleher took charge of the Wiesbaden Collecting Point The Dutch and French restitution representatives had gone home for the holidays. Joe had the spare time to examine some of the unopened cases. He asked Edith and me to come over one evening. He said that he might have a surprise for us. I said we'd come and asked if I might bring Colonel Kluss, Chief of the Restitution Control Branch. The colonel had never seen the Collecting Point.

We drove over in the colonel's car. After early dinner with Joe at the City Detachment, we went down to the Collecting Point. Joe unlocked the "Treasure Room" and switched on the lights. The colonel whistled when he looked around the room.

"Those are the Polish church treasures which the Nazis swiped," said Joe, pointing casually to the gold and silver objects stacked on shelves and tables. "There's something a lot more exciting in that box."

He walked over to a packing case about five feet square whidi stood in the center of the room. The lid had been unscrewed but was still in place. It was marked in black letters: "Kiste 28, Aegypt. Abteilung— Bunte Konigin—Tel-el-Amarna—NICHT KIPPEN!"—Case 28, Egyptian Department—Painted Queen—Tel-el-Amarna— DON'T TILT! Joe grinned with satisfaction as I read the markings. The Painted Queen—Queen Nefertiti. This celebrated head, the most beautiful piece of Egyptian sculpture in the world, had been one of the great treasures of the Berlin Museum. It was a momentous occasion. There was every reason to believe that the German museum authorities had packed the head with proper care. Even so, the case had been moved around a good deal in the meantime, first from the Merkers mine to the vaults of the Reichsbank in Frankfurt, and then from Frankfurt to Wiesbaden. There was not much point in speculating about that now. We'd know the worst in a few minutes.

Joe and I laid the lid aside. The box was filled with a white packing material. At first I thought it was cotton, but it wasn't. It was glass wool. In the very center of the box lay the head, swathed in silk paper.

Gingerly we lifted her from the case and placed her on a table. We unwound the silk paper. Nefertiti was unharmed, and as bewitching as ever. She was well named: "The beautiful one is here/'

While we studied her from every angle, Joe recounted the story of the Nefertiti, her discovery and subsequent abduction to Berlin. She was the wife of Akhnaton, enlightened Pharaoh of the fourteenth century B.C. This portrait of her was excavated in the winter of 1912 by Dr. Ludwig Borchardt, famous German Egyptologist, on the site of Tel-el-Amama, Akhnaton's capital. In compliance with the regulations of the Egyptian Government, Borchardt submitted a list of his finds at Tel-el-Amarna to M. Maspero of the Cairo Museum. According to the story, Maspero merely glanced at the list, to make certain that a fifty-fifty division had been made, and did not actually examine the items. The head was taken to Berlin and placed in storage until after the first World War. When it was placed on exhibition in 1920, the Egyptian Government protested loudly that Dr. Borchardt had deceived the authorities of the Cairo Museum and demanded the immediate return of the head. (The Egyptian Government was again pressing its claim in March 1946.)

After replacing Nefertiti in her case, Joe showed the colonel the collection of rare medieval treasures, including those of the Guelph Family—patens, chalices and reliquaries of exquisite workmanship dating from the eleventh and twelfth centuries. With a fine sense of showmanship he saved the most spectacular piece till the last: the famous Crown of St. Stephen, the first Christian king of Hungary, crowned by the Pope in the year 1000. It was adorned with enamel plaques, bordered with pearls and studded with great uncut gems. Joe said there was a difference of opinion among scholars as to the exact date and provenance of the enamels. The crown was surmounted by a bent gold cross. According to Joe, the cross had been bent for four hundred years and would never be straightened. During the sixteenth century, the safety of the crown was endangered. It was entrusted to the care of a Hungarian noblewoman, who concealed it in a compartment under the seat of her carriage. The space was small and when the lid was closed and weighted down by the occupant of the carriage, the cross got bent. The Hungarian coronation regalia included three other pieces: a sword, an orb, and a scepter. The scepter was extremely beautiful. The stalk was of rich gold filigree and terminated in a spherical ornament of carved rock crystal. The regalia was kept in a specially constructed iron trunk with three locks, the keys to which were entrusted to three different nobles. At the close of the present war, American troops apprehended a Hungarian officer with the trunk. Perhaps he was trying to safeguard the regalia as his predecessor in the sixteenth century had done. In any case, the American authorities thought they'd better relieve him of that grave responsibility.   -

A few days after our visit to Wiesbaden with Colonel Kluss, I received a letter from home enclosing a clipping from the December 7 edition of the *New York Times.* The clipping read as follows:

$80,000,000 PAINTINGS ARRIVE FROM EUROPE ON ARMY TRANSPORT

A valuable store of art, said to consist entirely of paintings worth upward of $80,000,000, arrived here last night from Europe in the holds of the Army transport *James Parker.*

Where the paintings came from and where they are going was a mystery, and no Army officer on the pier at Forty-fourth Street and North River, where the *Parker* docked with 2,483 service passengers, would discuss the shipment, or even admit it was on board. It was learned elsewhere that a special detail of Army officers was on the ship during the night to take charge of the consignment, which will be unloaded today.

Unusual precautions were taken to keep the arrival of the paintings secret. The canvases were included in more than forty crates and were left untouched during the night under lock and key.

Presumably the shipment was gathered at sites in Europe where priceless stores of paintings and art objects stolen by the Nazis from the countries they overran were discovered when Allied forces broke through into Germany and the dominated countries.

The White House announced in Washington two months ago that shipments of art would be brought here for safekeeping, to be kept in "trust" for the rightful owners, and the National Gallery of Art, through its chairman, Chief Justice Harlan Fiske Stone, was asked to provide storage and protection for the works while they are in this country. The gallery is equipped with controlled ventilation and expert personnel for the storage and handling of such works.

The White House announcement gave no listing of the paintings, but it is known that among the vast stores seized, including caches in Italy as well as Germany, and Hermann Göring's famous $200,000,000 art collection, [were] included many of the world's art treasures and works of the masters.

By coincidence, I received that same day a copy of the *New York Times Overseas Weekly* edition of December 9, which carried substantially the same story, except for the fact that it stated unequivocally that the paintings shipped to America were Nazi loot.

Edith and I were gravely disturbed by the inaccuracy of the statements in these articles. Our concern was increased by the fact that the articles had appeared in so reliable a publication as the *Times*. What could have happened to the official press release on the subject issued on the twenty-fourth of November when the *James Parker* was ready to sail?* And why all the mystery? I reread the December 7 clipping. To me there was the implication that we were shipping loot in wholesale lots to the United States. That would be alarming news to the countries whose stolen art works we were already returning as rapidly as possible.

The *Times* story most emphatically called for a correction. But if a statement from our office were sent through channels, it probably wouldn't reach New York before Easter. Edith looked up from her work. There was a glint in her eye. She asked, "Will you do me a favor? I'd like to write the letter of correction."*

I told her to go ahead. Ten minutes later she showed me the rough draft. It covered all the points. I reworked a phrase here and there but made no important changes and, as soon as it was typed and cleared, I signed and mailed it. As published in the *New York Times* two weeks later, on January 2, 1946, the letter read as follows:

TO THE EDITOR OF THE NEW YORK TIMES

On Dec. 7 The Times printed a report to the effect that $80,000,000 worth of paintings, presumably from the stores of art objects stolen by the Nazis, had arrived from Europe in the Army transport *James Parker*. Your Overseas Weekly edition of Dec. 9 repeated this information but stated categorically that the paintings were Nazi loot.

It is true that the *James Parker* brought to America some 200 paintings of inestimable value, but none of them is loot or of dubious ownership. They are the property of the Kaiser Friedrich Museum in Berlin. A press release from the Office of Military Government for

---

* See in this connection the statements released to the press by the White House on September 26, 1945, and by the War Department on December 6, 1945. They are printed in Magazine of Art for February. 1946.

Germany (U.S.), dated Nov. 24, states that these "priceless German-owned paintings, which might suffer irreparable damage if left in Germany through the winter, have been selected for temporary storage in the United States. These paintings have been gathered from various wartime repositories in the United States Zone of Germany and are being shipped to Washington to insure their safety and to hold them in trust for the people of Germany. The United States Government has promised their return to the German people."

It cannot be stated too emphatically that the policy of the American Military Government is to return all looted works of art to their owner nations with the greatest possible speed. Since the restitution in August of the famous van Eyck altarpiece, "The Mystic Lamb," to Belgium, a steady stream of paintings, sculpture, fine furniture and other art objects has poured from the highly organized collecting points of the United States Zone to the liberated countries. Few, if any, looted works of art of any importance are of unknown origin; and though, among the vast masses of material taken from the Jews and other "enemies of the state" for what was always described as "safekeeping" there will undoubtedly be many pieces whose ownership will be difficult to determine, it appears unlikely that these will be found to be of great value.

The shipment of German-owned paintings to the United States is thus a project entirely separate from the main objectives of the Monuments, Fine Arts and Archives Section of the Office of Military Government—namely, the restitution of loot and the reestablishment of the German museums and other cultural organizations. To confuse this shipment, which was directed by the highest national authority, with what is now the routine work of preservation, identification and restitution performed by trained specialist personnel is to mislead our Allies and to underrate the accomplishments of a small group of disinterested and hard-working Americans.

Thomas C. Howe Jr.
Lieut. Comdr., USNR, Deputy Chief;
Director on Leave, California Palace of the Legion of Honor,
San Francisco.
European Theatre, Dec. 18, 1945.

The main objectives of the Monuments, Fine Arts and Archives Section of American Military Government in Germany were defined in my letter to the New York Times as "the restitution of loot and the re-establishment of the German museums and other cultural institutions." Honorable and constructive objectives. And, as expressed in that letter, unequivocal and reassuring both to the liberated countries of Europe and to the Germans. Yet how difficult of attainment! How difficult even to keep those objectives clearly in mind when confronted simultaneously—as our officers often were—with a dozen problems of equal urgency!

At close range it was impossible to look objectively at the overall record of our accomplishments. But homeward bound in February I had that opportunity'. The pieces of the puzzle began to fit together and the picture took shape. It was possible to determine to what extent we have realized our objectives.

So far as restitution is concerned, the record has been a success. During the summer months our energies were devoted to obvious preliminary preparations. They included the establishment of Central Collecting Points at Munich, Marburg and Wiesbaden. Immediately thereafter, the contents of art repositories in the American Zone were removed to those central depots. The Central Collecting Points, organized and directed by Monuments officers with museum experience, were staffed with trained personnel from German museums. The one at Munich was primarily reserved for looted art, since the majority of the cultural booty was found in Bavaria. The Collecting Points at Wiesbaden and Marburg, on the other hand, housed German-owned collections brought from repositories in which storage conditions were unsatisfactory.

The process of actual restitution was inaugurated by token resti-tutions in the name of General Eisenhower to Belgium, Holland, France and Czechoslovakia. Circumstances beyond our control postponed similar gestures of good will to Poland and Greece. Representatives of the liberated countries were invited to the American Zone to identify and remove the loot from the collecting points. According to late reports, the restitution of loot was continuing without interruption.

Shortly after my return, there were disquieting rumors of drastic reductions in American personnel connected with cultural restitution in Germany. I earnestly hope that these rumors are without foundation. Such reductions would be disastrous to the completion of a program which has reflected so creditably on our government.

The re-establishment of German museums and other cultural institutions—our second main objective—has been, to a large extent, sacrified in the interests of restitution. This brings up again the urgent need for the immediate replenishment of our dwindling Fine Arts personnel in Germany. Our moral responsibility for the continuation of this phase of the MFA&A program is a grave one. It was understandably neglected during the first six months of our occupation in Germany. And it would be unfair to argue that the British have far outdistanced us in this field. That they have done so is undeniably true. However, the British found but little loot in their zone. Consequently, they have been able to make rapid strides in the reconstitution of German collections and cultural institutions, while we have been preoccupied with restitution.

Notwithstanding that preoccupation, our Monuments officers were instrumental in arranging a series of impressive exhibitions of German-owned masterpieces. The first of these was held at Marburg in November 1945. A second and more ambitious show, which included many of the finest treasures of the Bavarian State Galleries, opened at Munich in January 1946. A third, comprising paintings and sculptures from the museums of Berlin and Frank* furt, was presented at Wiesbaden in February.

All these exhibitions were accompanied by catalogues with German and English texts. Those of Munich and Wiesbaden were lavishly illustrated. The Munich catalogue contained several plates showing the rooms in which the exhibition was held—lofty, spacious galleries recalling the marble halls of our own National Gallery at Washington.

At the time of my departure from Germany, little was known of French and Russian procedures with regard to cultural rehabilitation in their respective zones of occupation. Their Military Governments have made provisions for personnel capable of carrying on work similar to ours and that of the British.

The caliber of the men drawn into the project from all branches of our Armed Forces has been cited as an important factor in the success of the Monuments, Fine Arts and Archives program. I would like to cite another factor which I consider equally important: There was no arbitrary drafting of personnel; participation was voluntary. The resulting spontaneity and its value to the spirit of the work cannot be exaggerated.

The blank wall at the Louvre in Paris, awaiting the return of Rembrandt's *Mona Lisa*. The painting was removed from the museum for safe-keeping dutring the war.

APPENDIX

The following is the complete list of the paintings transferred from Germany and now stored at the National Gallery, according to its News Release of December 14, 1945:

Albrecht Altdorfer: *Rest on the Flight into Egypt*
Albrecht Altdorfer: *Landscape with Satyr Family*
Albrecht Altdorfer: *Nativity*
Albrecht Altdorfer: *Christ's Farewell to His Apostles*
Christoph Amberger: *Cosmographer Sebastian Münster*
Jacopo Amigioni: *Lady as Diana*
Fra Angelico: *Last Judgment*
Austrian Master (ca. 1400): *Christ, Madonna, St. John*
Austrian Master (ca. 1410): *Crucifixion*
Hans Baldung Grien: *Altar of Halle*
Hans Baldung Grien: *Graf von Lowenstein*
Hans Baldung Grien: *Pietà*
Hans Baldung Grien: *Pyramus and Thisbe*
Giovanni Bellini: *The Resurrection*
Bohemian (ca. 1350): *Glatyer Madonna*
Hieronymus Bosch: *St. John on Patmos*
Botticelli: *Giuliano de Medici*, and frame
Botticelli: *Madonna of the Lilies*
Botticelli: *St. Sebastian*
Botticelli: *Simonetta Vespucci*
Botticelli: *Venus*
Dirk Bouts: *Madonna and Child*
Dirk Bouts: *Virgin in Adoration*
Peter Breughel: *Dutch Proverbs*
Peter Breughel: *Two Monkeys*
Angelo Bronzino: *Portrait of a Young Man*
Angelo Bronzino: *Portrait of a Young Man*

Angelo Bronzino: *Ugolino Martelli*
Hans Burgkmair: *Holy Family*
Giovanni Battista Caracciolo: *Cosmas and Damian*
Caravaggio: *Cupid as Victor*
Vittore Carpaccio: *Entombment of Christ*
Andrea del Castagno: *Assumption of the Virgin*
Chardin: *The Draughtsman*
Chardin: *Still Life*
Petrus Christus: *Portrait of a Girl*
Petrus Christus: *St. Barbara and a Carthusian Monk*
Joos van Cleve: *Young Man*
Cologne Master (ca. 1400): *Life of Christ*
Cologne Master (ca. 1350): *Madonna Enthroned, Crucifixion*
Correggio: *Leda and the Swan*
Francesco Cossa: *Allegory of Autumn*
Lucas Cranach, the Elder: *Frau Reuss*
Lucas Cranach, the Elder: *Lucretia*
Lucas Cranach, the Elder: *Rest on the Flight into Egypt*
Daumier: *Don Quixote*
Piero di Cosimo: *Mars, Venus and Cupid*
Lorenzo di Credi: *Young Girl*
Albrecht Dürer: *Madonna*
Albrecht Dürer: *Madonna with the Goldfinch*
Albrecht Dürer: *Young Woman*
Albrecht Dürer: *Hieronymus Hozschuher*

Albrecht Dürer: *Cover for Portrait of Hieronymus Holzschuher*
Adam Elsheimer: *The Drunkenness of Noah*
Adam Elsheimer: *Holy Family*
Adam Elsheimer: *Landscape with the Weeping Magdalene*
Adam Elsheimer: *St. Christopher*
Jean Fouquet: Etienne *Chevalier with St. Stephen*
French (ca. 1400): *Coronation of the Virgin*
French Master (ca. 1400): *Triptych*
Geertgen tot Sint Jans: *John the Baptist*
Geertgen tot Sint Jans: *Madonna*
Giorgione: *Portrait of a Young Man*
Giotto: *Death of the Virgin*
Jan Gossaert: *Baudouin de Bourbon*
Jan Gossaert: *Christ on the Mount of Olives*
Francesco Guardi: *The Balloon Ascension*
Francesco Guardi: *St. Mark's Piazza in Venice*
Francesco Guardi: *Piazzetta in Venice*
Frans Hals: *Hille Bobbe*
Frans Hals: *Nurse and Child*
Frans Hals: *Portrait of a Young Man*
Frans Hals: *Portrait of a Young Woman*
Frans Hals: *Singing Boy*
Frans Hals: *Tyman Oosdorp*
Meindert Hobbema: *Landscape*
Hans Holbein: *George Giesze*
Hans Holbein: *Old Man*
Hans Holbein: *Portrait of a Man*
Pieter de Hooch: *The Mother*
Pieter de Hooch: *Party of Officers and Ladies*
Willem Kalf: *Still Life*
Willem Kalf: *Still Life*
Philips Konninck: *Dutch Landscape*
Georges de la Tour: *St. Sebastian*
Filippino Lippi: *Allegory of Music*
Fra Filippo Lippi: *Adoration of the Child*

Pietro Lorenzetti: *St. Humilttas Raises a Nun*
Pietro Lorenzetti: *Death of St. Humilitas*
Claude Lorrain: *Italian Coast Scene*
Lorenzo Lotto: *Christ's Farewell to His Mother*
Bastiano Mainardi: *Portrait of a Man*
Manet: *In the Winter Garden*
Andrea Mantegna: *Cardinal Mezzarota*
Andrea Mantegna: *Presentation in the Temple*
Simon Marmion: *Altar of St. Omer* (two panels)
Simone Martini: *Burial of Christ*
Masaccio: *Birth Platter*
Masaccio: *Three Predelle*
Masaccio: *Four Saints*
Quentin Massys: *The Magdalene*
Master of the Darmstadt Passion: *Altar Wings*
Master of Flémalle: *Crucifixion*
Master of Flemalle: *Portrait of a Man*
Master of the Virgo inter Virgines: *Adoration of the Kings*
Hans Memling: *Madonna Enthroned with Angels*
Hans Memling: *Madonna Enthroned*
Hans Memling: *Madonna and Child*
Lippo Memmi: *Madonna and Child*
Antonello da Messina: *Portrait of a Man*
Jan Mostaert: *Portrait of a Man*
Aelbert Ouwater: *Raising of Lazarus*
Palma Vecchio: *Portrait of a Man*
Palma Vecchio: *Young Woman*
Giovanni Paolo Pannini: *Colosseum*
Giovanni di Paolo: *Christ on the Cross*
Giovanni di Paolo: *Legend of St. Clara*
Joachim Patinir: *Rest on the Flight into Egypt*
Sebastiano del Piombo: *Roman Matron*
Sebastiano del Piombo: *Knight of the Order of St. James*
Antonio Pollaiuolo: *David*

Nicolas Poussin: *St. Matthew*
Nicolas Poussin: *Amaltea*
Raphael: *Madonna Diotalevi*
Raphael: *Madonna Terranova*
Raphael: *Solly Madonna*
Rembrandt: *Landscape with Bridge*
Rembrandt: *John the Baptist*
Rembrandt: *Joseph and Potiphar's Wife*
Rembrandt: *Vision of Daniel*
Rembrandt: *Moses Breaking the Tablets of the Law*
Rembrandt: *Susanna and the Elders*
Rembrandt: *Tobias and the Angel*
Rembrandt: *Minervaı*
Rembrandt: *Rape of Proserpina*
Rembrandt: *Self Portrait*
Rembrandt; *Hendrickje Stoffels*
Rembrandt: *Man with Gold Helmet*
Rembrandt: *Old Man with Red Hat*
Rembrandt: *Rabbi*
Rembrandt: *Saskia*
Rubens: *Landscape (shipwreck of Aeneas)*
Rubens: *St. Cecilia*
Rubens: *Madonna Enthroned with Saints*
Rubens: *Andromeda*
Rubens: *Perseus and Andromeda*
Rubens: *Isabella Brandt*
Jacob van Ruisdael: *View of Haarlem*
Andrea Sacchi (?): *Allesandro del Boro*
Sassetta: *Legend of St. Francis*
Sassetta: *Mass of St. Francis*
Martin Schongauer: *Nativity*
Seghers: *Landscape*
Luca Signorelli: *Three Saints* (altar wing)
Luca Signorelli: *Three Saints* (altar wing)
Luca Signorelli: *Portrait of a Man*
Francesco Squarcione: *Madonna and Child*
Jan Steen: *Inn Garden*
Jan Steen: *The Christening*

Bemardo Strozzi: *Judith*
Gerard Terborch: *The Concert*
Gerard Terborch: *Paternal Advice*
Giovanni Battista Tiepolo: *Carrying of the Cross*
Giovanni Battista Tiepolo: *St. Agatha*
Giovanni Battista Tiepolo: *Rinaldo and Armida*
Tintoretto: *Doge Mocenigo*
Tintoretto: *Old Man*
Titian: *Venus with Organ Player*
Titian: *Self Portrait*
Titian: *Lavinia*
Titian: *Portrait of a Young Man*
Titian: *Child of the Strozzi Family*
Cosma Tura: *St. Christopher*
Cosma Tura: *St. Sebastian*
Adriaen van der Velde: *The Farm*
Roger Van der Weyden: *Altar with Scenes from the Life of Mary*
Roger Van der Weyden: *Johannes-alter Altar with Scenes from the Life of John the Baptist*
Roger Van der Weyden: *Bladelin Alta*
Roger Van der Weyden: *Portrait of a Woman*
Roger Van der Weyden: *Charles the Bold*
Jan Van Eyck: *Crucifixion*
Jan Van Eyck: *Madonna in the Church*
Jan Van Eyck: *Giovanni Arnolfini*
Jan Van Eyck: *Man with a Pink*
Jan Van Eyck: *Knight of the Golden Fleece*
Lucas van Leyden: *Chess Players*
Lucas van Leyden: *Madonna and Child*
Velasquez: *Countess Olivares*
Domenico Veneziano: *Adoration of the Kings*
Domenico Veneziano: *Martyrdom of St. Lucy*
Domenico Veneziano: *Portrait of a Young Woman*
Vermeer: *Young Woman with a Pearl*

Necklace

Vermeer: *Man and Woman Drinking Wine*

Andrea del Verrocchio: *Madonna and Child*

Andrea del Verrocchio: *Madonna and Child*

Watteau: *Fête Champêtre*

Watteau: *French Comedians*

Watteau: *Italian Comedians*

Westphalian Master (ca. 1250): *Triptych*

Konrad Witz: *Crucifixion*

Konrad Witz: *Allegory of Redemption*

On January 15, 1946, Mr. Rensselaer W. Lee, President of the College Art Association of America, sent the following letter to the Secretary of State:

My dear Mr. Secretary:

The members of the College Art Association of America, a constituent member of the American Council of Learned Societies, have been disturbed by the removal to this country of works of art from Berlin museums.

Information that we have received from abroad leads us to believe that the integrity of United States policy has been questioned as a result of this action. We have also been informed that adequate facilities and American personnel now exist in the American zone in Germany to assure the proper care of art treasures in that area.

We would therefore urge that the department of State clarify this action, and would strongly recommend that assurances be given that no further shipments are contemplated.

Copies of this letter were sent to members of the American Commission for the Protection and Salvage of Artistic and Historic Monuments in War Areas.

The State Department replied on January 25:

My Dear Mr. Lee:

Your letter of January 15, urging the Department to clarify the action taken in removing to the United States certain works of art from German museums, has been received. In the absence of the Secretary, I am replying to your letter and am glad to give you additional information on this question.

The decision to remove these works of art to this country was made on the basis of a statement by General Clay that he did not have adequate facilities and personnel to safeguard German art treasures and that he could not undertake the responsibility of their proper care.

You indicated in your letter that you have been informed that adequate facilities and personnel now exist in the American zone for the protection of these art treasures. I must inform you that our information, based upon three separate investigations, is precisely to the contrary. The redeployment program has, as you no doubt realize, reduced American personnel in Germany and this reduction is applied to arts and monuments and this personnel as well as to other branches.

The coal situation in Germany is critical and has made it impossible to provide heat for the museums. General Qay cannot be expected to provide heat for the museums if that means taking it away from American forces, from hospitals, or from essential utility needs.

We are furthermore advised that the security situation was not such as to ensure adequate protection in Germany. In short, the Department's information is such that it cannot agree with your premise.

It was realized that the "integrity of United States policy" might be questioned by some if these works of art were removed to this country. After a careful review of the facts, it was decided that the most important aspect was to safeguard these priceless treasures by bringing them to this country where they could be properly cared for. It was hoped that the President's pledge that they would be returned to Germany would satisfy those who might be critical of this Government's motives.

Sincerely yours,

For the Acting Secretary of State:
James W. Riddleberger Chief,
Division of Central European Affairs*

In April the author of this book received from Frederick Mortimer Clapp, director of the Frick Collection, New York, the following letter regarding the removal of German-owned works of art to this country. A copy of the resolution which accompanied this letter and a list of those who subsequently signed the resolution are also printed below.

1 East 70th Street
New York 21, New York
April 24, 1946

Dear

Since we believe that it is impossible to defend on technical, political or moral grounds the decision to ship to this country two hundred internationally known and extremely valuable pictures belonging indisputably, by prewar gift or purchase, to German institutions, notably the Kaiser Friedrich Museum of Berlin, we propose to memorialize the President in a resolution to be signed by a group of like-minded people interested in or associated with the arts.

We also intend to point out that no reason can be found for even temporarily

---

* These letters are printed on pages 83 and 84 of College Art Journal for January 1946; in Magazine of Art for February 1946, and in the New Yorfc Times of February 7, 1946.

alienating these works of art from the country to which legally they belong.

We represent no organized movement or institution. We merely wish as American citizens to go on record by appealing to our government to set right an ill considered action arising from an error of judgment which, however disinterested in intention, has already done much to weaken our national condemnation of German sequestrations of the artistic heritage or possessions of other nations under the subterfuge of "protective custody," or openly as loot.

The moral foundations of our war effort and final victories will be subtly undermined if we, who understand the implications, pass over in silence an action taken by our own officials that, in outward appearance at least cannot be distinguished from those, detestable to all right thinking people, which the Nazis* policy of pillage inspired and condoned.

The Monuments Officers attached to our armed forces with their specialized knowledge of the practical risks involved unanimously condemned the decision. Those Americans whose profession it is to study and preserve old paintings deplore it. On ethical grounds it is disapproved by the opinion of enlightened laymen.

We therefore consider the protest we will make to be our plain and simple duty, for it is our considered judgment that no explanation or excuse acceptable to the public conscience can be found for sending fragile old masters across the sea to this country. The physical hazards, the momentous responsibilities and the intellectual ambiguities inherent in such an act are only too grossly evident. The historical repercussions that will follow it can be imagined in the light of past situations of a similar kind. It is well known that the Nazis inculcated in the German mind a fanatical belief that we are destructive barbarians. All future deterioration of these pictures will now, rightly or wrongly, be laid at our door.

We should be glad if you would care to join us and others, who have already expressed to us their sense of the unjustified impropriety of the action to which we refer in demanding the immediate return to Germany of these panels and canvasses, the cancellation of all plans to exhibit them in this country and the countermanding at once of any contemplated further shipments.

The text of the proposed resolution is enclosed. As one of the principal reasons for submitting it to our government is to forestall further action of a similar kind with reference to pictures or objects of art belonging to German museums, as well as to rectify the existing situation, may I earnestly request you to signify your approval, if you are so minded, by signing the resolution and returning it to me before May 6.

Sincerely yours,

Signed: FREDERICK MORTIMER CLAPP

On May 9, 1946, Dr. Clapp and Mrs. Juliana Force, director of the Whitney Museum, sent President Truman the following resolution, a copy of which was enclosed with the above letter:

RESOLUTION

WHEREAS in all civilized countries one of the most significant public reactions during the recent war was the horrified indignation caused by the surreptitious or brazen looting of works of art by German officials in countries they had conquered;

AND WHEREAS that indignation and abhorrence on the part of free peoples was a powerful ingredient in the ardor and unanimity of their support of the war effort of democratically governed states in which the private opinions of citizens are the source and controlling directive of official action;

AND WHEREAS two hundred important and valuable pictures belonging to the Kaiser Friedrich and other Berlin museums have been removed from Germany and sent to this country on the still unestablished ground of ensuring their safety;

AND WHEREAS it is apparent that disinterested and intelligent people believe that this action cannot be justified on technical, political or moral grounds and that many, including the Germans themselves, may find it hard to distinguish between the resultant situation and the "protective custody" used by the Nazis as a camouflage for the sequestration of the artistic treasures of other countries;

BE IT THEREFORE RESOLVED that we, the undersigned, respectfully request the President to order the immediate safe return to Germany of the aforesaid paintings, the cancellation of any plans that may have been made to exhibit them in this country and the countermanding without delay of any further shipments of the kind that may have been contemplated.

This resolution was signed by:

Abbott, Jere, Director, Smith College Museum of Art Northampton, Mass.

Abbott, John E., Executive Vice-President, The Museum of Modern Art New York, N.Y.

Adams, Philip R., Director Cincinnati Museum Cincinnati, Ohio

Barber, Professor Leila, Vassar College Poughkeepsie, N. Y.

Baker, C. H. Collins, Henry E. Huntington Library and Art Gallery San Marino, Calif.

Barr, Alfred H., The Museum of Modern Art New York, N.Y.

Barzun, Jacques, History Department Columbia University New York, N.Y.

Baur, John I. H., Curator of Painting Brooklyn Museum Brooklyn, N. Y.

Biebel, Franklin, Assistant to Director Frick Collection New York, N. Y.

Breeskin, Mrs. Adelyn, Acting Director Baltimore Museum of Art Baltimore, Md.

Burdell, Dr. Edwin S., Director, The Cooper Union New York, N.Y.

Chase, Elizabeth Editor "Bulletin," Yale University Art Gallery New Haven, Conn.

Claflin, Professor Agnes Rindge, Vassar College Poughkeepsie, N. Y.

Clapp, Frederick Mortimer, Director Frick Collection New York, N. Y.

Cole, Grover, Instructor in Ceramics University of Michigan Ann Arbor, Mich.

Cook, Walter W. S., Chairman Institute of Fine Arts New York University, N. Y.

Courter, Miss Elodie, Dir. of Circulating Exhibitions, The Museum of Modern Art New York, N. Y.

Crosby, Dr. Sumner Assistant Professor, History of Art, Yale University New Haven, Conn.

Cunningham, Charles C., Director, Wadsworth Atheneum Hartford, Conn.

Dawson, John P., Professor of Law University of Michigan Ann Arbor, Mich.

Faisan, Professor Lane, Jr., Williams College Williamstown, Mass.

Faunce, Wayne M. Vice-Director, American Museum of Natural History New York, N.Y.

Fisher, H. H., Hoover Library, Stanford University Palo Alto, Calif.

Force, Mrs. Juliana, Director, Whitney Museum of American Art, New York, N. Y.

Goodrich, Lloyd, Research Curator Whitney Museum of American Art New York, N. Y.

Gores, Walter J., Professor and Chairman of Design, University of Michigan Ann Arbor, Mich.

Haight, Mary N., Assistant Curator of Ancient Art, Yale University Art Gallery, New Haven, Conn.

Hamilton, George Heard Curator of Paintings Yale University Art Gallery New Haven, Conn.

Hamlin, Talbot F., Librarian, Avery Architectural Library, Columbia University New York, N.Y.

Hammett, Ralph W., Professor of Architecture University of Michigan Ann Arbor, Mich.

Hancock, Walter, Director of Sculpture Pennsylvania Academy of the Fine Arts Philadelphia, Pa.

Hayes, Bartlett H., Jr., Director Addison Gallery of American Art, Andover, Mass.

Hebran, Jean, Professor of Architecture University of Michigan Ann Arbor, Mich.

Helm, Miss Florence, Old Merchant's House New York, N.Y.

Howe, Thomas Carr, Jr., Director California Palace of the Legion of Honor, San Francisco, Calif.

Hudnut, Joseph, Dean, Graduate School of Architecture, Harvard University Cambridge, Mass.

Hume, Samuel J., Director, Berkeley Art Association, Berkeley, Calif.

Ivins, William M., Jr., Counselor and Curator of Prints, The Metropolitan Museum of Art, New York, N.Y.

Janson, H. W., Assistant Professor Department of Art and Archaeology Washington University St. Louis, Mo.

Jewell, Henry A., Department of Art and Archaeology Princeton University Princeton, N. J.

Kaufmann, Edgar, Curator of Industrial Art The Museum of Modern Art New York, N. Y.

Keck, Sheldon, Restorer, The Brooklyn Museum Brooklyn, N. Y.

Kirby, John C., Assistant Administrator Walters Gallery Baltimore, Md.

Kirstein, Lincoln New York, N. Y.

Kubler, Professor George Yale University New Haven, Conn.

Lee, Rensselaer W., Princeton, N. J.

Marceau, Henri, Assistant Director, Philadelphia Museum of Art Philadelphia, Pa.

Mcllhenny, Henry, Curator of Decorative Arts Philadelphia Museum of Art Philadelphia, Pa.

McMahon, A. Philip, Chairman, Fine Arts Department, Washington

Square College New York University New York, N. Y.

Meeks, Everett V., Dean, Yale School of the Fine Arts New Haven, Conn.

Meiss, Millard, Professor, Columbia University New York, N. Y.

Miner, Miss Dorothy E., Librarian Walters Gallery, Baltimore, Md.

More, Hermon, Curator, Whitney Museum of American Art, New York, N. Y.

Morley, Dr. Grace McCann, Director San Francisco Museum of Art, San Francisco, Calif.

Morse, John D., Editor, Magazine of Art New York, N. Y.

Myer, John Walden Assistant Director, Museum of the City of New York New York, N. Y.

Myers, George Hewitt, President, Textile Museum of the District of Columbia Washington, D. C.

Nagel, Charles, Jr., Director, The Brooklyn Museum Brooklyn, N. Y.

O'Connor, John, Jr., Assistant Director, Carnegie Institute Pittsburgh, Pa.

Packard, Miss Elizabeth G., Walters Gallery Baltimore, Md.

Parker, Thomas G, Director, American Federation of Arts, Washington, D. C.

Peat, Wilbur D., Director, John Herron Art Institute, Indianapolis, Ind.

Phillips, John Marshall, Assistant Director and Curator of the Garvan Collections, Yale University Art Gallery New Haven, Conn.

Poland, Reginald, Director, Fine Arts Society of San Diego, San Diego, Calif.

Porter, Allen, Secretary, The Museum of Modern Art, New York, N. Y.

Porter, Vernon, Director, Riverside Museum New York, N. Y.

Post, Chandler, Fogg Museum of Art, Harvard University, Cambridge, Mass.

Rathbone, Perry T., Director, City Art Museum of St. Louis, St. Louis, Mo.

Reed, Henry Hope, New York, N. Y.

Rich, Daniel Catton, Director, The Art Institute of Chicago Chicago, Ill.

Riefstahl, Mrs. Elizabeth, Librarian, Wilbour Egyptological Library, The Brooklyn Museum Brooklyn, N. Y.

Ritchie, Andrew G, Director, Albright Art Gallery Buffalo, N. Y.

Robinson, Professor David M., Department of Art and Archaeology Johns Hopkins University Baltimore, Md.

Ross, Marvin Chauncey, Curator of Medieval Art, Walters Gallery Baltimore, Md.

Rowe, Margaret T. J., Curator, Hobart Moore Memorial Collection, Yale University Art Gallery New Haven, Conn.

Saint-Gaudens, Homer, Director, Carnegie Institute, Pittsburgh, Pa.

Scholle, Hardinge, Director, Museum of the City of New York, New York, N.Y.

Seize, Josephine, Assistant Curator of American Art, Yale University Art Gallery, New Haven, Conn.

Sexton, Eric Camden, Me.

Shelley, Donald A., Curator of Paintings New York Historical Society New York, N. Y.

Sizer, Theodore, Director, Yale University Art Gallery New Haven, Conn.

Slusser, Jean Paul, Professor of Painting and Drawing, University of Michigan Ann Arbor, Mich.

Smith, Professor E. Baldwin, Department of Art and \rchaeology Princeton Univ., Princeton, N. J.

Soby, James Thrall, New York, N. Y.

Spinden, Dr. Herbert J., Curator, Indian Art and Primitive Cultures, The Brooklyn Museum Brooklyn, N. Y.

Sweeney, James Johnson, Director, Department of Painting and Sculpture, The Museum of Modem Art New York, N. Y.

Sweet, Frederick, Associate Curator, Painting and Sculpture, The Art Institute of Chicago, Chicago, Ill.

Tee Van, John, Department of Tropical Research and Special Events, New York Zoological Park Bronx, N. Y.

Vail, R. W. G., Director, New York Historical Society New York, N. Y.

Walker, Hudson D., President American Federation of Arts, New York, N.Y.

Wall, Alexander J., New York

Historical Society, New York, N. Y.

Washburn, Gordon, Director, Museum of Art Rhode Island School of Design, Providence, R. I.

Weissman, Miss Polaire, Museum of Costume Art, New York, N. Y.

Wissler, Dr. Qark, American Museum of Natural History, New York, N. Y.

Wind, Edgar, Smith College, Northampton, Mass.

York, Lewis E., Chairman, Department of Painting, Yale University Art Gallery, New Haven, Conn.

Zigrosser, Carl, Curator of Prints and Drawings, Philadelphia Museum of Art, Philadelphia, Pa.

Stoddard, Whitney S., Assistant Professor of History and Art, Williams College Williamstown, Mass.

Dr. Clapp and Mrs. Force subsequently announced that they had received eight additional signatures which arrived too late to be affixed to the original copy of the resolution. They included: Frances A. Comstock, Donald Drew Egbert, Henry A. Judd, Sherley W. Morgan, Richard Stillwell—all of Princeton University; Robert Tyler Davis, Portland Museum, Portland, Maine; Frederick Hartt, Acting Director, Smith College Museum of Art; and George Rowley, Princeton Museum of Historic Art.

STATEMENT BY THE AMERICAN COMMISSION FOR THE PROTECTION AND SALVAGE OF ARTISTIC AND HISTORIC MONUMENTS IN WAR AREAS, OWEN J. ROBERTS, CHAIRMAN.

National Gallery of Art, Washington 25, D. C.

WASHINGTON, May 14, 1946: The members of the Commission have received copies of a resolution signed by Dr. Frederick M. Clapp, Director of the Frick Collection; Mrs. Juliana Force, Director of the Whitney Museum of American Art, and others who criticize the action of the United States Government, taken at the Direction of the President and the United States Army Command in Germany, in bringing to this country certain paintings from German museums for safekeeping until conditions in Germany warrant their return. The Clapp resolution compares the action taken by the United States Government to iooting operations carried on by the Nazis during the war.

The Commission has also noted the statements issued by the White House on September 26, 1945, and by the War Department on December 6, 1945, that the works of art of bona fide German ownership, which may be brought to this country for safekeeping, will be kept in trust for the German people and will be returned to Germany when conditions there warrant.

The Commission has also noted the statement issued by the late Chief Justice Stone, Chairman of the Board of Trustees of the National Gallery of Art, on December 14, 1945, that the Trustees of the National Gallery, at the request of the Secretary of State, had agreed to arrange for the storage space for such paintings as might be brought to this country by the United States Army for safekeeping, and that he felt the Army "deserved the highest praise for the care exercised in salvaging these great works of art and in making provisions for their safety until they can be returned to Germany."* The Commission accepts without reservation the promise of the United States Government, as voiced by its highest officials, that the works of art belonging to German museums and brought to this country for safekeeping, will be returned to Germany when conditions there warrant.

The Commission is strongly of the opinion that the resolution sponsored by Dr. Clapp, Mrs. Force, and others is without justification and is to be deplored.

Hon. Owen J. Roberts, Chairman, Philadelphia, Pa.

David E. Finley, Vice Chairman, Director, Nat. Gallery of Art, Washington, D. C.

Huntington Cairns, Secretary, Secretary, National Gallery of Art

Dr. William Bell Dinsmoor, Columbia University, New York New York

Hon. Herbert H. Lehman, New York

Paul J. Sachs, Professor of Fine Arts, Harvard University, Cambridge, Mass.

Francis Cardinal Spellman, Archbishop of New York

Francis Henry Taylor, Director, Metropolitan Museum, New York

The following letters were released on June 10, 1946:

THE WHITE HOUSE

Washington, May 22, 1946

Dear Mrs. Force: .

This is in acknowledgment of the letter to the President, signed by yourself and Dr. Frederick M. Clapp, Director, The Frick Collection, with which you enclosed a resolution signed by ninety-five of your colleagues in connection with the two hundred valuable paintings removed from Germany to this country for safekeeping.

These paintings were removed to this country last year on the basis of information to the effect that adequate facilities and personnel to ensure their safekeeping did not exist in Germany. Our military authorities did not feel that they could take the responsibility of safeguarding them under such conditions and it was therefore decided that they would have to be shipped to this country until such time as they could safely be returned to Germany. It was realized at the time that this action might lead to criticism but it was taken, nevertheless, because it was considered that the most important aspect was to safeguard these priceless treasures. It was hoped that the President's pledge that they would be returned to Germany, contained in a White House press release on September 26,1945, would satisfy those who might be critical of this Government's motives.

I know of no plans to make any further shipments of art objects from Germany to the United States nor of any plans for the exhibition of the two hundred paintings now in this country. While a definite date for the return of these pictures has not as yet been set, I can assure you that this Government will honor its pledge to effect their return as soon as conditions warrant.

> Very sincerely yours,
> (signed) William D. Hassett Secretary to the President.

DEPARTMENT OF STATE

Washington
May 22, 1946

My dear Mrs. Force and Dr. Clapp:

I have received your letter of May 9, 1946, and its enclosed resolution, signed by 95 of your colleagues, urging the President to order the immediate safe return to Germany of the 200 paintings which were brought to this country last year.

When these paintings were found by our forces in southern Germany every effort was made to assure their preservation. It soon became evident that adequate facilities and personnel to ensure their safe keeping could not be guaranteed. Consequently our military authorities, realizing the magnitude of their responsibility in preserving these priceless treasures, requested that they be relieved of this heavy responsibility and that the paintings be shipped to this country where they could be properly cared for. This Government reluctantly gave its approval to this request, knowing that such action would lead to criticism of its motives. The decision was taken because there seemed no other way to ensure preservation of these unique works of art. In order to dispel doubts as to the reasons for this action the White House released a statement to the press on September 26, 1945, which explained the situation and included a pledge that the paintings would be returned to their rightful owners. That pledge still holds good and while a definite date for the return of the paintings to Germany has not as yet been set, you may rest assured that this will be done as soon as conditions warrant.

The resolution also recommended that plans to exhibit these paintings in this country be cancelled and that further shipments of German works of art to this country be countermanded. I have never heard of any plans to make additional shipments of works of art from Germany to the United States nor do I know of any plans to exhibit the paintings which are now in this country.

Sincerely yours,

For the Secretary of State:
(signed) Dean Acheson
Under Secretary.

Following are Dr. Clapp's and Mrs. Force's replies, also released on June 10:

June 3, 1946

My dear Mr. President:

Permit us to thank you for your kind attention to the resolution, signed by us and ninety-five of our colleagues prominent on the staffs of museums or experts in the history and preservation of art, relative to the shipment to this country of two hundred famous paintings formerly in the Kaiser Friedrich and other museums of Berlin.

In addressing the resolution in question to you we felt that we were following the time-honored American custom of bringing to our government's attention a consensus of opinion on the part of those who have special practical familiarity with old pictures and personal, sometimes long, acquaintance with European history and culture in its emotional and intellectual aspects.

Should you, in the course of events, undertake further inquiries into the problem created by the shipment referred to in our resolution, we shall be happy to be so informed.

Respectfully yours,

June 3, 1946

Dear Mr. Hassett:

In reply to your letter of the twenty-second permit us to say that should the President make further inquiries into the subject covered by our resolution with reference to two hundred pictures selected chiefly from the collections of the Kaiser Friedrich Museum and brought to this country, we should be pleased to be kept informed.

We, and our ninety-five colleagues in museums and universities who have had long experience with old paintings and are interested in the history and preservation of works of art, would also be glad to know when the pictures referred to are returned to Germany since we are as yet uninformed whether the conditions which are held not to warrant their return are of a practical or a political nature.

This question obviously cannot but be uppermost in our minds in view of the fact that present conditions in Germany are apparently such as to warrant leaving there thousands of German-owned works of art of great moment which belong not only to the Kaiser Friedrich Museum but to the museums of other cities in the American zone, including the great collection of the Alte Pinakothek in Munich, where under satisfactory conditions and auspices an exhibition of early German art, including masterpieces by Dürer, Grünewald and others, is now being held.

It is in fact one of our perplexities that we have never been told why our officials discriminated against important pictures and art objects (many times the number of those urgently transported to this country for safekeeping) which were also formerly in the Kaiser Friedrich and other museums, not forgetting those which were in South German churches. Were they just left to their fate?

If it were convenient at any time to pass on to the President our continued anxieties on these important points we should be happy to have you do so.

Sincerely yours,

June 3, 1946

Dear Mr. Acheson:

In reply to your letter of the twenty-second with reference to our resolution supported by the signatures of ninety-five of our colleagues prominent in museums or experts in the history and preservation of old masters and other works of art, permit us to say that, in the absence of Secretary Byrnes, we took the liberty of sending you the resolution.

We are aware of the statement released by the White House on September 26, 1945 explaining the situation and promising to return the pictures to Germany when conditions there should warrant such action. We are, however, still uninformed why the unanimous advice of the monuments officers, who had special training and technical knowledge not only of the conditions required for the preservation of old masters but of the certain dangers to which journeys subject them, was disregarded.

We have also never been told whether the conditions believed to jeopardize the safety of these important pictures were of a practical or of a political nature. Neither do we know why, out of the great and extensive collections of the Kaiser Friedrich only two hundred pictures were selected nor by whom the selection was made. More serious still no official mention has ever been made of the fact that there were in the possession of the other museums of Berlin and other cities, including the famous collection of the Alte Pinakothek in Munich, as well as in the churches of the American Zone, art objects and pictures many times more numerous than the paintings actually brought to this country for safe-keeping. One cannot but ask: Were satisfactory conditions found for them or were they merely left to their fate?

These are questions that have given and still give rise to rumors, unhappy conjectures and ambiguous interpretations which we deplore. Unreasonably or otherwise the whole situation is confused by implications that we feel will not be laid until the pictures deposited in Washington have been sent back with the least possible delay to their rightful owners on whom devolves an unequivocable responsibility for their care and preservation.

Sincerely yours

29986495R00151

Made in the USA
Lexington, KY
14 February 2014